全国教学型本科院校商务英语系列规划教材

跨文化交际基础

An Introduction to Intercultural Communication

主编　单晓晖

对外经济贸易大学出版社

中国·北京

图书在版编目（CIP）数据

跨文化交际基础 / 单晓晖主编．—北京：对外经济贸易大学出版社，2015
全国教学型本科院校商务英语系列规划教材
ISBN 978-7-5663-1322-5

Ⅰ．①跨… Ⅱ．①单… Ⅲ．①商务-英语-高等学校-教材 Ⅳ．①H31

中国版本图书馆 CIP 数据核字（2015）第 065951 号

跨文化交际基础

An Introduction to Intercultural Communication

单晓晖 **主编**

责任编辑：胡小平 符梦醒

对外经济贸易大学出版社
北京市朝阳区惠新东街 10 号 邮政编码：100029
邮购电话：010-64492338 发行部电话：010-64492342
网址：http://www.uibep.com E-mail：uibep@126.com

唐山市润丰印务有限公司印装 新华书店北京发行所发行
成品尺寸：185mm×230mm 15.5 印张 311 千字
2015 年 7 月北京第 1 版 2015 年 7 月第 1 次印刷

ISBN 978-7-5663-1322-5
印数：0 001-3 000 册 定价：32.00 元

出版说明

随着经济全球化浪潮的日益高涨，中国与其他国家之间的经贸往来日益密切，既掌握娴熟英语又具有扎实商务专业知识的复合型人才已成为市场的主要需求。根据教育部发布的《国家中长期教育改革和发展规划纲要》中“建立高校分类体系，实行分类管理”的要求，对外经济贸易大学出版社专门针对教学型本科院校组织编写了这套“全国教学型本科商务英语系列规划教材”。

现在，我国的高等院校大致可分为研究型、教学研究型、教学型三大类。不同类型高等院校在人才培养类型、创新贡献和服务社会方面都应有各自的定位。与之相应的，其适用教材也各有不同。教学型高校作为我国高等教育的主力，量大面广、层次多、类型多，是培养应用型高级人才的主要力量。教学型高校以培养应用型、复合型人才为出发点，按“基础扎实，知识面宽，应用能力强，素质高，有较强的创新精神”的要求，以人为本，使学生“会学习”、“会创新”、“会做人”，既加强通识教育，同时也为终身教育作准备、打基础。

本系列教材面向全国教学型本科院校，目标群体明确。教材选题和内容均根据全国教学型本科院校课程设置而定，作者队伍选自全国教学型本科院校的优秀一线师资。本教材适用于全国教学型本科院校商务英语专业、财经专业和英语专业商务/应用/外贸外语方向的学生。

本套“全国教学型本科商务英语系列规划教材”包括《商务英语综合教程 1-4 册》《商务英语听说》《商务英语阅读》《商务英语写作》《商务英语函电》《商务英语翻译》《商务英语口译》《商务知识导读》《英语财经报刊阅读》《跨文化交际基础》《国际商务礼仪》《进出口贸易实务》《国际商务制单》和《国际贸易理论与实务》等。

本系列的编撰者们不仅具有丰富的语言教学经验，而且具备商务活动的实践经验，他们集教学经验和专业背景于一身，这是本套商务英语系列教材编撰质量的有力保证。

此外，本套教材配有辅导用书或课件等立体化教学资源，供教师教学参考（可登录我社网站 www.uibep.com 下载）。

对外经济贸易大学出版社
外语图书事业部
2014 年 3 月

前 言
Preface

跨文化沟通指本族语者与非本族语者之间的沟通交际,也指任何在语言和文化背景方面有差异的人们之间的沟通交际。由于不同的民族所处的生态、物质、社会及宗教等环境不同，因而产生了不同的语言习惯、社会文化、风土人情等语境因素。不同文化背景造成人们说话方式或习惯不尽相同。随着经济的全球化，跨文化沟通活动将越来越频繁，渗透面越来越广。但并非学好外语就可以成功有效地与外国人进行沟通，因为跨文化意识的缺乏和对具体文化差异认识的不足都可能导致沟通的失败。全面、系统地了解跨文化沟通的内涵、研究及应用是成功实现跨文化沟通的前提和基础。新颁布的《高等学校英语专业英语教学大纲》特别提出要培养适应社会需要的既有专业英语基础又有相关专业知识技能的外经贸、外事类复合型人才。在经济全球化和文化多样性并存的今天，如何培养和提高跨文化交际能力就成为英语教学面临的主要任务之一。

目前,深入浅出地介绍跨文化理论及其在商务领域的运用的教材并不多见。鉴于此，为满足广大教师、学生、从业人员的需要，我们尝试提供一套全方位的、综合性强的现代跨文化沟通教材。

本书的作者具有丰富的教学、研究和实践经验，且参编过相关书藉。在编著过程中，作者花了大量的时间做了大量的调查和案头工作，力求使理论性、实用性、可读性有机结合。本书内容新颖、概念清晰，理论性和实用性强，通俗易懂、层次分明，特别贴近生活，案例非常丰富。其读者对象虽定位于高等院校商务英语专业的学生，但对于其他专业学生、外贸工作人员、商务管理人员、外企文员等，也大有裨益。

本书分为六章：跨文化沟通概念导入；最有影响的跨文化沟通理论回顾；跨文化国际商务；跨文化国际谈判；跨文化国际营销；跨文化案例研究方法。本书的内容涵盖了当今国际跨文化沟通的最新观点和最新动态。它可以让读者了解在全球背景下跨文化商务活动的最新进展状况；并帮助读者做好准备，迎接新环境下跨文化国际商务研究和实践的新挑战。另外，每个章节后都附有丰富、多样的配套练习。由于其中绝大多数都是开放式题目，所以编者并未提供固定答案。读者还可以登录出版社网站（http://www.uibep.com）下载配套（PPT）课件。

本书在编辑过程中得到对外经济贸易大学出版社宋海玲和谭利彬编辑的无私热情帮助和专业技术指导，在此表示衷心感谢！

最后，由于编者水平有限，时间仓促，以及材料匮乏，不妥甚至错误之处难免，请各位见谅、指正。

编者

2014 年 3 月

目 录

Contents

Chapter 1

Culture and Intercultural Communication

I am not different from you, I am different like you.
Culture is a framework in which we communicate.

—Stephen Roberts

The basic difference between Chinese and western culture lies in the thinking pattern.

—Ji Xianlin

1. Lead-in

CASE 1:

Americans tended to be more exaggerated when applying figurative expressions than we Chinese did. For instance, as to the same scene of Tom's driving too fast, what a Chinese guy would say and what the American counterpart would say always differed from each other to a great extent. In such conditions, Chinese people prefer to compare this scene to flying, lightning or just compare the speed to velocity of light. However, an American would rather say: "Wow, Tom's just like a bat out of hell!" You see the difference? Whatever we Chinese may choose, the objects would be related to those existing in the real world. But as to the figurative expression "hell", it is something that does not actually exist in this three-dimensional space. (Source: <u>*Sarah's English BLOG*</u>)

CASE 2:

With regard to suppliers in Japan, workers have a clear comprehension of the production scale and necessary production time. Whether it be the person who places the order from the supplier, or those who deal with the transaction thereafter, from beginning to end the level of service is consistently high. If we look at Western business culture, incompletion of a task within the designated period often sees the worker placing the blame on the boss by claiming that his directions weren't clear. Thus, for the Western worker, one can, to some degree, avoid responsibility. Contrastingly, in Japan, if business doesn't go according to plan, it becomes the problem of the individual undertaking the task. What's more, the Japanese deliver a service that goes far beyond what was originally requested, leaving many customers very satisfied. The fact that they carry out the job with consistency means they are easy to work with. (Source: *Why Foreign Businessmen are Receiving Lessons on Doing Business the Japanese Way http://en.rocketnews24.com/2013/03/26/why-foreign-businessmen-are-receiving-lessons-on-doing-business-the-japanese-way/)*

CASE 3:

I was running at a good clip on my usual route down a narrow street in Nanjing. Cars were passing so I stayed over to the side. Behind me a bicycle bell rang and I motioned for the person to pass, as there was plenty of room. Again the bell rang and again I motioned. Then a man's voice rang out a two-syllable phrase. He didn't pass though, and kept ringing his bell nonstop. Now, I do run fast and in China faster than most bike riders, but to my mind this guy obviously wanted to cause a hassle. He could have passed easily. Instead, he yelled his two-syllable phrase over and over. The tone of it sounded to me like what we Americans say when someone cuts us off in traffic. So, I decided to return the sentiment and gave him one of our best two syllable invectives (abusive language), the one referring to body parts. He immediately followed with his, and we were off, speeding down the street both of us yelling back and forth to one another. Later I learned that the phrase he used was *jiayou* (加油), which is used to cheer someone. It's like saying, "Go for it." I wonder what he thought I was saying? (by Greg Brock, *http://source.mastvu.ah.cn/dzjxb/kwhjj/CCC_50cases.htm*)

CASE 4:

I remember before I came to America, family members and friends all said that I wouldn't experience any culture shock, since I like KFC, McDonald's, Pizza, steak and salad already, and the fact that I speak fluent English is going to make my life in America a lot easier. All those things my family said to me were true, my capability to speak fluent English undoubtedly make communication with local people a piece of cake for me. But the food was not as easy as I thought. Besides culture shock doesn't limit to food and language, there are a lot of other things which will be shocking to a foreigner.

Food is a big element in culture shock. A lot of times, when I go to a new country, the ethnic cooking can be very difficult to adjust. I indulged myself with the western food long before I came to America. But after I came here, I found the American food I had in China has few similarities compared to the real American food here. The way they cook the steak, the excessive sweetness of the cake, the bitter saltiness of popcorn, the deep fried sea food was beyond my imagination. I watched American people eat cheese with apple. I remember the combination of the two was very disturbing to my stomach at the time. One time I went to a restaurant wanting to have some mushroom. When the food came, I looked at my dish, puzzled and asked "What is this?" "Fried mushroom." The waitress said. I laughed hysterically. Does American have to fry everything? I am not complaining about American food, I am just pointing out the "shock" I experienced when I first came to this country. However after living here for almost 6 years, I love cheese and crackers, still unable to eat cheese with apple, somehow thinking the two together still make me sick a little bit. But who knows what will happen next year? I used to dislike American breakfast, now I love it so much. I had my first bagel this year, and it was delicious. I still don't like pan cakes, but everyone else seems to love them, maybe one of these days I will try it, you never know what will happen.

Manner is another culture shock for me. When I just came to America, I was living in a town of 2,000 people, which is very strange for me, due to the fact that I came from China which is extremely populous. I remember thinking that beggars wouldn't be able to make a living here. Everyone was so friendly to me, strangers would say Hi to me in supermarket, people would wave to me as they drive pass my car. I've never seen a person litter on the street since I came to this country. The fact that this country is so clean that they wear the shoes they walk on the street inside the house was astonishing to me, because in China I've never been to a house where I don't have to take off my shoes at the door. It is considered to be very rude to walk into people's house with your shoes on. So I learned to ask the host if they prefer me to take off my shoes. My mom always told me to be humble. When people say I am smart, I am supposed to say "Oh, no, I am not that smart." If I go to people's house and they offer me an apple, even if I want the apple, I am supposed to say "No, thank you." Unless they constantly offer it to me, then I can accept the apple. But in America, if a person comes to me and says "You are very pretty." I would say "Thank you so much!" And if a host offers me an apple and

I want it, I'd better say yes, because they won't ask me several times like a Chinese person would.

Living in another country can be very difficult. A lot of things are going to be different in another country. If you want to adjust yourself to the culture, you almost have to brainwash yourself, learning whole new ways of living and socializing. There were so many things strange to me, but now they seem so natural. I am not forgetting how to be a Chinese, I guess I am just Americanized a little bit. (Source: *From China to America: Culture Shock-living in a new country* by Kianna)

2. Main Text

2.1 Culture

The field of human communication is rich in its many principles and theories concerning relationships and their connection to messages. Over time, communication theorists recognized the vast influence of culture as a primary variable in the communication process. This emphasis has led to theories and principles which now trace culture's socializing patterns and imprints related to intercultural encounters. Of course, this book's aim is to introduce the many cultural elements that influence communication where intercultural situations develop.

DEFINING CULTURE

Definitions of culture cover a wide range of perspectives. When students are asked to describe culture, the following are words and phrases they use: *food, religion, language, music, region or geography, ethnicity, clothes*, and so on. Generally, there is always one person who raises his or her hand timidly and says, "I think culture is more than that. It's the things we don't see, like our beliefs or views about gender." Both are correct—culture represents the things we see, the tangible, as well as the intangible things. Someone describes and defines culture as "a monster", since it's so messy and sometimes it's too big to handle, and, it's scary because you don't know what you're dealing with.

Defining culture is not about positives or negatives—culture just is, and that is why it can be a challenge to describe it. Definitions of culture usually incorporate an expression of values and beliefs of groups, the learning that occurs in groups, and the expressions of those cultural norms. Edgar Schein (2010) said culture consists of the shared beliefs, values, and assumptions of a group of people who learn from one another and teach to others that their behaviors, attitudes, and perspectives are the correct ways to think, act, and feel. Cultures show up in many forms and are expressed differently. Yet all forms and levels of cultures express and share three fundamental aspects: values, assumptions, and symbols. Value systems are fundamental to understanding how culture expresses itself. Values often serve as principles that guide people in their behaviors and actions. Our values, ideally, should match up with what we say we will do, and our values are most evident in symbolic forms. Our values are supported by our assumptions of our world. They are beliefs or ideas that we believe and hold to be true. They come about through repetition. This repetition becomes a habit we form and leads to habitual patterns of thinking and doing. We do not realize our assumptions because they are ingrained in us at an unconscious level. We are aware of it when we encounter a value or belief that is different from ours,' when it makes us feel that we need to stand up for, or validate, our beliefs.

In his seminal work *The Interpretation of Cultures* (1973), Clifford Geertz outlined culture as "a system of inherited conceptions expressed in symbolic forms by means of which men communicate, perpetuate, and develop their knowledge about and attitudes toward life."

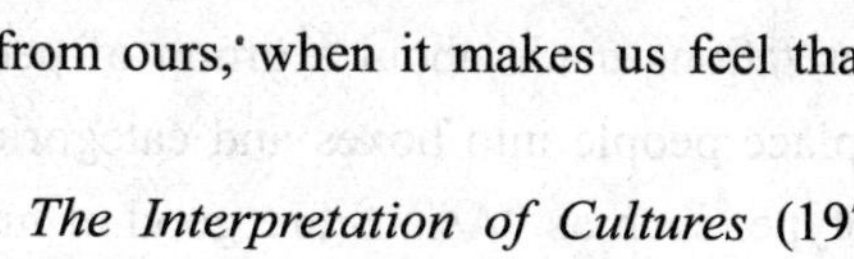

Figure 1.1 Different Layers of Culture
(*Source: http://www.buzzle.com/articles/what-is-culture.html*)

He believed that culture is a system based on symbols. He said that people use symbols to define their world and express their emotions. As human beings, we all learn, both consciously and unconsciously, starting at a very young age. What we internalize comes through observation, experience, interaction, and what we are taught. We manipulate symbols to create meaning and stories that dictate our behaviors, to organize our lives, and to interact with others. The meanings we attach to symbols are arbitrary. Looking someone in the eye means that you are direct and respectful in some countries, yet, in other cultural systems, looking away is a sign of respect. The meanings we attach to symbols can create a cultural havoc when we meet someone who believes in a different meaning or interpretation; it can give us culture shock. This shock can be disorientating, confusing, or surprising. It can bring on anxiety or nervousness, and, for some, a sense of losing control.

One of the things that can happen in the context of discussing culture is falling into the stereotypes and generalizations of a cultural group or norm. It is important to recognize the difference and the impact these factors have in cultural interactions. In general, stereotypes are negative statements and interpretations made about a group of people. Stereotypes, whether deemed positive or negative, place people into boxes and categories and limit them to those specific perspectives. A stereotype, such as "Asians are good at math," does not provide the complete picture someone needs to understand the Asian culture or the differences between Asian cultures. Similarly, just because you meet a 70-year old who does not know how to use current technology, it does not mean that other individuals in that generation do not know how to use it.

By contrast, generalizations of cultures are broad statements based on facts, experiences, examples, or logic. There are two kinds of generalizations, valid and faulty, and it is your role to determine which generalizations have validity. Broad characterization of cultural groups can serve as a framework for cultural interactions. For example, Hispanic societies have a high degree of machismo, or, in Middle Eastern cultures, women have a lesser status than men—these types of generalizations are helpful when engaging with people of those cultures. But in all cultural interactions, culturally intelligent leadership requires you to recognize that generalizations do not apply to everyone within a cultural group.

THE ORIGIN OF CULTURE

The origins, elements, and consequences of culture can be shown in the following Figure 1.2 at a glance.

TRAITS OF CULTURE

Culture is a powerful human tool for survival, but it is a fragile phenomenon. It is constantly changing and easily lost because it exists only in our minds. Our written languages, governments, buildings, and other man-made things are merely the products of culture. They are not culture in themselves. For this reason, archaeologists can not dig up culture directly in their excavations. The broken pots and other artifacts of ancient people that they uncover are only material remains that reflect cultural patterns—they are things that were made and used through cultural knowledge and skills.

For instance, an English person who values personal space very highly may consider it rude when a Mexican stands too close. A Japanese who values conformity may find it inappropriate when an American expresses too much of his or her own opinions. The relative importance of values within each culture can also be revealed through sayings, such as "Time is money" (American), "A zebra does not despise its stripes" (African) or "No need to know the person, only the family" (Chinese). Such sayings impart values that are important in each culture and can provide us with a better understanding of others' cultural beliefs.

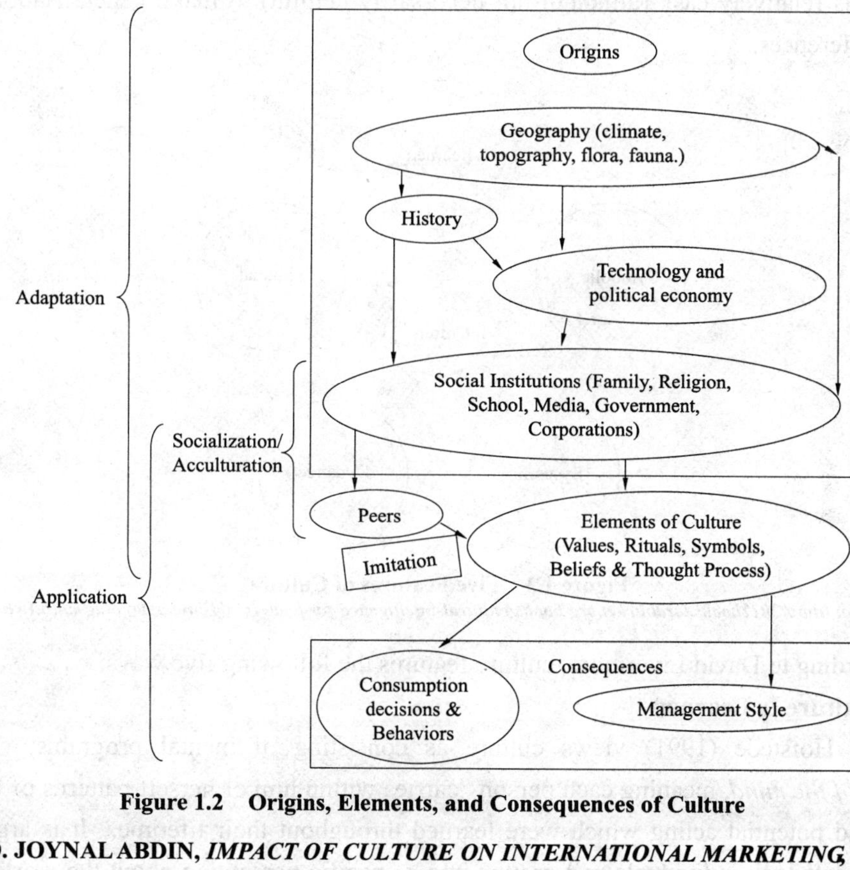

Figure 1.2 Origins, Elements, and Consequences of Culture

(MD. JOYNAL ABDIN, *IMPACT OF CULTURE ON INTERNATIONAL MARKETING*, 2008)

Wang et al., (2000:1-3) identify the essential features of culture. They are:

✧ Culture is the human-made part of the environment.

✧ Culture reflects widely shared assumptions about life.

✧ Culture is so fundamental that most people do not and cannot discuss or analyze it.

✧ Culture becomes evident when someone encounters someone from another country who deviates from his own cultural norms.

✧ Culture is transmitted from generation to generation.

✧ Even in new situations, people can make a judgment about what is expected in their own culture.

✧ Cultural values endure and change takes place over a number of generations.

✧ Violations of cultural norms have an emotional impact.

✧ It is relatively easy (although not necessarily helpful) to make generalisations about cultural differences.

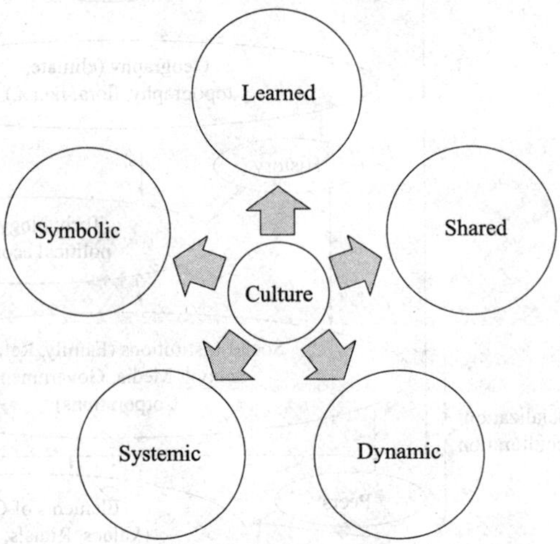

Figure 1.3 Five Features of Culture

(Source: http://2012books.lardbucket.org/books/cultural-intelligence-for-leaders/s04-understanding-culture.html)

According to David Livermore, culture features the following five ways:

1) Culture Is Learned

Geert Hofstede (1991) views culture as consisting of mental programs, calling it *softwares of the mind*, meaning each person "carries within him or herself patterns of thinking, feeling, and potential acting which were learned throughout their lifetime." It is argued that mental models lock individuals and groups into a specific perception about the world. Like a computer, we are programmed to act or behave in certain ways. The conscious and unconscious learning we undergo, over time, turns into beliefs that we consider to be valid. We then teach each other that these beliefs are cultural norms, and they are then expressed in our daily lives as behaviors and actions.

Think about your first day with your current organization or one you worked for in the past. Typically, your boss or a co-worker gave you an orientation to the company, describing its mission, products, and services. Most likely, you met your co-workers and received a tour of the office facilities. Perhaps you met and talked with co-workers to get a sense of how your job was related to their work. Maybe you spent time reading company materials, reviewing your department files, or talking with your supervisor about the details of your job responsibilities. Perhaps you had lunch with other staff members and were told about some parts of the organization such as, "Jane Doe should be fired but is still working here," "The CEO has control issues," or "The fax machine breaks down three times a day." Whatever you did in those first hours or days of orientation and training, you created an image of how you would fit into the company. In that moment, you told yourself a story of how you would work with the company and how it would work with you because others in that business culture told you how you needed to behave. This moment is so powerful that it shapes your experiences, including your thoughts, actions, behaviors, beliefs, and attitudes for the rest of your time with the company.

2) Culture Is Shared

Ming is a recent college graduate with a degree in accounting. She has taken a job with a large accounting firm. Although she gets along with members of her department and team, she tends to spend her free time with other colleagues who are of Asian descent, especially those who are in her generation. She feels that this group of co-workers understands her better and shares her values and ideas around work-life balance.

John has been with his state employer for thirty years, working up the ranks into seniority in his state agency. It's been customary for him and six co-workers of his age group to meet for lunch every day and discuss the latest sporting events. Once a week during the summer they meet up after work to play baseball at a local park and recreation site.

These two examples describe culture as a shared learning experience. Although you may think of yourself as an individual, you share beliefs, rituals, ceremonies, traditions, and assumptions with people who grew up or live in similar cultural backgrounds. It is easier for you to relate to someone who has shared value systems and ways of doing things than someone who does not share the same values.

The patterns of culture bind us together and enable us to get along with each other. Even though it feels good to be around people who think, act, and behave like you, shared learning can create blind spots. Shared cultures create a dynamic of in-groups, among which people segregate themselves from each other. Within teams in organizations, in-group blind spots can lead to "group think," meaning the ways in which groups ignore alternative solutions and take on actions and behaviors that discount the experiences of others.

3) Culture Is Dynamic

Culture is dynamic and thus complex. Culture is fluid rather than static, which means that culture changes all the time, every day, in subtle and tangible ways. Because humans communicate and express their cultural systems in a variety of ways, it can be hard to pinpoint exactly what cultural dynamics are at play. Consider, for example, a conversation about a person's attitude or feelings. In this type of conversation, Albert Meharbian (1971) found that people pay attention to (a) the words, or what is being said; (b) the tone, or how the words are said; and (c) the visual behind the words, often called the body language. All of these are aspects of culture that are interpreted differently depending on the cultural context. Add multiple layers of culture to the conversation—such as time, power and authority, emotion, age, gender, religion, nationality, and even previous intercultural interactions—and communication at a cross-cultural level becomes complex and hard to manage. The following is an example of the dynamism of cultures:

Sheila is the director of marketing for a social services agency. She provides feedback to one of her managers about how to improve services. Sheila sits behind a large executive desk and is leaning forward. The employee sits with her arms crossed, leaning away from Sheila.

If you were observing this scene, are you able to tell from the body language what each person is thinking? Why or why not? What cultural factors might be present?

In the example, Sheila's body language can be interpreted as any of the following: eager to assist or help, intensely interested in what the employee has to say, aggressive and wanting more information, or needing deeper engagement in the conversation. Her employee's body language could mean any of the following: protective, suspicious, not caring, or relaxed. To understand the dynamics of culture in this example, you would need to pay attention to the things you do not see such as:

- Is Sheila older or younger than her employee?
- What has been their working relationship?
- Does Sheila naturally lean forward when speaking with her employees?

◆ What is the tone of voice in the conversation?

"Cultures de facto no longer have the insinuated form of homogeneity and separateness. They have instead assumed a new form, which is to be called transcultural insofar that it passes through classical cultural boundaries. Cultural conditions today are largely characterized by mixes and permeations" (Welsch 1999: 197, italics in original)

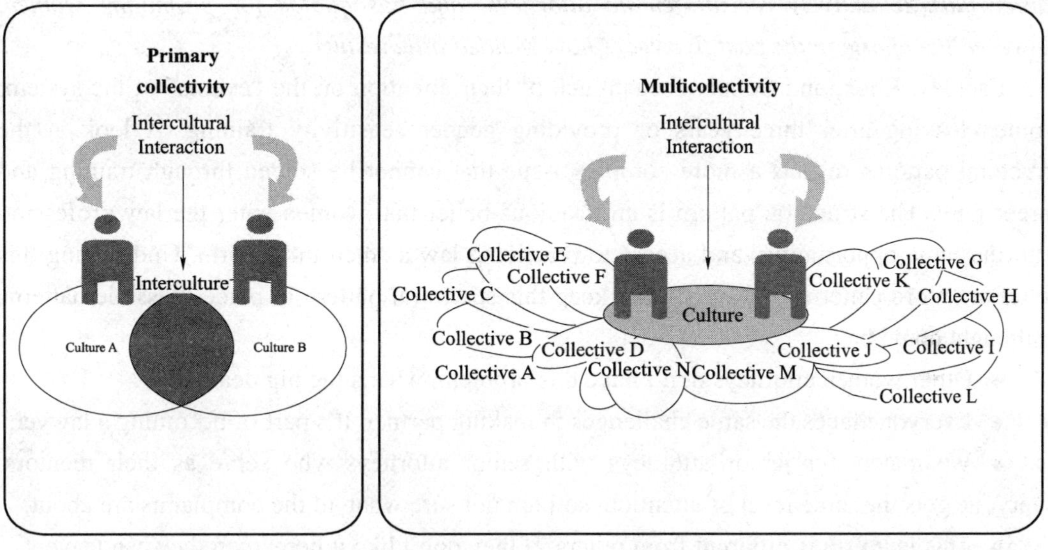

Figure 1.4 Primary Collectivity and Multi-collectivity (*Adapted after Hansen 2003, Rathje 2009*)

4) Culture Is Systemic

In systems theory, systems are interrelated, interconnected parts that create a whole. There are patterns of behavior, deeply rooted structural systems, which are beneath the waterline. What we see at the top of the iceberg are the behaviors; we do not see what contributes to those behaviors. Consider, for example, a white woman walking down a quiet street. She quickly clutches her handbag closer to her body as she passes a black man. Then, when she spots a white man walking toward her, she loosens her hold on the purse.

To address the system, one must be able to address the underlining patterns. These patterns, because they are deeply embedded in the system, will take up significant effort, time, and resources. Changes to the system are slow and gradual; visible changes may not appear until months, or even years, later.

Because most leaders spend their time evaluating and finding solutions to an "event," they revisit the issues over and over again, with no positive and sustainable results. The following case study illustrates the systemic nature of culture:

Langley, Knox, and Cooper, a law firm in the Midwest, knows that it has to do more to be inclusive to women attorneys. It has met challenges in retaining its female work force. The majority of women hired to work at the firm leave within a three year period. To address the issue, the firm provides gender sensitivity training to the entire company, attends graduate career fairs to actively recruit female attorneys, and has quotas for promoting women. However, the efforts in the past five years have yielded little results.

Langley, Knox, and Cooper focus much of their attention on the "events" of the system: women leaving after three years or providing gender sensitivity training. A look at the structural patterns reveals a more complex issue that cannot be solved through training and career fairs. The structural pattern is an insidious belief that women enter the law profession with the same opportunities and access to practicing law as men in the firm. Underlining this belief are more patterns of thought that keep this structural pattern in place. Possible patterns of thought could be:

◆ Other women attorneys don't have this problem, what's the big deal here?

◆ Everyone faces the same challenges in making partner. It's part of becoming a lawyer.

◆ We match our junior attorneys with senior attorneys who serve as their mentors. Everyone gets the same level of attention, so I am not sure what all the complaints are about.

◆ This law firm is different from others. If they don't like it here, then they can leave.

◆ We give the women in this firm more time off and flexibility than ever before, yet they still think it's not enough.

5) Culture Is Symbolic

Symbols are both verbal and nonverbal in form within cultural systems, and they have a unique way of linking human beings to each other. Humans create meaning between symbols and what they represent; as a result, different interpretations of a symbol can occur in different cultural contexts. Take, for example, a meeting of senior executives who need to make a decision about a new service. This group of leaders has a team culture that orients itself toward a democratic process: decision making is based on one vote from each member. Now imagine a similar group of leaders with the same task but, this time, the group of leaders is comprised of Native Americans. Leaders who are younger in the group ask their elders for advice. This is an example of how cultural systems differ in their interpretation and expressions of culture. In some cultural systems, voting is not an option. The symbol of a *vote* has different meanings and interpretations—or simply may not even exist in any practical sense—depending on the cultural background.

LAYERS OF CULTURE

Cultural systems have roots that are impacted by their surroundings. A culture's rituals, traditions, ceremonies, myths, and symbols provide it with the nutrients it needs to survive. Environmental changes impact cultural systems, forcing it to adapt and change to its surroundings or transition into death, creating new cultural stories that carry new life. But unlike trees and their roots, we get stuck in our cultural systems and do not budge even when our surroundings have changed. Change in cultural environments is inevitable and a part of the life cycle. Some cultural anthropologists would describe the cultural systems as "big C" (macroculture) and "little C" (microculture). The macroculture refers to a larger cultural system, for example, Catholicism is a culture that is not bounded by geography. Within the macroculture of Catholicism are smaller units of culture called *subcultures*. Change is constant in each cultural system, and transitions, renewal, and rebirth are endless cycles. As cultural shifts occur in the macro- and microcultures, small and large, gradual and disruptive, the entire system learns to adapt in different ways.

Exhibit: *Categories of Culture*

Culture	Category
Macro-cultures	Nations, ethnic and religious groups, occupations that exist globally
Organizational Cultures	Private, public, nonprofit, government organizations
Subcultures	Occupational groups within organizations
Micro-cultures	Micro-systems within or outside organizations

Culture could also relate to a country (national culture), a distinct section of the community (sub-culture), or an organization (corporate culture). One of the basic tenets of culture is that it consists of levels and sublevels. It is useful to think about culture in terms of five basic levels: national, regional, organizational, team, and individual. Within each of these levels are tangible and intangible sublevels of culture.

There are very likely three layers or levels of culture that are part of your learned behavior patterns and perceptions, National Culture, Subculture and Cultural Universals. Most obviously is the body of cultural traditions that distinguish your specific society. When people speak of Italian, Samoan, or Japanese culture, they are referring to the shared language, traditions, and beliefs that set each of these peoples apart from others. In most cases, those who share your culture do so because they acquired it as they were raised by parents and other family members who have it. So the first layer can be national culture.

- **National Culture**

The case below illustrates the national differences between two cultures: American and German.

Case study: Culture at Wal-Mart

By some measures, Wal-Mart is the largest corporation in the world. By other measures, it is the world's 14th largest economy. Indeed, the Arkansas-based retailer's annual revenue—over one-third of a trillion dollars—surpasses the total value of goods and services produced in many countries, such as Sweden.

Wal-Mart's rise to the status of an economic superpower has not been without criticism. Opponents have criticized its policy of shutting out labor unions, its lack of commitment to elevating women to managerial positions, its slowness to provide adequate health care benefits, and its negative impact on smaller retailers in the areas where its stores are located. Nonetheless, U.S. consumers have embraced Wal-Mart's "everyday low prices." The reaction has not been as positive when the discount giant has tried to enter countries where consumers hold different cultural values.

The company, now located in 15 countries, has not been an unqualified success abroad. In 2006 Wal-Mart pulled out of Germany, due in part to its failure to adjust to the national culture. German shoppers, accustomed to no-nonsense, impersonal service, found Wal-Mart employees' smiling, outgoing style off-putting. The company's "ten-foot attitude"—a salesperson who comes within 10 feet of a customer must look the person in the eye, greet the person, and ask if he or she needs help—simply did not play well there. Food shoppers, used to bagging their own groceries, were turned off by Wal-Mart's practice of allowing clerks to handle their purchases. Furthermore, German employees, who had grown up in a culture that accepts workplace romances, found the company's prohibition against on-the-job relationships bizarre.

Unfortunately, executives did not react quickly enough to the cultural clash. Despite their need for cultural know-how, they passed up the opportunity to install German-speaking managers in key positions. While the company struggled to adjust to unfamiliar cultural standards, fierce competition from German retailers cut into its profits. After an eight-year effort that cost the company one billion dollars, Wal-Mart's executives conceded defeat.

Wal-Mart's withdrawal from Germany was its second exit of the year. Earlier in 2006, the company sold all its facilities in South Korea, where its warehouse-style stores were not appreciated by shoppers accustomed to more elegant surroundings. Today, the successful U.S. retailer is learning not to impose its corporate culture on foreign customers and employees. No longer does the company plan to sell golf clubs in Brazil, where the game is rarely played, or ice skates in Mexico, where skating rinks are hard to find. More importantly, the corporate giant has begun to study the culture and social patterns of potential customers.

Wal-Mart's mistakes in Germany and South Korea are instructive. Even without a background in sociology, most businesspeople know that culture is fundamental to society. Yet they often fail to adjust to new cultures when they enter foreign markets. Today, as Wal-Mart prepares to enter China and India, two massive consumer markets, executives are determined to repeat the company's success in Latin America, rather than its failure in Germany and Korea.

National differences refer to the cultural influences of a nation that result in its national characteristics. Although nation-states have regional and political differences, national culture can be viewed as the values held by a majority of the population within the nation. These values are largely unconscious and developed throughout one's childhood. The values are pushed to a level of consciousness when in contrast to another nation's cultural values. Within national cultures, values are generally seen as stable over time. National values, because they reflect the traditions of the nation-state over time, will change slightly from generation to generation, but the overall values will remain the same. For example, a German who comes from a culture of punctuality and travels for business in Italy will notice a national cultural difference in how Italians view time (more leisurely and relaxed) as compared to their own national culture.

- **Subcultures**

Rodeo riders, residents of a retirement community, workers on an offshore oil rig—all are examples of what sociologists refer to as *subcultures*. A subculture is a segment of society that shares a distinctive pattern of customs, rules, and traditions that differs from the pattern of the larger society. In a sense, a subculture can be thought of as a culture existing within a larger, dominant culture. The existence of many subcultures is characteristic of complex societies such as the United States.

Members of a subculture participate in the dominant culture while engaging in unique and distinctive forms of behavior. Frequently, a subculture will develop an argot, or specialized language, that distinguishes it from the wider society. Athletes who play *parkour*, an extreme sport that combines forward running with fence leaping and the vaulting of walls, water barriers, and even moving cars, speak an argot they devised especially to describe their feats. Parkour runners talk about doing *King Kong vaults*—diving arms first over a wall or grocery cart and landing in a standing position. They may follow this maneuver with a tic tac—kicking off a wall to overcome some kind of obstacle. Such argot allows insiders—the members of the subculture—to understand words with special meanings. It also establishes patterns of communication that outsiders can't understand.

In complex, diverse societies in which people have come from many different parts of the world, they often retain much of their original cultural traditions. As a result, they are likely to be part of an identifiable subculture in their new society. The shared cultural traits of subcultures set them apart from the rest of their society. Examples of easily identifiable subcultures in the United States include ethnic groups such as Vietnamese Americans, African Americans, and Mexican Americans. Members of each of these subcultures share a common identity, food tradition, dialect or language, and other cultural traits that come from their common ancestral background and experience. As the cultural differences between members of a subculture and the dominant national culture blur and eventually disappear, the subculture ceases to exist except as a group of people who claim a common ancestry. That is generally the case with German Americans and Irish Americans in the United States today. Most of them identify themselves as Americans first. They also see themselves as being part of the cultural mainstream of the nation.

Sociologists associated with the interactionist perspective emphasize that language and symbols offer a powerful way for a subculture to feel cohesive and maintain its identity. In India, a new subculture has developed among employees at the international call centers established by multinational corporations. To serve customers in the United States and Europe, the young men and women who work there must be fluent speakers of English. But the corporations that employ them demand more than proficiency in a foreign language; they expect their Indian employees to adopt Western values and work habits, including the grueling pace U.S. workers take for granted. In return they offer perks such as Western-style dinners, dances, and coveted consumer goods. Significantly, they allow employees to take the day off only on U.S. holidays, like Labor Day and Thanksgiving—not on Indian holidays like Diwali, the Hindu festival of lights. While most Indian families are home celebrating, call center employees see only each other; when they have the day off, no one else is free to socialize with them. As a result, these employees have formed a tight-knit subculture based on hard work and a taste for Western luxury goods and leisure-time pursuits.

Another shared characteristic among some employees at Indian call centers is their contempt for the callers they serve. In performing their monotonous, repetitive job day after day, hundreds of thousands of these workers have come to see the faceless Americans they deal with as slow, often rude customers. Such shared understandings underpin this emerging subculture.

Functionalist and conflict theorists agree that variation exists within cultures. Functionalists view subcultures as variations of particular social environments and as evidence that differences can exist within a common culture. However, conflict theorists suggest that variations often reflect the inequality of social arrangements within a society. A conflict theorist would view the challenges to dominant social norms by African American activists, the feminist movement, and the gay rights movement as reflections of inequity based on race, gender, and sexual orientation. Conflict theorists also argue that subcultures sometimes emerge when the dominant society unsuccessfully tries to suppress a practice, such as the use of illegal drugs.

- **Countercultures**

By the end of the 1960s, an extensive subculture had emerged in the United States, composed of young people turned off by a society they believed was too materialistic and technological. The group included primarily political radicals and hippies who had dropped out of mainstream social institutions. These young men and women rejected the pressure to accumulate cars, homes, and an endless array of material goods. Instead, they expressed a desire to live in a culture based on more humanistic values, such as sharing, love, and coexistence with the environment. As a political force, this subculture opposed the United States' involvement in the war in Vietnam and encouraged draft resistance.

When a subculture conspicuously and deliberately opposes certain aspects of the larger culture, it is known as a counterculture. Countercultures typically thrive among the young, who have the least investment in the existing culture. In most cases, a 20-year-old can adjust to new cultural standards more easily than someone who has spent 60 years following the patterns of the dominant culture (Zellner 1995).

- **Regional Culture**

An interesting thing about living in the United States is the regional differences that make each part of the country unique. When I attended college in Boston, I heard the expression "wicked" used quite often. After asking my New England friends what "wicked" meant, I learned that it was used to emphasize a point. If I attended a concert that I really enjoyed, I would say, "That concert was awesome!" New Englanders would say, "That concert was wicked awesome." After living in the Boston area for 4 years, the word became a part of my vocabulary. When I used the word in conversations with my friends and family members in Minnesota, they did not understand what I meant.

Source: http://anthro.palomar.edu/culture/culture_1.htm

All national cultures consist of regional subcultures that influence the characteristics of one group from another in a nation state. The word "pop" refers to a soft drink in the Midwest, but if you go to the East Coast, it is referred to as "soda." In other regions of the United States, a soft drink is referred to as "Coke." The following is an example of regional cultural differences and one way the difference is expressed:

Dianne moves from Texas for a job opportunity in Georgia. She lives in Georgia for 25 years and feels that it is her home state. However, her neighbors and co-workers do not think that she is a Georgian. Even though Dianne thinks she is from the south, she is reminded by others that she is "not a southerner."

Dianne experiences a regional cultural shift that she did not know existed until her move. Although she considers herself a Georgian, she is constantly reminded that she is not a southerner. At a conscious and unconscious level, her regional cultural experiences will dictate her thoughts about herself and others. She may develop the following assumptions and beliefs as a result of the regional cultural influences:

◆ I better just tell people that I am from Texas.

◆ Georgians think that you have to be from certain states to be considered a "southerner."

◆ If you are from the south, you must have lineage or roots that directly link you to the south. A "transplant" is not considered a true southerner.

● **Organizational Culture**

Organizational culture speaks to the culture that is specific to an organization—the culture that makes it distinctive from competitors and non-competitors. Organizational cultures are often referred to as "corporate cultures" and reflect the beliefs, values, and assumptions of an organization. For example, the culture of one school in a school district can be different from the culture of another school located in the same district simply because of what the people in one school culture adhere and react to. Edgar Schein defines organizational culture as the basic assumptions and beliefs that are shared by members of an organization, that operate unconsciously and define in a basic taken-for-granted fashion an organization's view of itself and its environment. It is about the collective behaviors in an organization. It tends to consist of four layers.

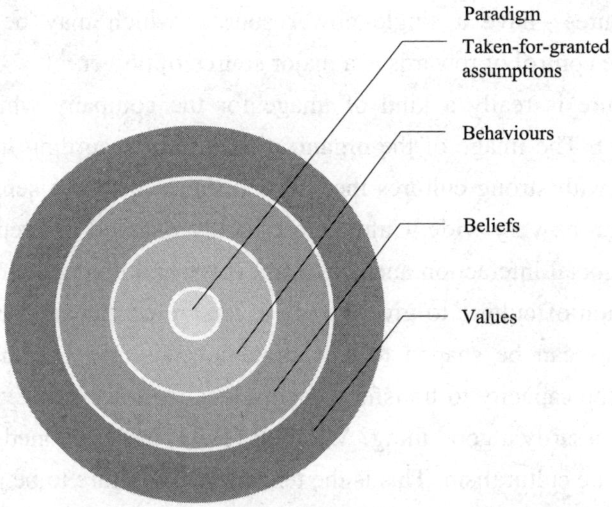

Figure 1.5 Four Layers of Organizational Culture
(*Source: http://www.innovationforgrowth.co.uk/Blog/what-is-the-cultural-web/*)

◆ Values—often easy to identify within an organization as they tend to be written down as statements about the organization's mission, objectives or strategies. They can often be vague.

◆ Beliefs—are more specific, but still are evident from corporate statements.

◆ Behaviors—these are the day-to-day way in which the organization operates. These include work routines and organizational structure.

◆ Taken-for-granted assumptions—are the core of an organizations' culture. They are often difficult to identify and explain. They are often referred to as the organizational paradigm, where the paradigm is the set of assumptions held in common and taken for granted. They represent collective experience without which, members of the organization would have to 'reinvent their world' for different circumstances that they face.

One way of exploring organizational cultures is to classify them into types. These types are usually tied to a particular structure and design of organization. A role culture has a typical pyramid structure. A task culture has flexible matrix structures. A power culture has web-like communications structure.

◆ Role Cultures—are highly formalized, bound with regulations and paperwork an authority and hierarchy dominate relations.

◆ Task Cultures—are the opposite; they preserve a strong sense of the basic mission of the organization and teamwork is the basis on which jobs are designed.

◆ Power Cultures—have a single power source, which may be an individual or a corporate group. The control of rewards is a major source of power.

Corporate culture is really a kind of image for the company which top management would like to project. The image of the organization differs according to where you view it. Even in companies with strong cultures the social distance between senior management and shop floor reality can be very wide. Cultures are hardly planned or predictable; they are the natural products of social interaction and they can evolve and emerge over time. So is it valid to allow such a notion of culture to give way to a version of managed consensus? Pettigrew believes that cultures can be shaped to suit strategic ends. He has in mind the idea that organizations have the capacity to transform themselves from within. Even if cultures can be managed, is this necessarily a good thing? Willmott (1993) has fashioned a tough challenge to what he calls corporate culturalism. This is the tendency for culture to be promoted as a device for increasing corporate effectiveness.

- **Team Culture**

Lupe oversees a business division that includes sales people, engineers, researchers, and customer service staff. All teams work in different ways to accomplish their business strategies, but they also have work that is cross functional, relying on each other to get their work completed. At times, Lupe is overwhelmed at the teams' cultural differences and the impact it has on productivity and sales. She knows that each team has their own working styles, but she didn't realize how much these styles could interfere in the day-to-day operations of the division.

The sales department seems more outgoing and energetic than her engineers, who as a whole seem introverted and serious. Her researchers are detailed and scientific in nature, always questioning the tactics of the sales people. Her customer service employees are by nature people-and service friendly and always wanting to make sure everyone gets along. These departments work well, but Lupe knows that silos in the organization can hinder growth and creativity.

The example above illustrates culture at the team level. The values, beliefs, and norms of culture are present in team environments, dictating the team's operations and efficiency. Cultural norms in teams guide members in their dress and appearance, their language, how they relate to one another, and how they get along. Some teams are very serious, while others use humor in their work life. Departments, teams, or workgroups can, and will, act very differently from each other even though they are located in the same building and in the same organization. Although you might not think about personality or temperament as cultural elements, they can and do shape a team's culture.

- **Cultural Universals**

Cultural universals are learned behavior patterns that are shared by all of humanity collectively. No matter where people live in the world, they share these universal traits. Examples of such "human cultural" traits include:

1) communicating with a verbal language consisting of a limited set of sounds and grammatical rules for constructing sentences
2) using age and gender to classify people (e.g., teenager, senior citizen, woman, man)
3) classifying people based on marriage and descent relationships and having kinship terms to refer to them (e.g., wife, mother, uncle, cousin)
4) raising children in some sort of family setting
5) having a sexual division of labor (e.g., men's work versus women's work)
6) having a concept of privacy
7) having rules to regulate sexual behavior
8) distinguishing between good and bad behavior
9) having some sort of body ornamentation
10) making jokes and playing games
11) having art
12) having some sort of leadership roles for the implementation of community decisions

Source: http://anthro.palomar.edu/culture/culture_1.htm

While all cultures have these and possibly many other universal traits, different cultures have developed their own specific ways of carrying out or expressing them. For instance, people in deaf subcultures frequently use their hands to communicate with sign language instead of verbal language. However, sign languages have grammatical rules just as verbal ones do.

- **Individual Culture**

Individual cultural differences relate to your preferences for things through your personal experiences that include the influence of your family, your peers, school, media, co-workers, and so on. You may share a national culture, such as being an American, with another person and live in the same regional culture, the Midwest. You may even work with the person in the same organization and department, thus sharing an organizational and team culture, and even though you share similar interests, you will likely have differences in individual culture based on who you are and your social upbringing. The following example illustrates these individual differences:

Bao, 31 years old and Hua, 32 years old, are both Chinese American managers living in San Francisco. They both grew up in the area as third generation Chinese Americans. Both attended universities on the East Coast in the same city and majored in public policy. Bao and Hua work for a national nonprofit that funds grassroots leadership projects in Chinese-American communities in the United States. Both work in the programming department of their organization and have been there four years each.

Bao and Hua, although similar in their cultural backgrounds, have different perspectives based on their individual cultures. Bao's mother passed away while she was very young and she was raised by her father and aunts. Her father was not around because of long work hours. Bao, with the help of her aunts, raised her younger siblings. Her mother's death was a significant event in her life as she felt she did not have the mother-daughter relationship that many of her peers did. As a result she is overly protective.

Hua is the youngest child in her family. Both her parents are still alive. Hua was raised around many of her relatives who took care of her while her parents were working. She has always been given what she wanted or needed. Whenever Hua had a problem, her older siblings took care of the situation. As a result, Hua is quite relaxed in her demeanor and approach to life.

When Bao and Hua make programming decisions, Bao approaches her decision-making process from a methodical and careful perspective, always looking out for the program's and organization's needs. Hua, on the other side, is more relaxed in her approach, more willing to allow for flexibility and ambiguity.

Bao and Hua's cultural experiences have shaped them into different individuals and have impacted their managerial and leadership styles. Even though they share many similar cultural experiences, their individual cultural experiences have strong influences on them. Bao's methodical and careful decision-making processes are a result of her having to be responsible at a very early age. Hua's relaxed approach comes about because of her experiences as the youngest child and always knowing that she would be taken care of—that everything would be okay in the end.

These levels or layers of culture are important to think about and recognize, but it should also be understood that each of these cultures can be expressed in subcultures or microcultures. Not everyone acts or behaves the same in a national culture such as the United States. There are regional, county, and city differences within the national culture of being an "American." There are religious differences as well as gender cultures, ability and disability cultures, cultures revolving around sexual orientation, and even cultures centered around concepts or states of being, for example, the culture of homelessness or the culture of juvenile delinquency.

ETHNOCENTRISM

Many everyday statements reflect our attitude that our culture is best. We use terms such as *underdeveloped, backward,* and *primitive* to refer to other societies. What "we" believe is a religion; what "they" believe is superstition and mythology.

It is tempting to evaluate the practices of other cultures on the basis of our perspectives. Sociologist William Graham Sumner (1906) coined the term **ethnocentrism** to refer to the tendency to assume that one's own culture and way of life represent the norm or are superior to all others. The ethnocentric person sees his or her group as the center or defining point of culture and views all other cultures as deviations from what is "normal." Westerners who think cattle are to be used for food might look down on India's Hindu religion and culture, which view the cow as sacred. Or people in one culture may dismiss as unthinkable the mate selection or child-rearing practices of another culture. In sum, our view of the world is dramatically influenced by the society in which we were raised.

Ethnocentrism is hardly limited to citizens of the United States. Visitors from many African cultures are surprised at the disrespect that children in the United States show their parents.

2.2 Intercultural Communication

DEFINING COMMUNICATION

Simply speaking, Communication is the act of transferring information from one place to another. The relationship between language, culture and communication is quite interrelated. Culture is usually carried by the language, and language is used to communicate. Intercultural Communication will fail without a good understanding of the different cultures, and understanding is not always easy.

Generally, communication can be defined as all messages disseminated within a context and a situation (Communication, n.d.). More specifically, communication is a process that involves a sender, a receiver and a message whereby a person or group (the sender) attempts to convey information (the message) to another person or group (the receiver) through both verbal and nonverbal cues (Harris, Moran, & Moran, 2004; Klopf, 1991).

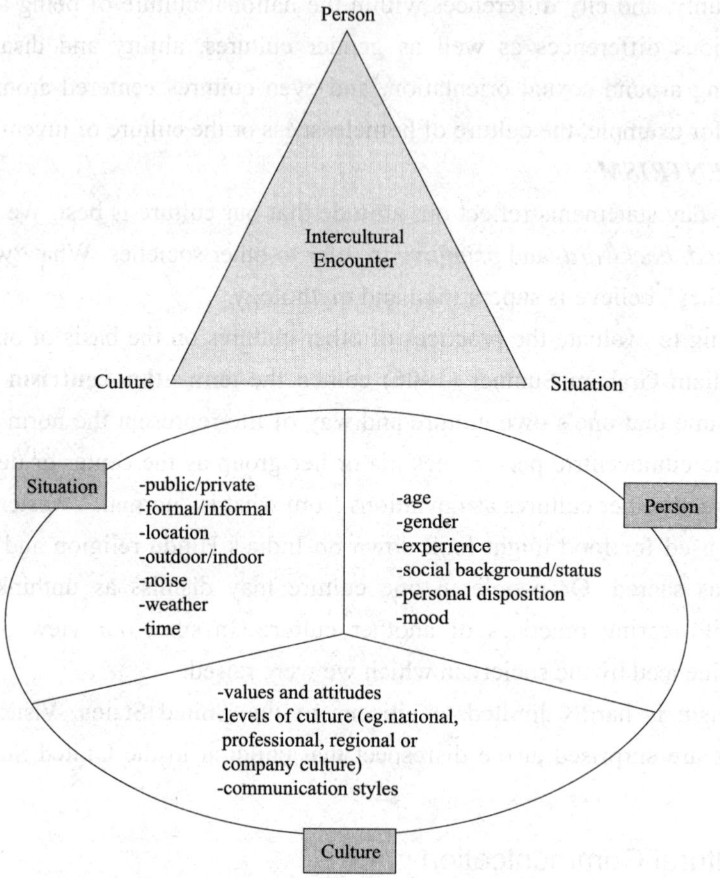

Figure 1.6 The C-P-S Model

In conceptualizing communication, Gundykunst & Kim (2003) identified at least eight assumptions involved in communication including (a) the use of verbal and non-verbal symbols to convey messages; (b) the transmission and interpretation of messages; (c) the creation of meaning; (d) different levels of awareness involved in the process; and (e) prediction of outcomes of their communication behavior.

Additionally, in writing of cross-cultural communication and communications within global organizations, Harris et al observed and emphasized that cross-cultural communication (a) occurs within a context; (b) is at the heart of all organizational operations and international relations; and (c) is "a process whereby individuals from different cultural backgrounds attempt to share meanings." Perhaps it is simplest and most useful to discuss communication by identifying its characteristics and what it is used for.

Communicating with others involves three primary steps:

◆ **Thought**: First, information exists in the mind of the sender. This can be a concept, an idea, information, or feelings.

◆ **Encoding**: Next, a message is sent to a receiver in words or other symbols.

◆ **Decoding**: Lastly, the receiver translates the words or symbols into a concept or information that he or she can understand.

As Leenen (2005: 91-92) argues, there are never purely "cultural encounters" as such, because it's not cultures that meet, but human individuals who are influenced by a complicated interplay of personal, situational and, of course, cultural factors. Therefore a particular difficulty with cultural overlap situations resides in precisely the structural uncertainty as to what the factor "culture" actually means.

CHARACTERISTICS OF COMMUNICATION

● **Process**

One characteristic of communication is that it is a process. If you have a conversation with your friend, you might think that it begins when you start talking with your friend and ends when you say good-by. However, this is not really accurate. Communication is influenced by the state of your relationship before the conversation. If, for some reason, you were angry with your friend before the conversation started, this would have an influence on the conversation. Many different aspects of the past can influence a communication event. Your past experiences in a relationship with a person may tell you whether you can believe what that person says, whether you can trust him/her to keep a secret, what topics you can discuss, and how much you need to explain.

The type of relationship before the conversation also has an effect on the way people communicate. A conversation with a stranger is very different from a conversation with a close friend. Two friends have common memories and experiences, and this affects the way they communicate. For example, you can say to your friend, "Remember the time we went ice skating?" and your friend would understand what you meant. Speaking to a stranger, much more explanation would be necessary. In some cases, close friends even invent words or uses for words, which they use as part of their private language.

In addition, your relationship after the conversation may change as a result of that very conversation. For example, if your friend apologizes for having made you angry, and you accept the apology, this will influence your future relationship. If you catch your friend in a lie, if he/she keeps a secret or is especially sympathetic over a death in your family, all of these will influence the future of your relationship. Therefore, communication even as simple as a conversation between two friends is influenced by the past and has an influence on the future, and so communication is a process.

The environment in which the communication takes place also influences the process. If you are in a noisy restaurant, you cannot have a serious, private conversation. At certain occasions, there are certain expressions that you should use. For example, at a wedding, you express congratulations and wish the couple happiness.

- **Two-way process**

Another characteristic of communication is that it is a two-way process. For simplicity, people sometimes talk about a "sender" and a "receiver" in communication. However, a sender receives messages as well as sending them, and a receiver sends messages, too. As the sender speaks, he/she adjusts the message, based on the receiver's reaction. For example, if you are explaining something and your listener looks confused, you will probably try to explain again in a different way or at least ask, "Do you understand?" If you are trying to convince your listener of something and your listener starts nodding, this will influence what you say, because you will assume that now your listener agrees with you. If your listener does not look convinced, you will continue to try to convince him/her, perhaps by giving another reason. Even a situation like public speaking or a television broadcast is, in some sense, two-way communication. If the public speaker senses that the audience is becoming restless, he/she might speak faster or go on to a new point. Though television and radio do not involve an immediate response from the listener, there are responses through letters from listeners and through ratings. As a result of the two-way nature of communication, both the speaker and the listener are responsible for the success of the communication. The listener must indicate whether he/she understands, and the speaker must adjust the message according to the listener's reactions.

- **Symbolic**

A third characteristic of communication is that it is symbolic. This means that in communication, we use one thing to stand for or represent another. Words are symbols. The word "dog" is not the dog itself; it is a symbol which represents the dog. Nonverbal communication can also involve symbols. The gesture that means "money" (a circle formed with the index finger and thumb) is a symbol for money. The symbolic nature of communication is very important. If we could not use symbols, we could not talk about objects or people that were not present. We could not talk about events that took place in the past or that would take place in the future. We could not talk about abstract concepts. Therefore, we use symbols to stand for all of these things.

PURPOSE OF COMMUNICATION

In a general sense, we use communication to achieve our goals. In order to achieve these goals, we use communication for three main purposes.

1) *Human contact* is one purpose of communication. It is important for all human beings to have contact with others. Without communication with other people, we can be very lonely.

2) *Controlling our environment* is another purpose of communication. We try to get people to do what we want (within limits) or arrange our situation the way we want it (balancing it with the desires of other people in the situation) by communicating. If you are unhappy with something another person is doing, you might complain to that person about that behavior, and you hope to control your environment that way. If you like something another person is doing, you might say so, which encourages the person to repeat or continue the behavior.

3) A third purpose of communication is *exchanging information*. Most human activities require us either to give information to others or to get information ourselves. Communication allows us to do this.

As you can see from these three functions, communication is crucial to our daily lives.

BARRIERS TO COMMUNICATION

There exist many barriers to communication and these may occur at any stage in the communication process. Barriers may lead to your message becoming distorted and you therefore risk wasting both time and/or money by causing confusion and misunderstanding. Effective communication involves overcoming these barriers and conveying a clear and concise message. A skilled communicator must be aware of these barriers and try to reduce their impact by continually checking understanding and by offering appropriate feedback.

Some common barriers to effective communication include:

- The use of jargon. Over-complicated or unfamiliar terms.
- Emotional barriers and taboos.
- Lack of attention, interest, distractions, or irrelevance to the receiver.
- Differences in perception and viewpoint.

◆ Physical disabilities such as hearing problems or speech difficulties.

◆ Physical barriers to non-verbal communication.

◆ Language differences and the difficulty in understanding unfamiliar accents.

◆ Expectations and prejudices which may lead to false assumptions or stereotyping. People often hear what they expect to hear rather than what is actually said and jump to incorrect conclusions.

◆ Cultural differences. The norms of social interaction vary greatly in different cultures, as do the way in which emotions are expressed. For example, the concept of personal space varies between cultures and between different social settings.

Language Barriers: Clearly, language and linguistic ability may act as a barrier to communication. However, even when communicating in the same language, the terminology used in a message may act as a barrier if it is not fully understood by the receiver(s). For example, a message that includes a lot of specialist jargon and abbreviations will not be understood by a receiver who is not familiar with the terminology used. Regional colloquialisms and expressions may be misinterpreted or even considered offensive.

Psychological Barriers: The psychological state of the receiver will influence how the message is received. For example, if someone has personal worries and is stressed, they may be preoccupied by personal concerns and not as receptive to the message as if they were not stressed. Stress management is an important personal skill that affects our interpersonal relationships. Anger is another example of a psychological barrier to communication. When we are angry it is easy to say things that we may later regret and also to misinterpret what others are saying. More generally people with low self-esteem may be less assertive and therefore may not feel comfortable communicating—they may feel shy about saying how they really feel or read negative sub-texts into messages they hear.

Physiological Barriers: Physiological barriers may result from the receiver's physical state. For example, a receiver with reduced hearing may not grasp to entirety of a spoken conversation especially if there is significant background noise.

Physical Barriers: An example of a physical barrier to communication is geographic distance between the sender and receiver(s). Communication is generally easier over shorter distances as more communication channels are available and less technology is required. Although modern technology often serves to reduce the impact of physical barriers, the advantages and disadvantages of each communication channel should be understood so that an appropriate channel can be used to overcome the physical barriers.

Systematic Barriers: Systematic barriers to communication may exist in structures and organisations where there are inefficient or inappropriate information systems and communication channels, or where there is a lack of understanding of the roles and responsibilities for communication. In such organisations, individuals may be unclear of their role in the communication process and therefore not know what is expected of them.

Attitudinal Barriers: Attitudinal barriers are behaviours or perceptions that prevent people from communicating effectively. Attitudinal barriers to communication may result from personality conflicts, poor management, resistance to change or a lack of motivation. Effective receivers of messages should attempt to overcome their own attitudinal barriers to facilitate effective communication.

VERBAL AND NONVERBAL COMMUNICATION

- **Verbal Communication**

Humans are pack animals. Our ancestors hunted and gathered as a collective, depending upon one another for protection, sustenance and companionship. Our success as a species and as individuals depends upon our ability to effectively communicate, both verbally and non-verbally. Verbal and non-verbal communication shapes our interactions with others in business and interpersonal relationships, as well as our financial and personal success, and our physical and psychological well-being. Understanding the different aspects of verbal and non-verbal communication, and the important roles they play in our interactions with others, is the first step to enhancing positive communication and nurturing relationships.

Verbal communication refers to the use of sounds and language to relay a message. It serves as a vehicle for expressing desires, ideas and concepts and is vital to the processes of learning and teaching. In combination with nonverbal forms of communication, verbal communication acts as the primary tool for expression between two or more people. Verbal communication encompasses any form of communication involving words, spoken, written or signed. The conversation we have with our coworker at lunch, the morning news or the sports page we read in the morning—even the text message you send to your spouse telling him to pick up some milk is a form of verbal communication. Our ability to communicate with a language that is based on an organized system of words, rather than merely sounds, is what sets us apart from lower species. Not only do we have language, but we also have the technology that enables us to communicate with one another no matter the physical distance.

We use verbal communication to inform, whether it is to inform others of our needs or to impart knowledge. Clarification is a key component of verbal communication. Often, we do not articulate ourselves clearly, or our words or actions are misconstrued. Verbal communication helps to clarify misunderstandings and provides missing information.

We can use verbal communication to correct a wrong. The power of the words, "I'm sorry," is often more effective than an action. Verbal communication can also be used as a tool of persuasion. It creates an opportunity for debate, stimulates thought and creativity, and deepens and creates new relationships. Robert M. Krauss explains that a species' survival depends critically upon its ability to communicate effectively, and the quality of its social life is determined in large measure by how and what it can communicate.

Interpersonal communication and public speaking are the two basic types of verbal communication. Whereas public speaking involves one or more people delivering a message to a group, interpersonal communication generally refers to a two-way exchange that involves both talking and listening. Signs and symbols are the major signals that make up verbal communication. Words act as symbols, and signs are secondary products of the underlying message and include things like tone of voice, blushing and facial expressions.

Verbal communication has many purposes, but its main function is relaying a message to one or more recipients. It encompasses everything from simple one-syllable sounds to complex discussions and relies on both language and emotion to produce the desired effect. Verbal communication can be used to inform, inquire, argue and discuss topics of all kinds. It is vital to teaching and learning, as well as forming bonds and building relationships with other people. Although all species communicate, language itself is a purely human phenomenon that allows for more precision than the communication methods of other beings.

A variety of challenges may arise when using verbal communication to express oneself. Misunderstandings can arise because of poor word choice, differing perspectives and faulty communication techniques, and subjective opinions regarding acceptable language may result in breakdowns in communication. Language barriers are a major cause of confusion when attempting to communicate verbally. According to the University of Louisville, differences in language influenced by geographic location, education and social status can create barriers even among those who speak the same language.

Although difficulties with verbal communication can't be completely avoided, it is possible to increase your chances of communicating successfully. Consider the message you wish to communicate before speaking and communicate with respect from the recipient's point of view. Pay attention to what you say and how you say it. Speak clearly and enunciate your words and be conscious of nonverbal aspects such as eye contact, posture and facial expressions.

Everyone has a unique style of communicating and perceiving messages. Although verbal communication is a primary means of expression, nonverbal actions such as body language can greatly affect the way a message is perceived.

- **Non-verbal Communication**

If you don't like the way a meeting is going, you might suddenly sit back, fold your arms, and turn down the corners of your mouth. When you see a friend in tears, you may give a quick hug. After winning a big game, you probably high-five your teammates. These are all examples of *nonverbal communication*—the use of gestures, facial expressions, and other visual images to communicate.

Like other forms of language, nonverbal communication is not the same in all cultures. For example, sociological research done at the micro level documents that people from various cultures differ in the degree to which they touch others during the course of normal social interactions. Even experienced travelers are sometimes caught off guard by these differences. In Saudi Arabia, a middle-aged man may want to hold hands with a partner after closing a business deal. In Egypt, men walk hand in hand in the street; in cafés, they fall asleep while lounging in each other's arms. These gestures, which would shock an American businessman, are considered compliments in those cultures. The meaning of hand signals is another form of nonverbal communication that can differ from one culture to the next. In Australia, the thumbs-up sign is considered rude. We are not born with these expressions. We learn them, just as we learn other forms of language, from people who share our same culture. This statement is as true for the basic expressions of happiness and sadness as it is for more complex emotions, such as shame or distress.

Verbal communication coexists alongside non-verbal communication, which can affect people's perceptions and exchanges in subtle but significant ways. Non-verbal communication includes body language, such as gestures, facial expressions, eye contact and posture. Touch is a non-verbal communication that not only indicates a person's feelings or level of comfort, but illustrates personality characteristics as well. A firm handshake or warm hug indicates something very different from a loose pat on the back or a timid handshake does. The sound of our voice, including pitch, tone and volume is also forms of non-verbal communication. The meaning behind someone's words is often entirely different from the literal translation, as is seen in instances of sarcasm and mockery. The clothing we wear and the way we design our living space are also forms of non-verbal communication that frequently shape people's judgments about others, regardless of whether or not the perceptions are true.

Think of how many relationships start with a man and woman making eye contact across a crowded room. A playful wink tends to be more effective than a well-thought out pick-up-line. There are five main functions of non-verbal communication: to express emotions, communicate interpersonal relationships, support verbal interaction, reflect personality and perform rituals, such as greetings and goodbyes. We can reinforce, contradict, substitute, complement or emphasize our verbal communication with non-verbal cues such as gestures, expressions and vocal inflection. Avoiding eye contact when we tell someone we love them communicates something far different than do spoken words, just as a bright smile when we say congratulations reinforces the sincerity of our words.

Verbal communication is enhanced when a person is an effective listener. Listening doesn't simply mean hearing; it necessitates understanding another person's point of view. Take the time to think before you speak to ensure that you articulate yourself clearly. Let other people interject and have the floor. Allow time for reflection on the subject at hand. Watching other people's body language, facial expressions and intonations, and being conscious of your own physicality and feelings can enhance non-verbal communication. Record yourself with both a video camera and an audio recorder to see how you communicate non-verbally. Are your gestures matching your words, or giving away what you're really thinking? Being aware of what we say and how we say it is the first step to successful communication. The ability to adapt quickly to the situation and form of communication at hand is a skill that people continue to hone for a lifetime.

When we communicate, non-verbal cues can have as great an impact on the listener as the spoken word. There are many different aspects of non-verbal communication including:

Body Movements (Kinesics): Body movements include gestures, posture, head and hand movements or whole body movements. Body movements can be used to reinforce or emphasise what a person is saying and also offer information about the emotions and attitudes of a person. However, it is also possible for body movements to conflict with what is said. A skilled observer may be able to detect such discrepancies in behaviour and use them as a clue to what someone is really feeling. Research work has identified the different categories of body movement that are detailed below with each category describing the purpose they commonly serve:

Emblems: Gestures that serve the same function as a word are called emblems. For example, the signals that mean "OK", "Come here!" or the hand movement used when hitch-hiking. However, be aware that whilst some emblems are internationally recognised, others may need to be interpreted in their cultural context.

Illustrators: Gestures which accompany words to illustrate a verbal message are known as illustrators. For example, the common circular hand movement which accompanies the phrase "over and over again", or nodding the head in a particular direction when saying "over there".

Affect Displays: These are facial expressions or gestures which show the emotions we feel. These are often unintentional and can conflict with what is being said. Such expressions give strong clues as to the true emotional state of a person.

Regulators: Gestures used to give feedback when conversing are called regulators, for example head nods, short sounds such as "uh-huh", "mm-mm", and expressions of interest or boredom. Regulators allow the other person to adapt his or her speech to reflect the level of interest or agreement. Without receiving feedback, many people find it difficult to maintain a conversation.

Adaptors: Non-verbal behaviours which either satisfy some physical need such as scratching or adjusting uncomfortable glasses, or represent a psychological need such as biting fingernails when nervous. Although normally subconscious, adaptors are more likely to be restrained in public places than in the private world of individuals where they are less likely to be noticed. Adaptive behaviours often accompany feelings of anxiety or hostility.

Posture: Posture can reflect people's emotions, attitudes and intentions. Research has identified a wide range of postural signals and their meanings, such as Open and Closed Posture, which may reflect an individual's degree of confidence, status or receptivity to another person. Someone seated in a closed position might have his/her arms folded, legs crossed or be positioned at a slight angle from the person with whom they are interacting. In an open posture you might expect to see someone directly facing you with hands apart on the arms of the chair. An open posture can be used to communicate openness or interest in someone and a readiness to listen, whereas the closed posture might imply discomfort or disinterest.

Mirroring: Notice the way a loving couple relate to each other. You might like to observe a close relationship in person or on television. You will see that the partners' postures will match, as if one partner is a mirror reflection of the other. For example, if one partner drapes an arm over the back of a chair this might be replicated in the other person's position. If one partner frowns, it could be reflected in the other partner's facial expression. This "mirroring" indicates interest and approval between people and serves to reassure others of interest in them and what they are saying.

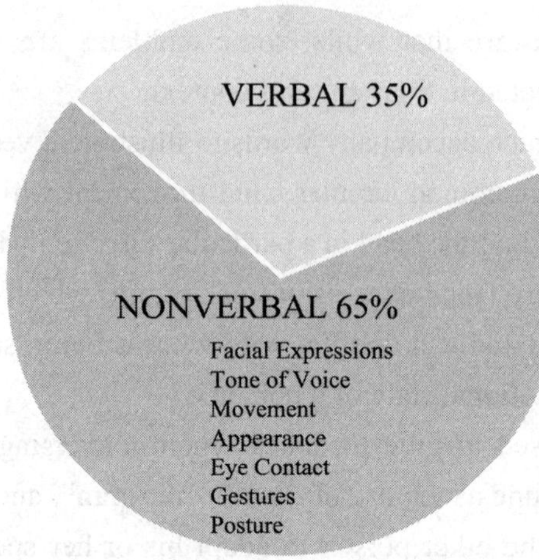

Figure 1.7 Verbal and Nonverbal Communication by Percentage
(***Source: http://kingpinlifestyle.com/5-classic-b e/ody-language-tips-are-you-forgetting-thes***)

Eye Contact: Eye contact is an important aspect of non-verbal behaviour. In interpersonal interaction, it serves three main purposes:

1) To give and receive feedback: Looking at someone lets them know that the receiver is concentrating on the content of their speech. Not maintaining eye contact can indicate disinterest. Communication may not be a smooth process if a listener averts their eyes too frequently.

2) To let a partner know when it is their "turn" to speak: This is related to the above point. Eye contact is more likely to be continuous when someone is listening, rather than speaking. When a person has finished what they have to say, they will look directly at the other person and this gives a signal that the arena is open. If someone does not want to be interrupted, eye contact may be avoided.

3) To communicate something about a relationship between people: When you dislike someone, you tend to avoid eye contact and pupil size is often reduced. On the other hand, the maintenance of positive eye contact signals interest or attraction in a partner.

Paralanguage: Paralanguage relates to all aspects of the voice which are not strictly part of the verbal message, including the tone and pitch of the voice, the speed and volume at which a message is delivered, and pauses and hesitations between words. These signals can serve to indicate feelings about what is being said. Emphasising particular words can imply whether or not feedback is required.

Closeness and Personal Space: Every culture has different levels of physical closeness appropriate to different types of relationship, and individuals learn these distances from the society in which they grew up. In today's multicultural society, it is important to consider the range of non-verbal codes as expressed in different ethnic groups. When someone violates an "appropriate" distance, people may feel uncomfortable or defensive. Their actions may well be open to misinterpretation.

In Western society, four distances have been defined according to the relationship between the people involved. The study of personal space is termed Proxemics. This term was used by the anthropologist Edward Twitchell Hall (1963).

1) Intimate Distance (touching to 45cm): It ranges from close contact (touching) to the "far" phase of 15-45cm. In British society, it tends to be seen as an inappropriate distance for public behaviour and, as mentioned above, entering the intimate space of another person with whom you do not have a close relationship can be extremely disturbing.

2) Personal Distance (45cm to 1.2m): The "far" phase of personal distance is considered to be the most appropriate for people holding a conversation. At this distance it is easy to see the other person's expressions and eye movements, as well as their overall body language. Handshaking can occur within the bounds of personal distance.

3) Social Distance (1.2m to 3.6m): This is the normal distance for impersonal business, for example working together in the same room or during social gatherings. Seating is also important; communication is far more likely to be considered as a formal relationship if the interaction is carried out across a desk. In addition, if the seating arrangements are such that one person appears to look down on another, an effect of domination may be created. At a social distance, speech needs to be louder and eye contact remains essential to communication, otherwise feedback will be reduced and the interaction may end.

4) Public Distance (3.7m to 4.5m): Teachers and public speakers address groups at a public distance. Exaggerated non-verbal communication is necessary if effective communication is to occur. Since subtle facial expressions are lost at this distance so clear hand gestures are often used as a substitute. Larger head movements are also typical of an experienced public speaker who is aware of changes in the way body language is perceived at longer distances.

These four distances are associated with the four main types of relationship—intimate, personal, social and public. Each of the distances are divided into two, giving a close phase and a far phase, thus making eight divisions in all. It is worth noting that these distances are considered the norm in Western Society.

Understanding these distances allows us to approach others in non-threatening and appropriate ways. People can begin to understand how others feel about them, how they view the relationship and, if appropriate, adjust their behaviour accordingly.

As you can see, non-verbal communication is an extremely complex yet integral part of overall communication skills. People are often totally unaware of the non-verbal behaviour they use. A basic awareness of these aspects of communication strategies, over and above what is actually said, can help to improve interaction with others. Knowledge of these signs can be used to encourage individuals to talk about their concerns and can lead to a greater shared understanding.

INTERCULTURAL COMMUNICATION

Intercultural communication is, literally, communication between people of different cultures. As the world becomes smaller, people of different countries come into contact more and more often, and the study of intercultural communication has become more important. In addition, within one country, there are often people of different subcultures, and so they are also included in the study of intercultural communication. For example, in the United States, Italian-Americans—Americans whose ancestors came from Italy—sometimes have patterns of communication that are different from those of other Americans, and a study of those differences would be included in intercultural communication.

In the study of intercultural communication, there are various areas of study. There is sometimes a distinction made between intercultural communication and cross-cultural communication. According to this distinction, cross-cultural communication involves the study of similar communication situations or behaviors in different cultures. Intercultural communication, in contrast, involves the study of the process of communication between people from different cultures. A study related to cross-cultural communication might be a study of how closely Japanese sit or stand when they talk with other Japanese people, and how closely Americans sit or stand when they talk with each other. In contrast, an intercultural communication study might look at how closely Americans and Japanese sit or stand when they talk with each other.

Approaches to studying intercultural communication can be divided into two types—culture specific and culture general. Culture-specific approaches to intercultural communication deal with communication between people of two specific cultures. For example, a course training American students who are preparing to go to Japan would deal specifically with Japanese culture and the types of problems Americans living in Japan might have. A culture-general approach, in contrast, would deal with intercultural communication in a more general way, looking at various theories of intercultural communication and the types of problems that are likely to come up when people of different cultures come into contact.

- **Message Transmission Between Cultures**

The problems in intercultural communication usually come from problems in message transmission. In communication between people of the same culture, the person who receives the message interprets it based on values, beliefs, and expectations for behavior similar to those of the person who sent the message. When this happens, the way the message is interpreted by the receiver is likely to be fairly similar to what the speaker intended. However, when the receiver of the message is a person from a different culture, the receiver uses information from his or her culture to interpret the message. The message that the receiver interprets may be very different from what the speaker intended.

Whether the message is misinterpreted depends, in part, on how different the cultures are. An American and an English-speaking Canadian are likely to have a lot of cultural beliefs, values, and knowledge in common—though there are differences between them. An American and a French-speaking Canadian come from cultures that are slightly more different. An American and a German are more different, and an American and a person from China even more so. However, the situation is not really so simple. A Chinese farmer and an American farmer may have many differences between them—language, religion, philosophy, and social attitudes, for example—but they would also be likely to have things in common. In fact, they would probably have things in common that the American farmer would not have in common with, for example, an American doctor.

Differences in culture can cause difficulties in communication. While not all of these difficulties are avoidable, there are some possible solutions to these problems.

1) It is important for the people from different cultures involved in communication to have a sincere desire to understand each other. They must also avoid thinking of cultures as being superior or inferior.

2) It is also important to know about the other culture when communicating with a person of that culture. Knowing, for example, something about what gestures mean and what some of the general beliefs and values of the culture are can help reduce communication problems.

3) It is also useful to understand something about one's own culture and one's own basic cultural assumptions in order to see where they might be different from those of the people of another culture.

- **Models of Intercultural Communication**

Models are very useful in helping us to understand intercultural communication in general. They serve several functions, including: providing a visual representation of a process so that we can better understand it (descriptive function); summarizing research in an area, especially if the model is "theoretical" or is based on actual research (for example, a model on communication accommodation theory that shows which factors might lead one to adjust behavior); helping to understand where or how a communication breakdown has occurred (the troubleshooting function). Several influential models are introduced below.

Neuliep (2008) proposes a new line of argument with respect to contextualising intercultural communication but no new conceptualisation of basic concepts. His model presents a series of mutually dependent contexts, graphically represented by a series of concentric circles. Neuliep commences his presentation with the outermost circle of the model—the cultural context—and moves inward, chapter by chapter, towards more specific contexts of communication: microcultural, environmental, and then, within this last, two perceptual contexts. These refer to the individual characters of communicators from different cultures. The shared area between the two represents socio-relational context, the relationship between the communicators. The model argues that intercultural communication is defined by the interdependence of these various contexts.

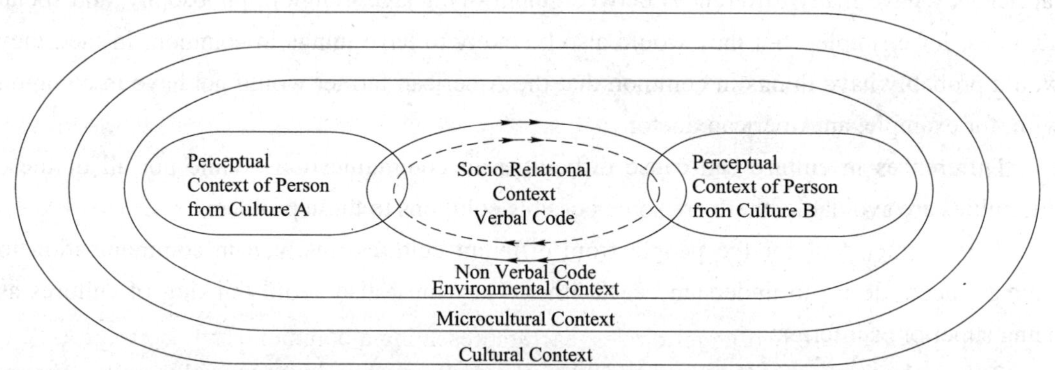

Figure 1.8 Neuliep's Contextual Model of Intercultural Communication

A dialectical approach emphasizes the processual, relational, and contradictory nature of intercultural communication. In other words, you will encounter many different kinds of intercultural knowledge. For example, some culture-specific information will tell you how closely people in that culture tend to stand to each other. Other studies will give you historical background that might help explain certain antagonisms felt toward and by members of that culture. A dialectical approach to intercultural interaction emphasizes the processual character of understanding. Cultures change and so do individuals. In this dynamic mixture, we cannot assume that someone has particular characteristics simply because he or she belongs to a certain culture. We change over our lifetime, and this dynamic nature of personhood needs to be considered in intercultural communication. It also emphasizes the relational rather than individual, the relationship between aspects of intercultural communication, and the importance of viewing these holistically and not in isolation. Besides it stresses the importance of relationship in intercultural communication encounters. A more challenging aspect of the dialectical approach is that it requires holding two contradictory ideas simultaneously. In contrast, a dialectical approach recognizes a need to transcend these dichotomies.

- Cultural ←→ Individual
- Personal ←→ Social-Contextual
- Differences ←→ Similarities
- Static ←→ Dynamic
- Present-future ←→ History-past
- Privilege ←→ Disadvantage

Figure 1.9 Martin & Nakayama's Dialectical Approach to Intercultural Communication

Gudykunst & Kim's Model of Intercultural Communication

William Gudykunst felt that the central issue in intercultural and intergroup communication was the ability for people to control ("manage") their levels of uncertainty ("cognitive" ability to explain and predict the behavior of the other person) and anxiety ("affective" or "emotional" apprehension, fear of different things that might occur in the interaction, such as looking stupid, being rejected and so on). If one could control these, one would have better shared understanding (which Gudykunst calls effectiveness) and will be better able to adapt. In G&K model, there are two larger circles, each representing a communicator. Between the two individuals are lines of sending and receiving verbal and nonverbal messages. Gudykust and Kim argue that when we create or process messages, we use four different filters. (1) Cultural: it refers to all elements of shared perception, including Values, Beliefs, World View, Rules, Norms, and Definitions. (2) Sociocultural: it regards aspects of group identity, specifically things like: Roles and Social identities. (3) Psychocultural: it regards aspects of the individual mind, includes Prejudice, stereotypes, Uncertainty, anxiety, Mood, attitude, perception of the other. (4) Environmental: all of the communication occurs in an environmental context. This includes Situation/location, Geography/climate, and "Interaction potential".

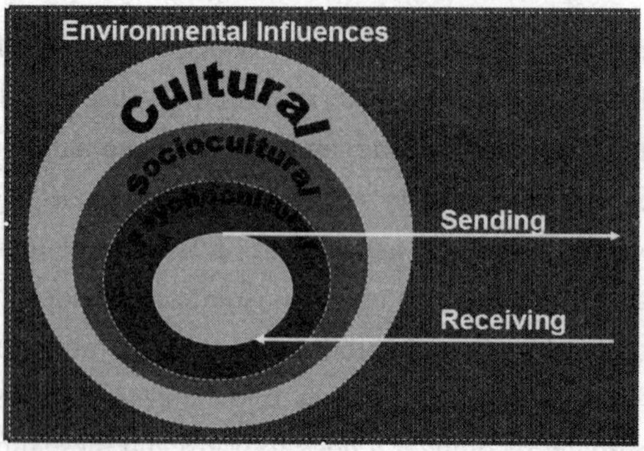

Figure 1.10 Gudykunst & Kim's Model of Intercultural Communication

Samovar & Porter (1997) point out that as cultures differ from one another, the communication practices and behaviors of people will inevitably vary as a result of their different perceptions of the world. Intercultural communication, more precisely then, is defined as the study of communication between people whose "cultural perceptions and symbol systems are distinct enough" to alter their communication. In their model of intercultural communication, they illustrate the process of how the meaning of a message changes when it is encoded by a person in one culture and decoded by a person in another culture in the context of his or her own cultural background. In some cases, the message may be interpreted to carry a different meaning than was intended.

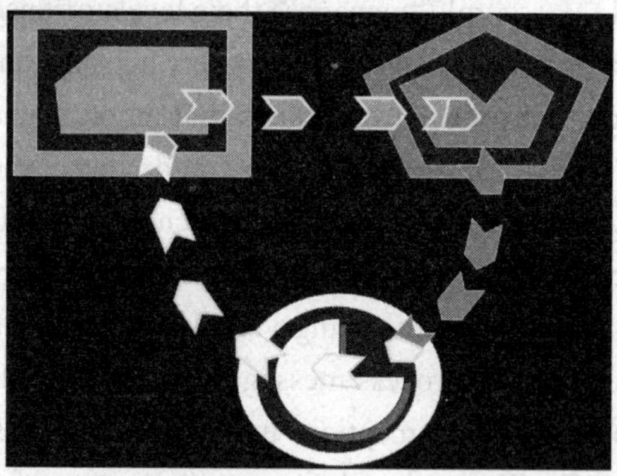

Figure 1.11 Samovar & Porter's Model of Intercultural Communication

Baldwin & Hecht (2003). Baldwin (Baldwin & Hunt, 2002; Baldwin & Hecht, 2003) argue that intercultural communication (where real differences in values, beliefs, behaviors, etc., impinge upon the interaction, regardless of the communicators' awareness of the effect of culture) and intergroup communication (where communicators perceive there to be differences, based on perceptions of in-groups, outgroups, including stereotypes and prejudice) should be teased apart and treated separately. Instead, Baldwin and Hecht conceive of interactions where: One can perceive there to be differences (for example, because the person looks different), when in fact there are no real cultural differences (high intergroup, low intercultural). Or one might perceive there to be no differences, because the partners look alike and see each other from the same group, when in fact, there are cultural differences they are not aware of (such as from different regions of the U.S., or from urban and rural cultures). They, instead, propose a 3-axis model. It is actually 3-dimensional, and is difficult to draw on paper, but the dotted axis would be perpendicular to the other three:

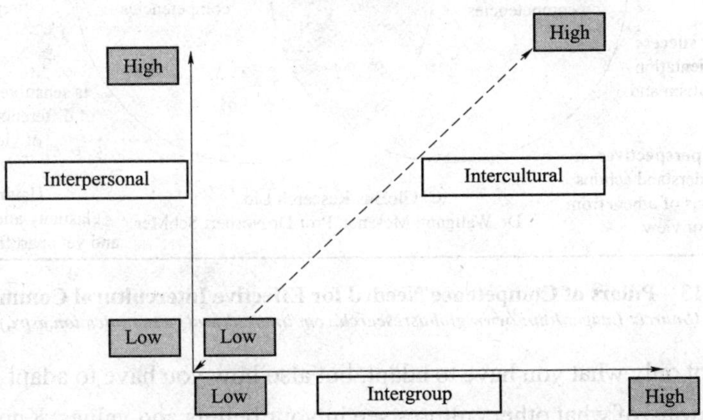

Figure 1.12 Baldwin's Model of Intercultural Communication

- **Pillars of Competence Needed for Effective Intercultural Communication**

In order for the intercultural communication to be effective, one has to evolve his affective, behavioural and cognitive competences, as illustrated on the following image. The three pillars of competences can each be further decomposed into sub-branches. These branches are all linked to cultural beliefs and values which will be different depending on the culture that is being applied. However, the image also visualizes how cultural differences can be overcome and how they can be turned into advantages.

Affective Competencies: The first important aspect that will determine the modification of one's affective competencies starts with self-awareness. This self-awareness involves two aspects. First of all you have to know what you have to adapt. In other words, it is important that you are above all fully aware of your own values and beliefs. This knowledge is necessary in

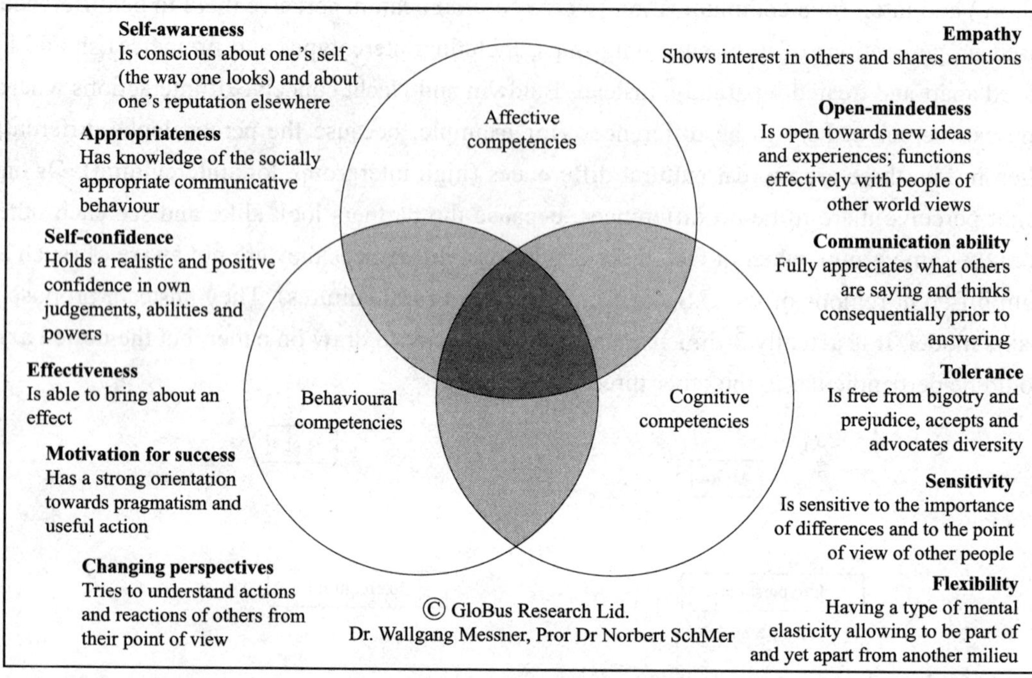

Figure 1.13 Pillars of Competence Needed for Effective Intercultural Communication
(*Source: Image: http://www.globusresearch.com/intercultural communication.aspx,*)

order to know not only what you have to adapt, but also how you have to adapt it. Secondly, you also have to be aware of what other cultures see in your beliefs and values. Knowing this, it will be easier to know the extent to which one has to adapt its affective competencies. Important to mention is the fact that self-awareness has to go in combination with self-confidence. When cultures collide one cannot has the intention of having one culture completely dominating the other culture. This will not lead to effective intercultural communication. These personal affective competences have to be in combination with the affective competences focusing on the other culture. In order to have effective intercultural communication, the personal affective competences have to be "radiated" to the outside. This can be fulfilled through empathy and open-mindedness. Showing a high level of empathy will help creating interest towards the beliefs and values of the other culture. However, empathy alone is not enough, it has to go in hand with open-mindedness. Being open-minded means not only that you show interest in others' beliefs and values, but also that you are willing to open yourself to personally learn from these new ideas and experiences. This open-mindedness will be the first step to follow in order to communicate effectively with people of a different culture.

Cognitive Competencies: The cognitive competencies form the second pillar of personal competences for intercultural communication. The first important branch is the ability of communication. Being able to communicate is not simply being able to say what you have to say towards the other. In order to have effective intercultural communication, your words have to show respect and appreciation towards the thoughts and expression of the other person. This communication ability is based on tolerance, sensitivity and flexibility. Being tolerant towards another culture means avoiding prejudices and opening your mind towards diversity. The higher your level of sensitivity, in other words your understanding of the point of view of others and its ground reasons, the easier you will find the achieving of tolerance. All these will lead to you being a flexible partner of communication, which brings us back to the first branch of cognitive competences: the ability of communication.

Behavioural Competencies: The affective and cognitive competences concerning self-awareness, open mindedness and the communication ability will affect and maybe even form the base for one's general behaviour in the situation of intercultural communication. The behaviour shown will determine to a great extent the effectiveness of intercultural communication. The correct behaviour should be growing out of a motivation for changing perspectives and success. The meaning of effective communication is creating an action reaction situation. If you respect the changing perspectives created in this situation, in other words if you understand the action of the other person because of his point of view, this can have another effect on your reaction will be.

3. Exercises

I. How many cultural components from the list below can you identify in these six photos?

Religion	Language	Architecture	Cuisine	Technology	Music
Dance	Sports	Medicine	Dress	Gender roles	Law
Education	Government	Agriculture	Economy	Sport	Marriage
Friends	Family	Trade	Holiday	Pets	Dining
Values	Work ethic	Etiquette	Courtship	Recreation	Gestures

II. Try to Identify Regional Cultural Differences and Similarities.

Regional Culture Names	Cultural Expression	Regional Differences	Regional Similarities
	Food		
	Dress code		
	Language		
	Housing		

continued

Regional Culture Names	Cultural Expression	Regional Differences	Regional Similarities
	Music		
	Sports		
	Friendship		
	Business		
	Marriage		

III. Try to explain the following terms in your own words.

1. Intercultural communication
2. Culture (from intercultural communication perspective)
3. Verbal/Non-verbal Communication
4. Acculturation
5. Euphemism

IV. Translation

It has been argued that when cultures and subcultures interact, they (not always peacefully) *negotiate* meanings and values in a way that facilitates co-existence, adaptation and, eventually, mutual cooperation. The degrees of interaction between dominant and minority cultures would go from the simple diffusion of innovations (a single artifact or cultural practice is adopted by the "receiving" culture) to cultural domination (a whole set of beliefs, norms and cultural values is imposed by the dominant to the minority culture). In the case of contact resulting from immigration, one might encounter cultural processes occurring in intermediary stages, such as acculturation, assimilation, integration, separation and marginalization.

Acculturation, for one, is an umbrella term that encompasses the different processes (and stages) resulting from the contact between two different cultural groups. Acculturation happens "when two independent groups come into continuous first-hand contact over an extended period of time, resulting in changes in either or both cultural groups". In each case, groups and individuals would have to answer the questions: "Is it considered to be of value to maintain contact with other groups?" and "Is it considered to be of value to maintain cultural identity and characteristics?" By answering yes or no to those questions, the acculturation process could take four different routes: assimilation, integration, separation and marginalization.

Assimilation happens when the group (or individual) does not value retention of its own identity, but instead values assimilation of the other group's values. Integration happens when the group considers both identities equally important. Separation means considering one's own culture important, but avoiding contact with other groups. And marginalization refers to saying no to your own culture, as well as to the host culture. Immigrant groups have provided researchers with a myriad of patterns and cultural characteristics that exemplify all of the acculturation routes outlined here. The difference in acculturation patterns has been related to education, socioeconomic status, mastery of the host language, and consumption of both ethnic and host mass media.

V. Group Discussion

In the following case, what mistakes have been made regarding the gift?

Lin Bao recently moved to Los Angeles as a sales representative for an international conglomerate. He has already been able to bring new business to the company by developing professional relationships with several new clients. He knows it's important to do a good job and provide good service to these clients so they will continue doing business with him rather than the competitors.

It's early December and Lin Bao knows this is the season many businesses give gifts to their clients. The gifts are usually not extravagant, but a gesture to show appreciation for a client's business. Lin Bao has one client named Ann in Beverly Hills who's been very nice to work with, and he wants to buy her a nice gift. So he buys a bottle of perfume, has it gift wrapped in paper that's red with pictures of Santa Clause, then takes it back to his office and places it on his desk so he can deliver it to Ann the next day.

Lin Bao's manager enters his office:

Manager: Lin Bao who's the gift for?

Lin Bao: It's for my client Ann.

Manager: That's nice of you to buy her a holiday gift, but we haven't known Ann very long so I recommend you re-wrap it in different paper. It's best to select either a plain color without any Christmas artwork, or one with a winter scene, perhaps gold or silver metallic. And, by the way what did you buy as the gift? Remember we have a price limit on gifts we can purchase for clients.

Lin, Bao: Yes, I read the company regulations and the gift doesn't exceed the price limit. I bought a small bottle of perfume.

Manager: I'm afraid you'll have to return it to the store and select another gift.

4. References

1. Clifford, J G. The Interpretation of Cultures: Selected Essays [M]. New York: Basic, 1973.
2. David, L. Leading with Cultural Intelligence: The New Secret to Success [M]. Los Angles: AMACOM, 2009.
3. Edward, G W. The Importance of Effective Communication, Ph.D. paper, Boston: Northeastern University, 2012.
4. Edgar, H S. Organizational Culture and Leadership [M]. San Francisco: Jossey-Bass, 4th Edition, 2010.
5. Gudykunst, W. & Kim, Y. Y. Communicating With Strangers: An Approach to Intercultural Communication [M]. 4th ed. New York: McGraw-Hill Humanities/Social Sciences/Languages, 2002.
6. Myron, W. L. & J. Koester. Intercultural Competence: Interpersonal Communication Across Cultures [M]. New York: HarperCollins College Publishers, 1996.
7. Chen, G. M. & W. J. Starosta. Foundations of Intercultural Communication [M]. 2nd ed. Lanham: University Press of America, 2005.
8. Hall, E. T. A System for the Notation of Proxemic Behavior [J]. *American Anthropologist* 65 (5). 1963: 1003-1026.
9. Harris, R. M. & Moran, S. Managing Cultural Differences: Global Leadership Strategies for the Twenty-First Century, 6e. [M] Burlington, MA: Elsevier Butterworth- Heinemann, 2004.
10. Hofstede, G. H. Culture's Consequences: International Differences in Work-Related Values. Beverly Hills [M]. CA: Sage Publications, 1980.
11. Hofstede, G. H. Cultures and Organizations: Software of the Mind [J]. *Administrative Science Quarterly* (Johnson Graduate School of Management), Ithaca: Cornell University, 1993.
12. Hugh, W. Strength Is Ignorance; Slavery Is Freedom: Managing Culture in Modern Organizations [J]. Manchester School of Management, UMIST, *Journal of Management Studies* 30:4. 1993: 0022-2380.
13. James, W. N. Intercultural Communication: A Contextual Approach [M]. 4th edition. Thousand Oaks: Sage Publications, 2008.
14. Jenkins, G. Klopf, D. & Park, M-S. Argumentativeness in Korean and American college

students. Paper presented at the World Communication convention, Jyvaskyla, Finland, 1991.

15. Leenen, Wolf-Rainer, H. Grosch & A. Groß, eds. Bausteine zur interkulturellen Qualifizierung der Polizei [M]. Münster: Waxmann, 2005.
16. Martin, J.N., & Nakayama, T.K. Intercultural Communication in Contexts [M]. Mountain View, CA: Mayfield, 1997.
17. Meharbian, A. Silent Messages [M]. Belmond, CA: Wadsworth, 1971.
18. Pettigrew, AM, Woodman, RW, & Cameron, KS. Studying Organizational Change and Development: Challenges for Future Research [J]. *The Academy of Management Journal,* Vol. 44, No. 4, 2001.
19. Robert M. K. The Psychology of Verbal Communication [J]. *The International Encyclopedia of Social and Behavioral Sciences*, Amsterdam: Elsevier Science Ltd, 2002.
20. Samovar, L.A., & Porter, R.E. Communication between Cultures [M]. Belmont, CA: Wadsworth, 1991.
21. Samovar, L.A., & Porter, R.E. (Eds.) Intercultural Communication: A Reader [M]. eighth ed. Belmont, CA: Wadsworth, 1997.
22. Wang, M. M., Brislin, R., Wang, W., Williams, D., & Chao, J. H. Turning bricks into jade: Critical incidents for mutual understanding among Chinese and Americans [M]. Yarmouth, ME: Intercultural Press, 2000.

Chapter 2

Theories and Research on Intercultural Communication

Culture hides more than it reveals, and strangely enough what it hides, it hides most effectively from its own participants.

—Edward T. Hall

Culture provides people with an implicit theory about how to behave and how to interpret the behavior of others. People from different cultures learn different implicit theories. These theories are learned through socialization. And through socialization, individuals also learn the dominant values of their particular culture and their self-identities.

—Australian anthropologist Roger Keesing

1. Lead-in

CASE 1

Remember the joke about the cruise ship captain who has to convince the passengers of his sinking ship to jump overboard? He has to use a different approach with each nationality—He tells the English it would be unsporting of them not to jump, the French that it would be the smart thing to do, the Germans that it is an order, the Japanese that it is a matter of honor and the Italians that jumping overboard is forbidden.

CASE 2

To raise awareness of different cultures, Dr. Kaminsky (the founder and President of MALKAM Cross-Cultural Training in Canada) used a "diversity quiz" which challenged participants to think about differences in culture between people of different nations, religions, working and family structures. One of a number of examples used was:

Q: Why do not mothers in cultures such as Indian, Thai, some African or South American want somebody to compliment their new baby?

A: In these cultures this can be seen to bring bad luck.

The challenge was neatly described in the words of one participant: "The *culture quiz* really made me aware of how much I do not know."

2. Main Text

A brief review of some influential intercultural scholars and theories.

2.1 Edward T. Hall's Value Orientations

An Intercultural Conversation: In the following exchange, Mr. Hutchinson is the head of Information Technology within his organization. Mr. Wong is lead computer programmer. Mr. Wong was born and raised in Malaysia, a high-context culture. The two are discussing when Mr. Wong will put a computer program into production. Note that Mr. Hutchinson's speech is direct and to the point while Mr. Wong's is indirect and subtle. In simple frequency, Mr. Hutchinson uses four times as many words as Mr. Wong.

Hutchinson: *The program looks good and passed the test run with only minor errors. When do you think you can put it into production? I don't see any production schedule here. The changes need to go into the system by the end of the month. Is that possible? When do you want to go with this?*

Wong: *Maybe I should review the requirements.*

Hutchinson: *The errors were minor. Quality Control needs to know when it will go into production. Let's set the production date now. Just tell me when you'll fix the errors. I'll tell QC.*

Wong: *Perhaps I can e-mail you an estimate. I'll talk to the team.*

Hutchinson: *Couldn't you just tell me when you'll have them fixed? Here, it's no big deal.*

	(Hands Mr. Wong the program) Don't they seem like easy fixes?
Wong:	*(Looks at the program but says nothing—as if not hearing Mr. Hutchinson's suggestion)*
Hutchinson:	*Mr. Wong? Just give me a date.*
Wong:	*Yes. Whenever you prefer is fine. (Hands the program back to Mr. Hutchinson)*
Hutchinson:	*I don't need this. (Hands it back to Mr. Wong) Well, it's got to go in by the first of next month. OK?*
Wong:	*Yes, that is fine.*

In the above dialogue, Mr. Hutchinson misses the hint that Mr. Wong is unable to set a production date. When Mr. Wong indicates that setting a date is difficult and will require some expertise, he is indirectly telling Mr. Hutchinson that he is not in a position to make the decision on his own and would prefer to discuss it with the team. Mr. Wong further signals his discomfort by telling Mr. Hutchinson that he could e-mail him the date. Mr. Hutchinson ignores Mr. Wong's status in the organization and further complicates the issue by handing Mr. Wong the program. Trying to avoid any disagreement, Mr. Wong simply asks Mr. Hutchinson to set the date for production and agrees to whatever he says.

HIGH-AND LOW-CONTEXT CULTURE

In order to distinguish among cultures, high-context culture and the contrasting low-context culture are terms presented by the anthropologist Edward T. Hall in his 1976 book *Beyond Culture*. High-context culture refers to a culture's tendency to use high-context messages over low-context messages in routine communication. This choice of communication styles translates into a culture that will cater to in-groups, an in-group being a group that has similar experiences and expectations, from which inferences are drawn. In a high-context culture, many things are left unsaid, letting the culture explain. Words and word choice become very important in higher-context communication, since a few words can communicate a complex message very effectively to an in-group (but less effectively outside that group), while in a lower-context culture, the communicator needs to be much more explicit and the value of a single word is less important. Highly mobile environments where people come and go need lower-context culture. With a stable population, however, a higher-context culture may develop. An individual moving to a higher- or lower-context culture may need to adapt and/or be accommodated in ways different than moving within cultures of similar context.

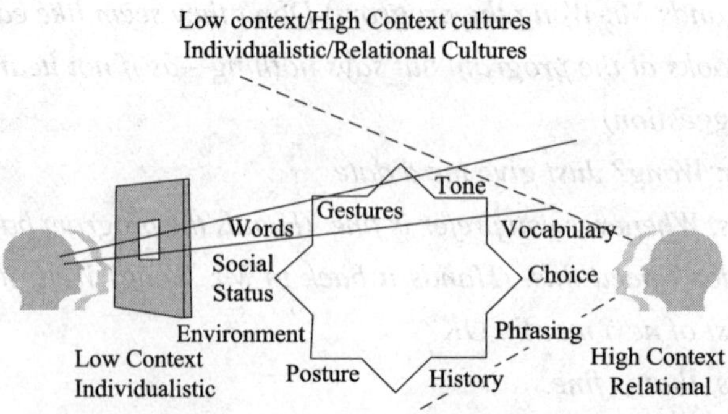

Figure 2.1 Adapted from *Managing Intercultural Difference by Claire B. Anderson*

High-context cultures (including much of the Middle East, Asia, Africa, and South America) are relational, collectivist, intuitive, and contemplative. This means that people in these cultures emphasize interpersonal relationships. Developing trust is an important first step to any business transaction. According to Hall, these cultures are collectivist, preferring group harmony and consensus to individual achievement. And people in these cultures are less governed by reason than by intuition or feelings. Words are not so important as context, which might include the speaker's tone of voice, facial expression, gestures, posture—and even the person's family history and status. Examples:

✧ A Japanese manager explained his culture's communication style to an American: "We are a homogeneous people and don't have to speak as much as you do here. When we say one word, we understand ten, but here you have to say ten to understand one." High-context communication tends to be more indirect and more formal. Flowery language, humility, and elaborate apologies are typical.

✧ Small religious congregations, a party with friends, family gatherings, expensive gourmet restaurants and neighborhood restaurants with a regular clientele, undergraduate on-campus friendships, regular pick-up games, hosting a friend in your home overnight are all examples of high-context situation.

Low-context cultures (including North America and much of Western Europe) are logical, linear, individualistic, and action-oriented. People from low-context cultures value logic, facts, and directness. Solving a problem means lining up the facts and evaluating one after another. Decisions are based on fact rather than intuition. Discussions end with actions. And communicators are expected to be straightforward, concise, and efficient in telling what action is expected. To be absolutely clear, they strive to use precise words and intend them to be taken literally. Explicit contracts conclude negotiations. This is very different from communicators in high-context cultures who depend less on language precision and legal documents. High-context business people may even distrust contracts and be offended by the lack of trust they suggest. Examples: large US airports, a chain supermarket, a cafeteria, a convenience store, a motel, sports where rules are clearly laid out.

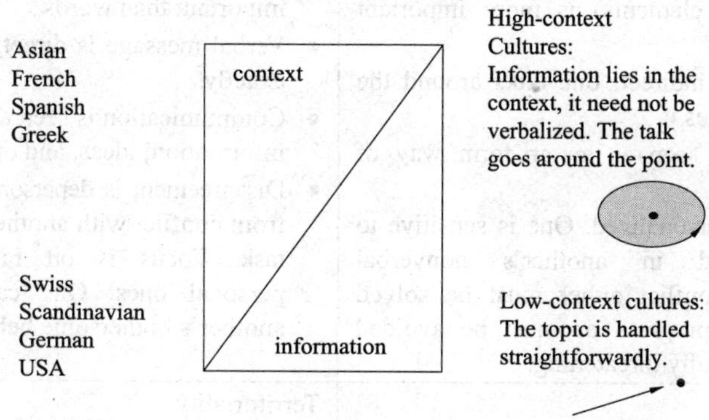

Figure 2.2 Cultures at the opposite ends of the high- and low-context continuum.

The list below shows the kind of behavior that is generally found in high- and low-context cultures within five categories: how people relate to each other, how they communicate with each other, how they treat space, how they treat time, and how they learn. One thing to remember is that few cultures, and the people in them, are totally at one end of the spectrum or the other. They usually fall somewhere in between and may have a combination of high and low context characteristics.

Table 2.1 High-and Low-Context Culture in Comparison

HIGH CONTEXT (HC)	LOW CONTEXT (LC)
Association	Association
• Relationships depend on trust, build up slowly, are stable. One distinguishes between people inside and people outside one's circle.	• Relationships begin and end quickly. Many people can be inside one's circle; circle's boundary is not clear.
• How things get done depends on relationships with people and attention to group process.	• Things get done by following procedures and paying attention to the goal.
• One's identity is rooted in groups (family, culture, work).	• One's identity is rooted in oneself and one's accomplishments.
• Social structure and authority are centralized; responsibility is at the top. Person at top works for the good of the group.	• Social structure is decentralized; responsibility goes further down (is not concentrated at the top).

continued

HIGH CONTEXT (HC)	LOW CONTEXT (LC)
Interaction • High use of nonverbal elements; voice tone, facial expression, gestures, and eye movement carry significant parts of conversation. • Verbal message is implicit; context (situation, people, nonverbal elements) is more important than words. • Verbal message is indirect; one talks around the point and embellishes it. • Communication is seen as an art-form way of engaging someone. • Disagreement is personalized. One is sensitive to conflict expressed in another's nonverbal communication. Conflict either must be solved before work can progress or must be avoided because it is personally threatening.	Interaction • Low use of nonverbal elements. Message is carried more by words than by nonverbal means. • Verbal message is explicit. Context is less important than words. • Verbal message is direct; one spells things out exactly. • Communication is seen as a way of exchanging information, ideas, and opinions. • Disagreement is depersonalized. One withdraws from conflict with another and gets on with the task. Focus is on rational solutions, not personal ones. One can be explicit about another's bothersome behavior.
Territoriality • Space is communal; people stand close to each other, share the same space.	Territoriality • Space is compartmentalized and privately owned; privacy is important, so people are farther apart.
Temporality • Everything has its own time. Time is not easily scheduled; needs of people may interfere with keeping to a set time. What is important is that activity gets done. • Change is slow. Things are rooted in the past, slow to change, and stable. • Time is a process; it belongs to others and to nature.	Temporality • Things are scheduled to be done at particular times, one thing at a time. What is important is that activity is done efficiently. • Change is fast. One can make change and see immediate results. • Time is a commodity to be spent or saved.
Learning • Knowledge is embedded in the situation; things are connected, synthesized, and global. Multiple sources of information are used. Thinking is deductive, proceeds from general to specific. • Learning occurs by first observing others as they model or demonstrate and then practicing. • Groups are preferred for learning and problem solving. • Accuracy is valued. How well something is learned is important.	Learning • Reality is fragmented and compartmentalized. One source of information is used to develop knowledge. Thinking is inductive, proceeds from specific to general. Focus is on detail. • Learning occurs by following explicit directions and explanations of others. • An individual orientation is preferred for learning and problem solving. • Speed is valued. How efficiently something is learned is important.

Source: *The 1993 Annual: Developing Human Resources*. Pfeiffer & Company.

ASSESSING HIGH-AND LOW-CONTEXT COMMUNICATION

Communication researcher William Gudykunst and his colleagues have developed a survey designed to measure low- and high-context communication styles. The instrument that follows is an adaptation of Gudykunst's scale.

Low-and High-Context Communication Scale

Directions: *Below are 32 statements regarding how you feel about communicating in different ways. In the blank to the left of each item, indicate the degree to which you agree or disagree with each statement. If you are unsure or think that an item does not apply to you, enter a 5 in the blank.*

Strongly Disagree	1	2	3	4	5	6	7	8	9	Strongly Agree

_____ 1. I catch on to what others mean, even when they do not say it directly.

_____ 2. I show respect to superiors, even if I dislike them.

_____ 3. I use my feelings to determine whether to trust another person.

_____ 4. I find silence awkward in conversation.

_____ 5. I communicate in an indirect fashion.

_____ 6. I use many colorful words when I talk.

_____ 7. In argument, I insist on very precise definitions.

_____ 8. I avoid clear-cut expressions of feelings when I communicate with others.

_____ 9. I am good at figuring out what others think of me.

_____ 10. My verbal and nonverbal speech tends to be very dramatic.

_____ 11. I listen attentively, even when others are talking in an uninteresting manner.

_____ 12. I maintain harmony in my communication with others.

_____ 13. Feelings are a valuable source of information.

_____ 14. When pressed for an opinion, I respond with an ambiguous statement/position.

_____ 15. I try to adjust myself to the feelings of the person with whom I am communicating.

_____ 16. I actively use a lot of facial expressions when I talk.

_____ 17. My feelings tell me how to act in a given situation.

_____ 18. I am able to distinguish between a sincere invitation and one intended as a gesture of politeness.

_____ 19. I believe that exaggerating stories makes conversation fun.

_____ 20. I orient people through my emotions.

_____ 21. I find myself initiating conversations with strangers while waiting in line.

_____ 22. As a rule, I openly express my feelings and emotions.

_____ 23. I feel uncomfortable and awkward in social situations where everybody else is talking except me.

_____ 24. I readily reveal personal things about myself.

_____ 25. I like to be accurate when I communicate.

_____ 26. I can read another person "like a book."

_____ 27. I use silence to avoid upsetting others when I communicate.

_____ 28. I openly show my disagreement with others.

_____ 29. I am a very precise communicator.

_____ 30. I can sit with another person, not say anything, and still be comfortable.

_____ 31. I think that untalkative people are boring.

_____ 32. I am an extremely open communicator.

Scoring: *Reverse your score for Items 4, 6, 7, 10, 16, 19, 21, 22, 23, 24, 25, 28, 29, 31, and 32. If your original score was 1, reverse it to a 9; if your original score was a 2, reverse it to an 8; and so on. After reversing the score for those 15 items, simply sum the 32 items. Lower scores indicate low-context communication. Higher scores indicate high-context communication.*

SOURCE: Reprinted from Gudykunst, Matsumoto, Ting-Toomey, Nishida, Kim, & Heyman, "The Influence of Cultural Individualism-Collectivism, Self Construals, and Individual Values on Communication Styles Across Cultures," in Human Communication Research, 22, 1996, pp. 510-543. Reproduced with permission of Oxford University Press, Inc. via Copyright Clearance Center.

2.2 Kluckhohn's and Strodtbeck's Value Orientations

Hall provides a distinctive starting point for his analysis—namely, identifying communication as the underlying factor in explaining culture and culture difference—it is evident that his work has produced some findings similar to those of the other writers. Indeed the underlying issues dealt with in Hall's work could be seen to have their antecedents in Kluckhohn and Strodtbeck's fundamental problems, *like how to conceptualize time* and *how to deal with others*.

People's attitudes are based on the relatively few, stable values they hold. Kluckhohn and Strodtbeck's (1961) Values Orientation Theory proposes that all human societies must answer a limited number of universal problems, that the value-based solutions are limited in number and universally known, but that different cultures have different preferences among them. They set out to operationalise a theoretical approach to the values concept developed by Florence's husband, Clyde Kluckhohn (1949, 1952). He argued that humans share biological traits and characteristics which form the basis for the development of culture, and that people typically feel their own cultural beliefs and practices are normal and natural, and those of others are strange, or even inferior or abnormal. He defined a value as: "A conception, explicit or implicit, distinctive of an individual or characteristic of a group, of the desirable which influences the selection from available modes, means and ends of action." (Kluckhohn, 1951, p395). Kluckhohn and Strodtbeck described the value orientation profiles of five SW USA cultural groups. Their theory has since been tested in many other cultures, and used to help negotiating ethnic groups understand one another, and to examine the inter-generational value changes caused by migration.

Florence Kluckhohn and Fred Strodtbeck suggested five basic types of problem to be solved by every society:

1) What is the character of *human nature (*good, bad ("Evil") or a mixture*)*?

2) What is the relation of humankind to *nature (*mastery, submission or harmony*)*?

3) What is the orientation toward *time (*primarily focus—past, present or future*)*?

4) What is the orientation toward *activity (*the prime motivation for behaviour—to express one's self ("Being"), to grow ("Being-in-becoming"), or to achieve?*)*?

5) What is the relationship of *people* to each other (hierarchically (which they call "Lineal"), as equals ("Collateral"), or according to their individual merit)?

They also suggested a sixth value dimension of Space (Here, There, or Far Away) but did not explore it further. Nonetheless, it should be recognized that the sixth problem—how to relate to space—was not fully incorporated into their findings (French, 2008).They then spelled out the possible answers to each of the questions, arguing that the preferred answer in any society reflects the basic *orientation* of the society to that aspect of its environment. There are three possible responses for each question:

Table 2.2 **Five Basic Types of Problems**

Range of Values	Response 1	Response 2	Response 3	Description
Human nature	Basically good	Mixture of good and evil	Basically evil	What do people assume about the basic nature and beliefs about other people? "Good" here is in the traditional sense of being socially oriented and basically pretty good at heart. A bad person is thus considered selfish. Most people can't be trusted. People are basically bad and need to be controlled. Mixture means there are both evil people and good people in the world, and you have to check people out to find out which they are. People can be changed with the right guidance. How you think about other people in this way will have significant effect on how you respond to them. It also affects how you think about yourself.
Relationship between humans and nature	Humans dominate	Harmony between the two	Nature dominates	What do people think about nature and their responsibilities and rights around it? Some people believe that we should live in harmony with nature, preserving and supporting it and exercise partial but not total control by living in a balance with the natural forces. Others (and perhaps a majority now) see nature as our servant and supplier. This view allows us to plunder it without concern. In other parts of life this translates into the use of all kinds or resource and whether it is used up or sustained and we are subject to the higher power of these forces.
Time orientation	Future-oriented	Present-oriented	Past-oriented	Which is more important: past, present or future? Some societies focus on the past, ancestors and traditionalism. Others are focused on the hedonism of today, accommodating changes in beliefs and traditions, whilst still others plan carefully for the future, seeking new ways to replace the old.

continued

Range of Values	Response 1	Response 2	Response 3	Description
Activity orientation	"Doing": stress on action	"Growing": stress on spiritual growth	"Being": stress on who you are	What is the primary mode of activity in an organization or a society? In some societies, there is an internal focus on "being", where *who you are* is more important than *what you do*, emphasising activity valued by ourseloes but not necessarily by others in the group. Being-in-becoming Motivation is to develop and grow in abilities which are valued by us, although not necessarily by others. Achievement ("Doing") motivation is external to us, emphasising activity that is both valued by ourselves and is approved by others in our group.
Relation-ships between people	Individual	Group-oriented	Collateral	What duty do we have towards others? Should we act first to support others or can we just focus only on ourselves? Considering the group first supports a society, but it also is limiting on the freedom of the individual. It also raises the question about who chooses what is right for the group. Hierarchical ("Lineal") Emphasis on hierarchical principles and group benefits and deferring to higher authority or authorities within the group. Equal ("Collateral") Emphasis on consensus within the extended group of equals. Individualistic Emphasis on the individual or individual families within the group who make decisions independently from others.
Space Orientation	Here/ private	There/ Public	Far away Private-mixed-public	How is space treated in a society? Who owns it? What rights do people have to occupy it? One approach is that space is owned by individuals and privacy is important. Meetings are held behind closed doors and are by invitation only. The alternative is open ownership, where people can go where they please and meetings are open to all who want to attend.

2.3 Geert Hofstede's National Value Dimensions

Starting with IBM 1970s: If all engineers are working in the same company and having the same education but still behave very differently, there must be cultural differences.

Geert Hofstede has operated in an international environment since 1965, and his curiosity as a social psychologist led him to the comparison of nations, first as a traveling international staff member of a multinational (IBM) and later as a visiting professor at an international business school in Switzerland. His 1980 book *Culture's Consequences* combined his personal experiences with the statistical analysis of two unique data bases. The first and largest comprised answers of matched employee samples from 40 different countries to the same attitude survey questions. The second consisted of answers to some of these same questions by his executive students who came from 15 countries and from a variety of companies and industries. Systematic differences between nations in these two data bases occurred in particular for questions dealing with values. Values, in this case, are "broad preferences for one state of affairs over others", and they are mostly unconscious.

In December 1980, just after the first edition of *Culture's Consequences* had been published. Hofstede met Michael Harris Bond from the Chinese University of Hong Kong. Bond and a number of his colleagues from the Asia-Pacific region had just finished a comparison of the values of female and male psychology students from each of 10 national or ethnic groups in their region. They had used an adapted version of the Rokeach Value Survey developed by US psychologist Milton Rokeach on the basis of an inventory of values in US society around 1970. When Bond analyzed the RVS data in the same way as Hofstede had analyzed the IBM data, he also found four meaningful dimensions. Across the six countries that were part of both studies, each RVS dimensions significantly correlated with one of the IBM dimensions (Hofstede & Bond, 1984, 1988). The discovery of similar dimensions in completely different materials represented strong support for the basic nature of what was found. With another questionnaire, other respondents (students instead of IBM employees), at another point in time (data collected around 1979 instead of 1970), and a restricted group of countries, FOUR similar dimensions emerged. Subsequent work by Bond and the Chinese Cultural Connection (1987) developing the Chinese Values Survey and the Long-term/Short-term (LTO/STO) dimension is well known. LTO/STO was originally named "Confucian Dynamism" but was subsequently identified in non-Confucian heritage societies and officially renamed in Hofstede (1991) and further developed in Minkov and Hofstede (2012).

Cultural value dimensions help you to understand culture and to be able to make sense of culture. These dimensions provide you with a perspective of culture for yourself as well as a perspective of how others perceive their culture. All cultures experience these dimensions of difference in many ways, and different cultures solve these differences in many ways. Becoming aware of these concepts helps you to figure out the experiences you have in relation to your culture. It helps to make that experience less ambiguous and threatening. Cultural value dimensions provide clarity and a starting place for cultural awareness. However, they are often seen as intangible and under the waterline, but once you adapt to the cultural dimensions, you become more comfortable and do not see the cultural difference.

These dimension are acquired through "mental programming", learned patterns of thinking, feeling and potential acting.

Three level of uniqueness are distinguished:

1) The inherited universal human nature,

2) The learned culture specific to certain societies or groups within a society, and

3) The inherited and learned individual personality.

The first four dimensions are listed below.

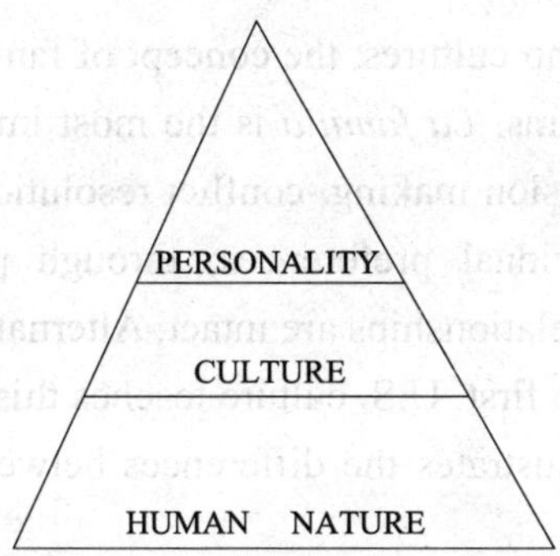

Table 2.3 Four Cultural Value Dimensions

Value Dimensions	One Extreme	Other Extreme
Identity	Group	Individual
Power	Egalitarian	Hierarchical
Gender	Feminine	Masculine
Uncertainty	Ambiguity	Structure

IDENTITY

The value dimension of identity refers to the attention of groups or individuals toward group needs versus individual needs as well as toward individual achievement and interpersonal relationships. On a continuum, you see the identity value dimension expressed as such in Figure 2.3 "Dimension of Identity".

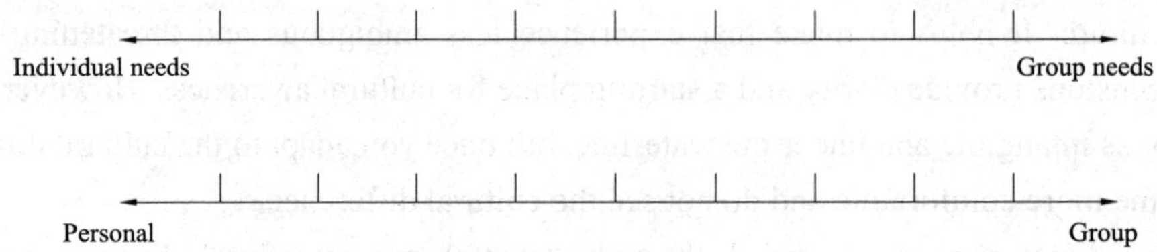

Figure 2.3 Dimension of Identity

On one spectrum, there is an expectation of doing things for the group rather than for oneself. On the other side, achievements and needs are individualized. Hofstede (2001) found that cultures placing a high value on individualism and a low value on collectivism valued individual rights; cultures placing a high value on collectivism valued relationships and harmony. This orientation, he argued, can have a large affect on managing organizations and people.

For example, in many Latino cultures, the concept of family, *la familia*, is critical to their cultural history and social systems. *La familia* is the most important social unit and includes extended family members. Decision making, conflict resolution, and negotiation are based on group needs rather than individual preferences; through paying attention to group and collective needs, harmony and relationships are intact. Alternatively, in individualistic cultures, the need of the individual comes first. U.S. culture teaches this to children at a young age. The following is an example that illustrates the differences between individualist and collectivist cultures:

Mary takes her eight-year-old, Johnny, to the store to buy ice-cream. She asks him to choose what ice-cream flavor he would like. Over time he learns to tell his mother about his personal likes and dislikes. Every time his mother responds to his decisions with encouragement. Over time he learns that he can and should be able to express himself.

By encouraging her child to make decisions and choices on his own, Mary raises a child that considers his personal needs and wants. If Johnny was in a group that operated more collectively, he might become quite upset when told that the whole group must agree to a specific ice cream flavor, that is, that his personal choice does not matter in the group decision.

Individualism and collectivism refer to the extent of which an individual is free to express himself or herself independently of their group or cultural society (Olausson et al, 2009, p. 3; Fowler p. 3). "A high IDV score indicates a loose connection with people [whereas] a society with a low IDV score would have strong group cohesion, and there would be a large amount of loyalty and respect for members of the group" (Mindtools).In short this cultural dimension looks at how much a culture does or does not value hierarchical relationships and respect for authority.

Positive words for an individualistic culture are positive connotation: self, friendship, "do your own thing," contract, litigation, self-interest, self-respect, self-actualizing, individual, dignity, I, me, pleasure, adventure, guilt, and privacy. These same words have a negative connotation in a collectivist culture. The words with a positive connotation for a collectivist culture (and negative for an individualistic culture) are: harmony, face, obligation, sacrifice, family, tradition, decency, honor, duty, loyalty, and shame.

The following are some other examples that illustrate the value differences between collectivist and individualist cultures:

✧ *An American history teacher gives a lesson on the Bill of Rights to her students. She explains that everyone has individual rights and liberties. Sahara is a student in the class. She is thirteen years old and a recent immigrant from Somali. She learns that she has individual rights and to the disappointment and frustration of her parents, her behaviors begin to change at home. She comes home late from school, she stops doing her chores, and she talks back to her mother. She says, "I can do whatever I want. In America, I am free!"*

✧ *Sahara comes from a culture that is collective and tribal in nature. Her parents express confusion when they hear her say, "I can do whatever I want." They do not understand what she means and why she says what she says. They begin to think that she is losing her cultural values.*

✧ *Tabitha is 22 years old and moves in with her college boyfriend, Randy, to an apartment near her parents. Tom and Susan, Tabitha's parents, are excited that she is able to be independent and to live on her own.*

✧ *Xioli is Tabitha and Randy's friend from college. She is Chinese American and wants to move out of her parents' house. Randy and Tabitha have offered the second bedroom space for Xioli in their apartment. Xioli's parents think she is too young to live on her own. They also think it is a sign of disrespect to them if she, as a single woman, lives with a man.*

Individualist cultures include the United States and much of Western Europe, where personal achievements are emphasised. Collectivist cultures, such as China, Korea, and Japan, emphasize the group such as the family and at work this manifests in a strong work group mentality.

So how does this manifest in a culture or country?

In a country that scores highly on the individualism scale the following traits are common:

◆ A person's identity revolves around the "I".

◆ Personal goals and achievements are strived for.

◆ It is acceptable to pursue individual goals at the expense of others.

◆ "Individualism" is encouraged whether it be personality, clothes or music tastes.

◆ The right of the individual reign supreme; thus laws to protect choices and freedom of speech.

In a country that scores low on the individualism scale the following traits are common:

◆ "We" is more important than "I".

◆ Conformity is expected and perceived positively.

◆ Individual's desires and aspirations should be curbed if necessary for the good of the group.

◆ The rights of the family (or for the common good) are more important.

◆ Rules provide stability, order, obedience.

POWER

Power distance (PD) refers to the degree or extent that members of a certain society tolerate inequality in power distribution (Olausson Stafstrom, and Svedin, 2009, p. 9; Fowler, p. 2). A high PD score indicates that society accepts an unequal distribution of power and people understand "their place" in the system. Low PD means that power is shared and well dispersed. It also means that society members view themselves as equals. (Mindtools, 2009). On a continuum, you see the power value dimension expressed as such in Figure 4 "Dimension of Identity".

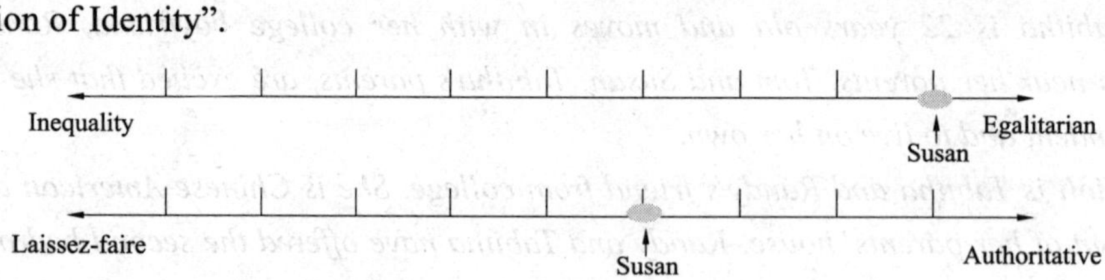

Figure 2.4 Power Value Dimension

Positive words for high power distance culture are "respect, father, master, servant, older brother, younger brother, wisdom, favor, protect, obey, orders, and pleasing." These same words have a negative connotation for a low power distance index culture. The words with a positive connotation for a low power distance index culture (and negative for high power distance index culture) are "rights, complain, negotiates, fairness, necessity, codetermination, objectives, question, and criticize."

Examples of cultures with high PDI scores include Arabic speaking countries, Russia, India and China. Those with low scores include Japan, Australia and Canada.

So how does this manifest in a culture or country?

In a high power distance culture the following may be observed:

◆ Those in authority openly demonstrate their rank.

◆ Subordinates are not given important work and expect clear guidance from above.

◆ Subordinates are expected to take the blame for things going wrong.

◆ The relationship between boss and subordinate is rarely close/personal.

◆ Politics is prone to totalitarianism.

◆ Class divisions within society are accepted.

In a low power distance culture:

◆ Superiors treat subordinates with respect and do not pull rank.

◆ Subordinates are entrusted with important assignments.

◆ Blame is either shared or very often accepted by the superior due to it being their responsibility to manage.

◆ Managers may often socialise with subordinates.

◆ Liberal democracies are the norm.

◆ Societies lean more towards egalitarianism.

An Intercultural Conversation between Large and Small Power Distance Cultures:

Different power distance orientations manifest themselves in interaction. In the dialogue below, Jim Neuman is a U.S. high school exchange student in Guatemala. Coming from a smaller power distance culture, Jim is accustomed to interacting with his teachers. Raising one's hand in a U.S. classroom is not only acceptable but encouraged. In Guatemala, a larger power distance culture, the classroom is teacher centered. In Mr. Gutierrez's classroom, there is strict order, with Mr. Gutierrez initiating all the communication. Teachers are to be treated with deference.

Mr. Gutierrez: This morning I will be discussing some points about Guatemala's geography. Guatemala is the northernmost country of Central America. (Jim Neuman raises his hand) To the north it borders the countries of El

Salvador and Honduras. To the west, its natural border is the Pacific Ocean. In the east is another natural border, the Atlantic Ocean, as well as the country of Belize.

Jim Neuman: *(Raising his hand and waving it slightly) Mr. Gutierrez?*

Mr. Gutierrez: *Guatemala is called the "Land of the Eternal Spring." There are all the same kinds of natural land forms as in Mexico but are (Jim Neuman interrupts)—*

Jim Neuman: *Mr. Gutierrez, I have a question.*

Mr. Gutierrez: *Jim, stop interrupting, please.*

Jim Neuman: *May I ask a question?*

Mr. Gutierrez: *No! If you continue to disobey, I will punish you! Be quiet!*

In the above dialogue, Jim does not understand Mr. Gutierrez's harsh reprimand. Coming from a small power distance culture, Jim recognizes that teachers have more power than students but does not see their power as absolute. Jim sees himself as an active participant of the class. After all, for most of his life Jim's teachers have encouraged him to speak up in class. Mr. Gutierrez, on the other hand, sees the classroom as his domain, one that he rules absolutely. By raising his hand, Jim demonstrates his insolence toward Mr. Gutierrez. To some extent, a certain degree of power distance is essential if cultures are to survive. Legitimate power is a necessity of civil life. Yet independence from power, liberation, and freedom of choice are politically attractive alternatives. Perhaps the ideal situation is one where individual families operate with internally driven large power distances while the larger cultural milieu restricts overbearing, omnipotent, and intimidating governments.

GENDER

Hofstede (2001) describes the value dimension of gender as representing two paradigms of thinking and practice about the world in relation to traditional values associated with gender roles. Gender refers to the culture's tendencies or orientation toward enforcing or reinforcing masculine and feminine roles in work. Masculine cultures tend to emphasize ambition, control, competition, assertiveness, and achievement, whereas feminine cultures emphasize nurture, care, sharing, quality of life, and relationships. Sometimes these values are expressed as the "quantity of life" and the "quality of life."

Positive words for masculine cultures are "career, competition, fight, aggressive, assertive, success, winner, deserve, merit, excel, force, big, fast, tough, quantity, total, power and action". These words have a negative connotation for a feminine culture. The words with a positive connotation for feminine cultures (and negative for masculine culture) are "caring, solidarity, modesty, compromise, help, love, grow, small, soft, slow, tender, and touch."

Masculinity is one of the least understood cultural dimensions as many people tend to associate it with masculinity literally. In essence it looks at the degree to which "masculine" values like competitiveness and the acquisition of wealth are valued over "feminine" values like relationship building and quality of life. This cultural factor refers to how much a society sticks with, and values, traditional male and female roles. High masculinity scores are found in countries where men are expected to be tough, to be the provider, to be assertive and to be strong. If women work outside the home, they have separate professions from men. Low masculinity scores do not reverse the gender roles. In a low masculinity society, the roles are generally blurred. You see women and men working together equally across many professions. Men are allowed to be sensitive and women can work hard for professional success. (Mindtools, p. 1; Fowler, p. 3; Dimensions, p. 171).

Hofstede never meant to describe how gender empowerment differs in a culture but rather uses the term "masculinity" to capture certain propensities. If one looks at the cultures with a low masculinity rating they will notice that many also have low gender equality, i.e. Middle East. The terms relate to nurturing (feminine) versus assertive (masculine) behaviours and ideals. In his findings, Hofstede indicated that cultures that rate high in masculinity, such as Japan, Austria, Venezuela, and Italy, revealed a high proportion of males in dominant structures; in low masculine cultures, such as Denmark, Norway, Netherlands, and Sweden, women were treated more equally in their social systems.

So how does this manifest in a culture or country?

Below are some of the common traits found in countries that score low on the masculinity scale:

- In life the main priorities are the family, relationships and quality of life.
- Conflicts should ideally be solved through negotiation.
- Men and women should share equal positions in society.
- Professionals "work to live", meaning longer vacations and flexible working hours.

Below are some of the common traits found in countries that score high on the masculinity scale:

- Life's priorities are achievement, wealth and expansion.
- It is acceptable to settle conflicts through aggressive means.
- Women and men have different roles in society.

◆ Professionals often "live to work", meaning longer work hours and shorter vacations.

It is important that you recognize that these values are not associated with being male or female. In other words, this does not mean that men cannot be part of feminine cultures or that women do not orient themselves toward "masculine" cultural values. Finally, like other value dimensions, gender dimensions can vary greatly within any culture. You can think about the value dimension of gender in the ways displayed in Figure 2.5 "Gender Dimensions".

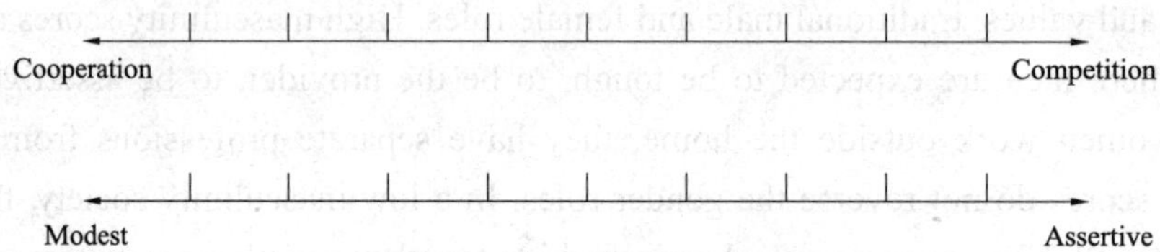

Figure 2.5 Gender Dimensions

UNCERTAINTY

Uncertainty avoidance refers to the degree to which members of a particular culture can handle uncertain or ambiguous situations (Hofstede, House et al, 2004; Gundykunst & Kim, 2003). More specifically, uncertainty avoidance points to the extent to which members of a particular culture seek orderliness, consistency, structure, formalized procedures, and laws to cover situations in their daily lives. Members of societies characterized as high in uncertainty avoidance have less tolerance for ambiguity than those characterized as low in uncertainty avoidence (Gundykunst & Kim, 2003). In high uncertainty avoidance cultures, aggressive behavior of self and other is acceptable; however, individuals prefer to contain aggression by avoiding conflict and competition. Furthermore, cultures high in uncertainty avoidance show a strong tendency for consensus, making deviant behavior or voicing dissent against the group unacceptable (Gundykunst & Kim). In essence this cultural dimension measures a country or culture's preference for strict laws and regulations over ambiguity and risk.

The dimension of uncertainty emphasizes cultures that are either oriented toward uncertainty or toward creating certainty and stability. Hofstede described this as a society's tolerance for ambiguity (Hofstede 2001). Societies that are in *high uncertainty avoidance* are rule-bound and pay more attention to written procedures, rules, or goals. Individuals who have a higher need for formalized structures, procedures, or diplomacy tend to minimize their uncertainty levels in order to cope with the unknowns of their situations. Someone who is on the other extreme of the dimension is more relaxed about the rules and procedures; they are more flexible in their attitudes toward rules and policies. The value dimension can be expressed in the ways shown in Figure "Uncertainty Value Dimension".

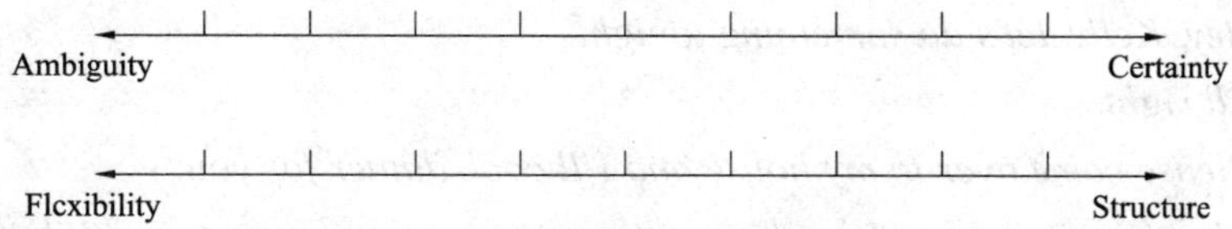

Figure 2.6 Uncertainty Value Dimension

According to Hofstede's findings Greece is the most risk-averse culture while Singapore the least. Generally speaking Protestant countries and those with Chinese influences score low. Catholic, Buddhist and Arabic speaking countries tend to score high in uncertainty avoidance.

So how does this manifest in a culture or country?

Below are some of the common traits found in countries that score highly on the uncertainty avoidance scale:

- Usually countries/cultures with a long history.
- The population is not multicultural, i.e. homogenous.
- Risks, even calculated, are avoided in business.
- New ideas and concepts are more difficult to introduce.

Positive words for high uncertainty avoiding culture are "structure, duty, truth, law, order, certain, pure, clear, secure, safe, predictable, and tight." These same words have a negative connotation for a low uncertainty avoiding culture. The words with a positive connotation for a low uncertainty avoiding culture (and negative for a high uncertainty avoiding culture) are "maybe, creative, conflict, tolerant, experiment, spontaneous, relativity, insight, unstructured, loose, and flexible."

Some of the common traits found in countries that score low on the uncertainty avoidance scale include:

- Usually a country with a young history, i.e. USA.
- The population is much more diverse due to waves of immigration.
- Risk is embraced as part of business.
- Innovation and pushing boundaries is encouraged.

An Intercultural Conversation between Weak and Strong Uncertainty Avoidance:

One's uncertainty avoidance orientation may manifest itself in interaction in any number of ways. In the dialogue presented below, Kelly and Keiko are interacting about a dinner invitation. Kelly, from the United States, possesses a relatively weak uncertainty avoidance index, while Keiko, from Japan, comes from a culture with a relatively strong uncertainty avoidance index.

Keiko: Hey, Kelly, let's do something tonight.

Kelly: All right.

Keiko: Please come over to my house and I'll cook dinner for you.

Kelly: I have invited some friends over to my house for dinner tonight, but I don't know if they're coming.

Keiko: Well... as soon as you know if they're coming, let me know.

Kelly: I won't know until tonight.

Keiko: What time?

Kelly: I won't know until they call me. They'll probably call later this afternoon.

Keiko: How will you know whether or not to cook enough for everyone?

Kelly: Oh, I'll make up something on the spot. I like to cook. I'll whip up something fast.

Keiko: But... what if they don't come? Won't they call and let you know?

Kelly: No... if they don't come, I'll know that something else came up. I'll let you know as soon as I can.

Keiko: Maybe we should plan my dinner for some other night.

In the above dialogue, Keiko is confused by Kelly's easygoing attitude toward the evening's plans. Coming from a strong uncertainty-avoidant culture, Keiko would prefer to plan ahead to avoid uncertainty and prepare her script for the evening. Kelly, on the other hand, is perfectly comfortable making plans based on how the evening progresses. Without a plan, how will Keiko know how to act? Although the feelings associated with uncertainty are personal and subjective, they can be shared by whole cultures. Although anxiety creates the same physiological responses in humans, what triggers anxiety and one's level of tolerance for it is learned. A culture's orientation toward uncertainty can be found in its families, schools, and institutions. But uncertainty avoidance ultimately manifests itself in human interaction.

TIME

The fifth dimension is Long-Term Orientation (LTO).Research by Michael Bond and colleagues among students in 23 countries led him in 1991 to adding a fifth dimension called Long- versus Short-Term Orientation. In 2010, research by Michael Minkov allowed to extend the number of country scores for this dimension to 93, using recent World Values Survey data from representative samples of national populations. Long-term oriented societies foster pragmatic virtues oriented towards future rewards, in particular saving, persistence, and adapting to changing circumstances. Short-term oriented societies foster virtues related to the past and present such as national pride, respect for tradition, preservation of "face", and fulfilling social obligations.

Positive words for long-term orientation cultures are "work, save, moderation, endurance, duty, goal, permanent, future, economy, virtue, invest, afford, and effort." These same words have a negative connotation for a short-term orientation culture. The words with a positive connotation for a short-term orientation culture (and negative for long-term orientation culture) are "relation, gift, today, yesterday, truth, quick, spend, receive, grand, tradition, show, image, and the bottom line".

Time is also a reference to a culture's orientation toward tasks or relationships. For example, a manager from the United States who travels to India to negotiate a business contract needs to know that meetings will occur whenever people show up to the meeting, which could be hours after it is scheduled. A task-oriented leader is certain to be frustrated when he meets up with an Indian who is more time-oriented toward relationships. In the American perspective, promptness is professionalism; yet, in the other perspective, the concept of time is more loose and flexible. The value of time is illustrated in Figure 2.7 "Time Value Dimension".

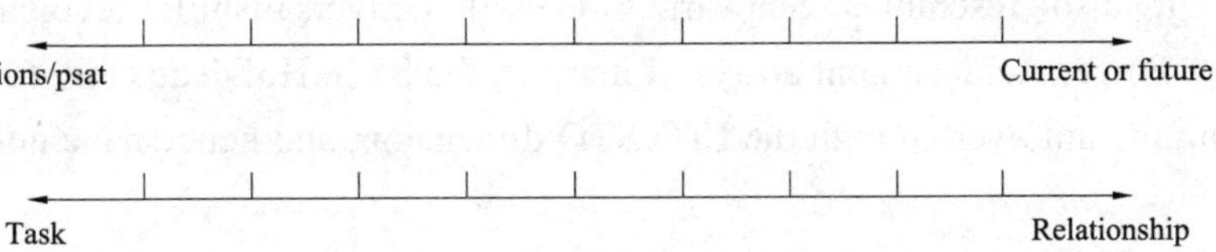

Figure 2.7 Time Value Dimension

NEED

The sixth dimension is Indulgence versus Restraint (IVR).In the same book a sixth dimension, also based on Minkov's World Values Survey data analysis for 93 countries, has been added, called Indulgence versus Restraint. Indulgence stands for a society that allows relatively free gratification of basic and natural human drives related to enjoying life and having fun, especially those that have to do with leisure, merrymaking with friends, spending, consumption, and sex. Restraint stands for a society that suppresses gratification of needs and regulates it by means of strict social norms. Indulgence is analogous to Schwartz's (1992) Hedonism; inspection of the Schwartz Value Survey (SVS) items opposite Hedonism in the Multidimensional Scaling Smallest Space Analysis reveals items similar to those defining Restraint. Minkov relates the dimension to Gelfand's "tight vs. loose" (Gelfand, Nishii, &

Raver, 2006). Indulgence vs. Restraint has been "officially" added to Hofstede's model (Hofstede, Hofstede & Minkov, 2010: 277-298).

Theory development is a continuous process, at least until it is disproven or until it develops into a set of laws. Research on the theory directs changes. Hofstede has been open to change and development in his theoretical model since the beginning, e.g., the early collaboration with Bond. Further research, development, and recalculation of this dimension resulted from Minkov's work with the World Values Survey data, discussed in Hofstede et al. (2010: 252-259) and Minkov and Hofstede (2012).

Minkov (2007) also identified the Monumentalism vs. Flexumility (a created word, with the dimension name changed to Self Effacement in the VSM 08, but not added to the model in Hofstede et al., 2010) dimension. Monumentalism is related to pride in self, national pride, making parents proud, and believing religion to be important, similar to McClelland's (1961) concept of need for achievement, which is also a theoretical basis of the GLOBE dimensions. The Flexumility pole identifies societies valuing humility, with members seeing themselves as not having a stable, invariant self-concept, and a flexible attitude toward Truth. Minkov reports similarities between this dimension and Hofstede's Masculinity-Femininity role-based dimension. It also resembles Schwartz's (1992) Universalism/Benevolence/Conformity/Tradition vs. Power/Achievement arrays of items in the SVS. Hofstede et al. (2010: 252) see it as having significant overlap with the LTO/STO dimension, and hence have not added it to the model.

Gert Jan Hofstede (personal communication, 2011) states that the two dimensions reallocate the composition of Hofstede's uncertainty avoidance and short-term/long-term orientation. However, in Littrell (2008), dimension scores are relative. The country scores on these dimensions are relative-societies compared to other societies. These relative scores have been proven to be quite stable over decades. The forces that cause cultures to shift tend to be global or continent-wide—they affect many countries at the same time, so that if their cultures shift, they shift together, and their relative positions remain the same.

2.4 Fons Trompenaars's Value Dimensions

We have already presented the findings of Hall and Hofstede and today we will review Fons Trompenaar, who has done very influential and insightful studies into Culture. Based on his seminars and training programmes Fons Trompenaars created a database which consists of 50,000 participants today. Along with Charles Hampden-Turner, Trompenaars developed the

"Seven Dimensions of Culture Model" for the analysis of cultural differences. With this model he wants to make executive personnel more sensitive for the features of foreign cultures. These are the 7 criteria of cultural differentiation which have an impact on the management trends. He shows how to manage complexity in a heterogeneous environment, which is a major challenge for today's international managers and corporate leaders as well as a critical component of long term success. He explains how to reconcile cultural differences, which will lead to competitive advantage. He often co-authored with Hampden-Turner; together they wrote their seminal work *Riding the Waves of Culture*; in 1997, he built the model around three key principles illustrated in below. And from this they developed a series of scenario based questions to test out how individuals react in these three areas, which led to 7 pairs of dichotomies described as dimensions.

- Five Dimensions in Relationships between People
  - ◆ universalism/particularism
  - ◆ individualism/collectivism
  - ◆ neutral/affective
  - ◆ specific/diffuse
  - ◆ achievement/ascription
- Time orientation
  - ◆ past, present, future
  - ◆ sequential/synchronous
- One Dimension in Relationship to Nature
  - ◆ internal/external

UNIVERSALISM versus PARTICULARISM

Universalism vs. particularism describes how people judge other people's behavior and the degree of importance a culture assigns to either the law or to personal relationships. In a universalistic culture, people share the belief that general rules, codes, values and standards take precedence over the needs and claims of friends and other relationships. In a pluralistic culture, people see culture in terms of human friendship and intimate relationships. While rules do exist in a pluralistic culture, they merely codify how people relate to one another.

Countries which can be seen as universalism societies: USA, Australia, Germany, Switzerland, Sweden, United Kingdom, Netherlands, Czech Republic, Slovakia, Belgium, France. Countries which can be seen as particularism societies: Brazil, Italy, Japan, Argentina, Mexico and Thailand.

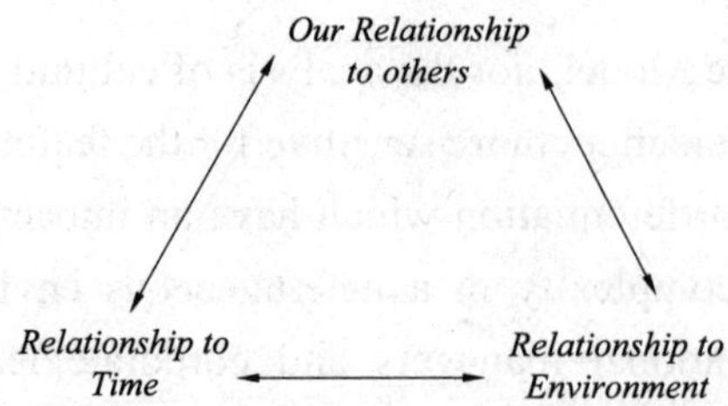

Figure 2.8 Trompenaars and Hampden-Turner (1997) Areas of Culture

INDIVIDUALISM versus COMMUNITARISNISM (COLLECTIVISM)

The degree to which people see themselves function more as a community or more as individuals. In a principally individualistic culture, people place the individual before the community. This means that individual happiness, fulfillment and welfare prevail and people take their own initiative and take care of themselves. In a principally communitarian culture, people place the community before the individual. Thus, it is the responsibility of the individual to act in ways which serve society. In doing so, individual needs are automatically attended.

Typical individualist cultures include the U.S., Canada, the U.K, Scandinavia, New Zealand, Australia, and Switzerland. Typical communitarian cultures include countries in Latin-America, Africa, and Japan.

SPECIFIC versus DIFFUSE

This dimension is sometimes referred to as "concern-/commitment-dimension", which is expressed at the level of an individual affected by a particular situation or action. It means the degree to which responsibility is specifically assigned or is diffusely accepted. In specific-oriented cultures areas of life such as work and family are recognized widely. A member of a specific-oriented culture is more open in the public space but very closed in the private one. Other characteristics of people in such a culture are directness, being to the point and purposeful in relating. There are often principles and consistent moral stands independent of the person being addressed. In diffuse-oriented cultures areas of life such as work and family are closely linked. A diffuse-oriented person is more closed in public space but is very open in private space. In contrast to the specific-oriented persons, diffuse-oriented are indirect, circuitous and seemingly aimless in forms of relating. High situational morality depends upon the person and context, which is encountered.

Typical specific cultures include the U.S., the U.K., Switzerland, Germany, Scandinavia, and the Netherlands. Typical diffuse cultures include Argentina, Spain, Russia, India, and China.

AFFECTIVITY versus NEUTRALITY

This dimension refers to the degree to which individuals display their emotions. In an affective culture, people display their emotions and it is not deemed necessary to hide feelings. However, in a neutral culture, people are taught not to display their feelings overtly. The degree to which feelings become manifested is therefore minimal. While emotions are felt, they are controlled. Instrumentality and rationality are of action in the foreground. People in such a culture are not necessarily cold or unfeeling, nor are they emotionally constipated or repressed. The emotions they show are often the result of convention. In neutral cultures, where emotions are controlled, irrepressible joy or grief will still signal loudly.

Typical neutral cultures include the U.K., Sweden, the Netherlands, Finland, and Germany. Typical emotional cultures include Poland, Italy, France, Spain, and countries in Latin-America.

INNER DIRECTED versus OUTER DIRECTED

This dimension refers to the degree to which individuals believe the environment can be controlled versus believing that the environment controls them. In an inner-directed culture, people have a mechanistic view of nature; nature is complex but can be controlled with the right expertise. People believe that humans can dominate nature, if they make the effort. In an outer-directed culture, people have an organic view of nature. Mankind is viewed as one of nature's forces and should therefore live in harmony with the environment. People therefore adapt themselves to external circumstances.

Typical internal-direction cultures include Israel, the U.S., Australia, New Zealand, and the U.K. Typical outer-direction cultures include China, Russia, and Saudi Arabia.

ACHIEVEMENT versus ASCRIPTION

This dimension refers to the question of whether the status of an individual results from his religion, origin or age or the status has mainly to do with his own performance. In achievement-oriented cultures a title is used only when it is relevant to the competence an individual brings to the task. Respect for managers is based on the individual's knowledge and skills. Decision-making is challenged on technical and functional grounds. In this kind of dimension the status of an individual refers mainly to his own performance. In ascription-oriented cultures a title is extensively used when these clarify one in an organization. Respect for a manager is based on seniority and hierarchy. Decision-making is challenged by people with higher authority. In an ascription-oriented culture a status refers to the religion, origin or age of the individuals. In addition there is a different way in which societies look at time.

Typical achievement cultures include the U.S., Canada, Australia, and Scandinavia. Typical ascription cultures include France, Italy, Japan, and Saudi Arabia.

SEQUENTIAL TIME versus SYNCHRONIC TIME

This dimension deals with the question of how people in different cultures manage time. Therefore Trompenaars defines in this dimension two ways of managing time. For him there is a sequential and a synchronic way to manage time. The degree to which individuals do things one at a time versus several things at once. Cultures developed their own response to time. Time orientation has two aspects: the relative importance cultures assign to the past, present and future, and their approach to structuring time. In a sequential culture, people structure time sequentially and do things one at a time. In a synchronic time culture, people do several things at once, believing time is flexible and intangible.

Typical sequential-time cultures include Germany, the U.K., and the U.S. Typical synchronous-time cultures include Japan, Argentina, and Mexico.

The seven dimensions help managers better understand the "other side", e.g. when trying to make trans-national projects or mergers work. Better understanding reduces the number of cultural driven misunderstandings and conflicts thereby reducing coordination costs. The model also helps marketers understand how consumers in different countries behave differently towards the same product.

2.5 Triandis's Cultural Dimensions

Although Hofstede's work was concerned primarily with cultural differences, subsequent researchers have become interested in individualism-collectivism at the individual level as well. Harry Triandis, from the University of Illinois, is well known for his work on individualism and collectivism. Triandis discusses four defining attributes of individualism-collectivism:

1) How individuals perceive themselves (e.g., "I am distinct and unique" vs. "I am a member of a family, tribe").

2) How individuals relate to others (e.g., "How/what do I gain from this act?" vs. "How will this act affect others?").

3) The goals they follow (e.g., "I want to win" vs. "I'm a team player to help the group win").

4) What drives their behavior (e.g., "It is my right to do this" vs. "My duty is to my group").

To account for some of these finer distinctions among individualistic and collectivistic cultures, Singelis, Triandis, Bhawuk and Gelfand (1995) made a further distinction between individualism and collectivism (IC), arguing that both individualism and collectivism may be either horizontal (H)—that is emphasizing equality—or it may be vertical (V)—that is emphasizing hierarchy. A brief description of the four patterns at the individual level is as follows:

1) Horizontal individualist (HI) assesses the extent to which individuals strive to be distinct without desiring special status. People want to be unique and self-reliant, but they are not especially interested in becoming distinguished or having high status. *I often "do my own thing."*

2) Vertical individualist (VI) assesses the extent to which individuals strive to be distinct and desire special status. People try to compete with others for distinction and status. *It annoys me when other people perform better than I do.*

3) Horizontal collectivist (HC) assesses the extent to which individuals emphasize interdependence but "do not submit easily to authority." People perceive themselves as an aspect of in-group and emphasize common goals with others. *The well-being of my co-workers is important to me.*

4) Vertical collectivist (VC) assesses the extent to which individuals emphasize interdependence and competition with out-groups. People sacrifice their personal goals for the sake of in-group goals, but the members of the in-group are different from each other, some having higher status than others. *I would sacrifice an activity that I enjoy very much if my family did not approve of it.*

The Horizontal & Vertical Individualism & Collectivism scale was designed to assess cultural orientation. It distinguishes between 4 components of cultural orientation:

1) Horizontal orientation emphasizes equality.

2) Vertical orientation emphasizes hierarchy.

3) Individualism emphasizes independent self-construals, exchange relationships, attitudes, and personal goals.

4) Collectivism emphasizes interdependent self-construals, communal relationships, norms, and in-group goals.

MEASURING HORIZONTAL AND VERTICAL INDIVIDUALISM-COLLECTIVISM

Consider the following situations. Place a check next to the response that most closely fits how you would act.

1) You and your friends decided spontaneously to go out to dinner at a restaurant. What

do you think is the best way to handle the bill?

A. ____ Split it equally, without regard to who ordered what.

B. ____ Split it according to how much each person makes.

C. ____ The group leader pays the bill or decides how to split it.

D. ____ Compute each person's charge according to what that person ordered.

2) Which of the four books are you more likely to find the most interesting?

A. ____ How to make friends

B. ____ How to succeed in business

C. ____ How to make sure you are meeting your obligations

D. ____ How to enjoy yourself inexpensively

3) When you buy clothing for a major social event, you would be most satisfied if...

A. ____ your friends like it.

B. ____ it is so elegant it will dazzle everyone.

C. ____ your parents like it.

D. ____ you like it.

4) When people ask me about myself, I...

A. ____ talk about my friends and what we like to do.

B. ____ talk about my accomplishments.

C. ____ talk about my ancestors and their traditions.

D. ____ talk about what makes me unique.

5) Suppose your boy/girlfriend and your parents do not get along very well. What would you do?

A. ____ Tell my boy/girlfriend that he/she should make a greater effort to "fit in with my family".

B. ____ Tell my boy/girlfriend that I need my parents' financial support and he/she should learn to handle them.

C. ____ Remind my boy/girlfriend that my parents and family are very important to me and he/she should submit to their wishes.

D. ____ Nothing

6) Suppose you had one word to describe yourself. What would it be?

A. ____ Cooperative B. ____ Competitive C. ____ Dutiful D. ____ Unique

7) Happiness is attained by...

A. ____ linking with a lot of friendly people.

B. ____ winning in competition.

C. ____ gaining a lot of status in the community.

D. ____ keeping one's privacy.

8) You are at a pizza restaurant with a group of friends. How should you decide what kind of pizza to order?

A. ____ We select the pizza that most people prefer.

B. ____ We order the most extravagant pizza available.

C. ____ The leader of the group orders for everyone.

D. ____ I order what I like.

Scoring: Indicate the number of times you selected letters A, B, C, and D. The frequency that is the highest represents your general HC, VI, VC, or HI orientation.

A. ____ Horizontal Collectivism (HC) B. ____ Vertical Individualism (VI)

C. ____ Vertical Collectivism (VC) D. ____ Horizontal Individualism (HI)

DISCUSSION

To be sure, one's individualistic or collectivistic disposition will affect communication. In the following exchange, Mr. Patterson, an American manager working in Korea, is meeting with his supervisor, Mr. Wyman, who is also American. The United States is considered more individualistic than Korea. In this scenario, Mr. Patterson reports to Mr. Wyman about some changes he has made within several of his sales teams. Later, Park Young Sam, their Korean counterpart, enters into the dialogue.

Mr. Patterson: *Good morning, Mr. Wyman, thanks for meeting with me this morning. As you know, our division has been doing very well this quarter. In fact, our numbers are up across the board.*

Mr. Wyman: *Yes, I've seen your quarterly reports. Nice job!*

Mr. Patterson: *Thanks. In order to recognize their hard work, I've made some changes in our sales teams. I've created team leaders in each group. In our product group, I promoted Lee Young-sam. In the marketing group, I promoted Chun Tae-woo, and in the technology group, I promoted Choi Mino. All of them have been real leaders. I think this idea will really motivate them. In fact, I met with the groups individually and announced the promotions.*

Mr. Wyman: *Good job, Patterson. I can see you're really on top of things. Good work.*

Two Months Later

Mr. Patterson, Mr. Wyman, and Park Young Sam, a Korean manager, are discussing the poor performance of Mr. Patterson's sales teams.

Mr. Wyman: *Well, just look at these dismal results. The numbers for this quarter are way down from last quarter. What's happened?*

Mr. Patterson: *I don't know. Ever since I introduced the team leader concept, the groups' productivity has really plummeted. I thought it was a great idea. I guess I chose the wrong people to lead the teams. I'll assign new leaders tomorrow.*

Park Young Sam: *Well... you may select new leaders if you desire, but the men you chose were all very capable. However, by elevating them, you made them stand out and disrupted the harmony of each group. In Korea, we all work hard for the group... not just one person.*

Mr. Patterson: *I guess I should have just left things as they were.*

TIP: Following their individualistic orientations, Mr. Patterson and Mr. Wyman were perfectly comfortable with the idea of appointing team leaders within the individual sales groups. However, as Park Young Sam mentioned, doing so upset the harmony of the groups, which in turn led to poor performance. In the United States, workers are often motivated by the opportunity for promotion and advancement, as this serves the individualistic drive for individual achievement. In less individualistic cultures, however, workers may be motivated by being a part of a cohesive and productive team. Mr. Patterson and Mr. Wyman could have consulted with Mr. Sam prior to making the promotions. He probably would have advised against it.

2.6 Shalom H. Schwartz's Universal Value Orientations

A different approach to finding (cultural) value differences has been taken by Shalom Schwartz. Using his "SVI" (Schwartz Value Inventory), Schwartz did not ask for preferred outcomes, but asked respondents to assess 57 values as to how important they feel these values are as "guiding principles of one's life". Schwartz's work is separated into an individual-level analysis and a culture-level analysis, a major difference compared to the works of Hofstede and Trompenaars and Hampden-Turner who sometimes fail to clearly distinguish between the two levels, although generally claim to work at the culture-level.

All societies have developed certain common practices and beliefs, known as cultural universals. Many cultural universals are, in fact, adaptations to meet essential human needs, such as the need for food, shelter, and clothing. Schwartz took Maslow's thinking of Hierarchy of Needs and pushed it further to determine a map that demonstrates values states. Schwartz also proposes that these values sit opposite one another in a wheel like configuration. Schwartz's goal is to create a comprehensive classification scheme of the substantive content of human values that are shared across cultures. From data collected in 63 countries, with more than 60,000 individuals taking part, Schwartz derived a total of 10 distinct value types at an individual-level analysis. These individual level value types each represent a number of values which can be combined in a joint "idea".

POWER

Attainment of social status. (social power, wealth, authority, preserving my public image, social recognition)

This takes value from social status and prestige. The ability to control others is important and power will be actively sought through dominance of others and control over resources.

ACHIEVEMENT

The need and value of personal success and prestige. (ambitious, influential, capable, successful, intelligent, self-respect)

Value here comes from setting goals and then achieving them. The more challenge, the greater the sense of achievement. When others have achieved the same thing, status is reduced and greater goals are sought.

HEDONISM

The need and motivation for pleasure. (pleasure, enjoying life)

Hedonists simply enjoy themselves. They seek pleasure above all things and may, according to the view of others, sink into debauchery.

STIMULATION

The goal is derived from the need for variety and stimulation in order to maintain an optimal level of activation. Some of these needs are biological, while others are learned/cultural. (an exciting life, a varied life, daring)

The need for stimulation is close to hedonism, though the goal is slightly different. Pleasure here comes more specifically from excitement and thrills and a person with this driver is more likely to be found doing extreme sports than propping up a bar.

SELF-DIRECTION

The defining goal of this value type is independent thought and action. (freedom, creativity, independent, choosing own goals, curious, self-respect)

Those who seek self-direction enjoy being independent and outside the control of others. They prefer freedom and may have a particular creative or artistic bent, which they seek to indulge whenever possible.

UNIVERSALISM

The value of understanding, appreciation, tolerance, and protection for the welfare of all people and for nature. (equality, unity with nature, wisdom, a world of beauty, social justice, broad-minded, protecting the environment, a world at peace)

The universalist seeks social justice and tolerance for all. They promote peace and equality and find war anathema except perhaps in pursuit of lasting peace.

BENEVOLENCE

The need and motivation for positive interaction and affiliation. (helpful, respon sible, forgiving, honest, loyal, mature love, true friendship)

Those who tend towards benevolence are often giving, seeking to help others and provide general welfare. They are the "earth mothers" who nurture all.

TRADITION

The value of religious rites, beliefs, and norms of behavior that, over time, are valued and passed on by a collective. (respect for children, devout, accepting of my portion in life, humble, moderate)

The traditionalist respects that which has gone before, doing things simply because they are customary. They are conservatives in the original sense, seeking to preserve the world order as it is. Any change makes them uncomfortable.

CONFORMITY

Restraint of actions, inclinations, and impulses. (obedient, self-discipline, politeness, honoring of parents and elders)

The person who values conformity seeks obedience to clear rules and structures. They gain a sense of control through doing what they are told and conforming to agreed laws and statutes.

SECURITY

Need for safety, harmony, and the stability of society and relationships. (national security, reciprocation of favors, family security, sense of belonging, social order, healthy, clean)

Those who seek security seek health and safety to a greater degree than other people (perhaps because of childhood woes). Although they may worry about the potential of military force, they welcome the comfort that their existence brings.

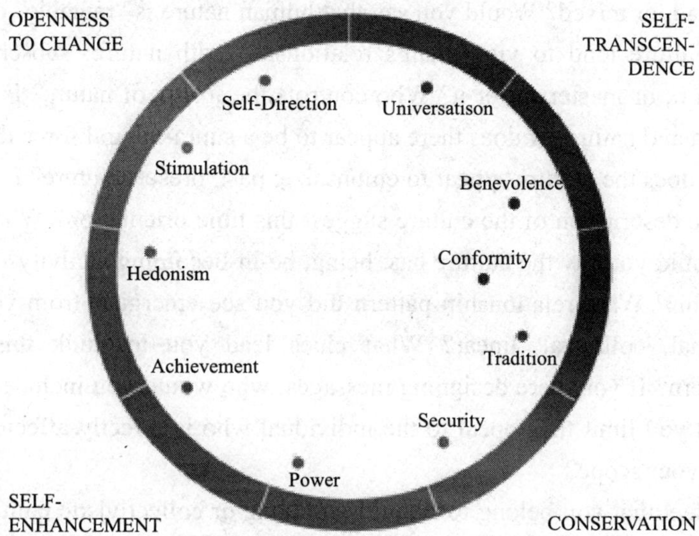

Figure 2.9 Model of Value Priorities Taken from Schwarz & Boehnke (2005)

3. Exercises

I. Discussion

1) Do you believe Hall is correct in his assumptions? If so, what examples can you give that demonstrate high- and low-context cultures? What are some of the ways that you use high-context communication? What are some of the ways that you use low-context communication? Which do you prefer? How would context help explain instances of miscommunication between North Americans and Japanese? How could you become a better international communicator?

2) Define a value. Explain how a value affects human behavior. What are the most important values you hold? Can you rank them? Where do you think your values came from? How do the values you hold compare with those of others? Your friends? Your family? Most other people in your community? Most psychological research has relied on questionnaires to study people's values. What other methods of measuring values might be feasible? Two ways are reported in which value measurement has been practically useful. Can you think of other situations in which understanding and measuring people's values might be useful?

3) Would you say that the culture you are profiling tends to view human nature as basically good, bad, or mixed? Would you say that human nature is "mutable" or "immutable"? How does the culture tend to view man's relationship with nature: subservient to nature, harmonious with it, or mastery over it? Who controls the forces of nature? Is the relationship just between man and nature, or does there appear to be a supra-natural force that controls both? What dimension does the culture appear to emphasize: past, present, future? How can you tell? What clues in the description of the culture suggest this time orientation? What self-definition or orientation would you say the culture has: being, be-in-becoming, activity? What clues lead you to suggest this? What relationship pattern did you see emerging from your study of the culture: individual, collateral, linear? What clues lead you to think this might be the relationship pattern? If you were designing messages, who would you include in your "target" audience? Could you limit the appeal to the individual who is directly affected or would you need to broaden your scope?

4) Do you feel that you belong to an individualistic or collectivistic culture? Why? What are the signs? Is your relationship with your professors indicative of large or small power distance? Is your relationship with your parents indicative of large or small power distance? If you have no plans for the upcoming weekend, does that make you feel anxious, or are you comfortable with not knowing? Depending on your answer, are you certainty or uncertainty oriented?

II. Case Study

1) A Case Study on Cross-cultural Partnerships, Intercultural Communication and High-context versus Low-context Communication

Mark is an American living in Delhi and is meeting with Ajay, who is a government official that frequently deals with the public. Mark is interested in forming a partnership with Suresh, a local businessman with whom Ajay has worked in the past. Mark wants to know if Ajay thinks partnering with Suresh is a good idea.

Mark: Do you happen to know Suresh?

Ajay: Of course, I have worked closely with him on a number of projects over the past 10 years. I know him very well.

Mark: I was thinking about meeting him and seeing if there might be a possibility for collaboration. What do you think?

Ajay: Yes, you should meet with him, and you should also meet with others.

Mark: Thanks. Who else should I meet with?

Ajay: You know there are some girls who fall in love with a boy who is very popular, well dressed, and good looking. After they get married, they realize that they made a mistake because the boy has no substance. Other girls will look for a guy with good character—checking out his family situation and talking with his friends about him. When she gets married, she is much happier than the girl who married the popular guy.

✧ Should Mark meet with Suresh? Why or why not?

✧ Why does Mark ask about other people to meet with?

✧ Why does Ajay talk about a hypothetical marriage?

2) Identify the Cultural Differences in the Following Cross-cultural Case with the High and Low Context Communication Theory

✧ *On a sunny day in March 2002, Lilan, an 18-year old Chinese girl, was flying to Tokyo on a Boeing 747. She was very excited because this was her first trip to Tokyo and the first time she had traveled such distance alone. She had an uncle who had lived in Japan for 10 years, but was worried that he might not be at the airport to meet her when she arrived.*

The girl sitting alone in the seat next to Lilan was Angela, an American who was also 18 years old. She told Lilan this was a vacation and her first trip to Japan too. She also said she had previously traveled alone to several different countries on vacations. Lilan was very surprised to hear this.

Finally the plane landed at the airport, and the girls were at the arrival gates of Tokyo International Airport. Lilan was thrilled to see her uncle's family waving their hands at her. In the meantime, she felt sorry for Angela who had to walk out of the airport alone, holding a map and disappearing among the strangers...

✧ *In September 2002, Esmeralda Simpson, an English scholar, was coming to Zhejiang Medical College in China for one year. Since it would be a new exciting experience for her, she read books about China, and even bought a guidebook before she left England.*

When she arrived at XiaoShan International Airport in Hanghzou, she was greeted by Minghua, a young teacher from the college, who had just been assigned to this city from another province. Minghua would be responsible for Esmeralda's daily affairs during her stay in Hangzhou, including sightseeing.

Since Minghua was also new to the city, she was very excited about the sightseeing opportunities with Esmeralda during their weekends. However, it turned out that it was Esmeralda who was the tour guide for the two of them. She would use her guidebook to plan

their trips to the different scenic spots in the city.

Minghua was surprised to find out that Esmeralda knew so much about China, even more than she did.

3) A Case Study on the Dimension of Individualism and Collectivism

Ma Pin works in a joint-venture company as an executive in China. His boss is an American named Steve. They are good friends. Once, at a meeting with mostly Chinese participants including Ma Pin, Steve didn't hear much disagreement when asking for any suggestions on his new project. So he took it for granted that his new project would be quite satisfactory to everyone present at the meeting. But to his great surprise and puzzlement, after the meeting, Ma Pin came to his office and told him that the project might not work properly. This time, to Ma Pin's surprise, Steve didn't seem happy but even annoyed with this.

✧ What would Steve expect from the participants on his new project at the meeting?

✧ What proper explanation could you give for Ma Pin's behavior?

✧ Suppose you are the person who knows both of them quite well, could you please give some advice to both of them so that they could understand each other well?

4) A Case Study on the Dimension of Power Distance

A works as a secretary in a company. A's boss often tells her how he wants his time scheduled, and A then makes his appointments based on his instructions. A translates memos and other documents. If the manager doesn't think A has done well on an assignment, he tells her right away. He's very demanding, but A feels that she knows what her duties are and knows what her manager expects. She is confident that she's doing a good job.

✧ Does the boss come from a large or small power distance country? Why?

5) A Well-known Case from Trompenaars' Research Material Referring to the Dimension of Universalism/Particularism: "The Car and the Pedestrian" (Trompenaars 1993:34):

"You are driving in a car driven by a close friend. He hits a pedestrian. You know he was going at least 35 miles per hour in an area of the city where the maximum allowed speed is 20 miles per hour. There are no witnesses. His lawyer says that if you testify under oath that he was only driving 20 miles per hour it may save him from serious consequences. What right has your friend to expect you to protect him? (a definite right, some right, no right)."

✧ What would you do in that kind of situation?

III. Project Presentation

Each student should find a person from a country not presented in the course (Bulgaria, China, Germany) and do the self-image, image, perceived image test with him/her. The *own* culture is the culture of the test person, the *other* culture is the culture of the student. Please discuss, if possible, the results with the test person.

(*Example: A Chinese student is asking an Italian person: The three lists should be: Characteristics of the Italians, Characteristic of the Chinese, Perceived Image of the Italians by the Chinese*)

Each student should present his findings in a short (5-7 min.) presentation.

4. References

1. Bhawuk, Dharm & Triandis, Harry. The role of culture theory in the study of culture and intercultural training. In Dan Landis & Richard W. Brislin (Eds.), Handbook of intercultural training [M]. Thousand Oaks: Sage, 1996: 17-34.
2. Brislin, Richard; Lonner, Walter & Thorndike, Robert. Cross-cultural Research Methods [M]. New York: John Wiley, 1973.
3. De Mooij, M. Global Marketing and Advertising: Understanding Cultural Paradoxes [M]. Thousand Oaks, CA: Sage, 1998.
4. Gudykunst, W. B., & Ting-Toomey, S. Culture and Interpersonal Communication [M]. Newbury Park, CA: Sage, 1988.
5. Gudykunst, William. Intercultural communication theory: Current perspectives [M]. Newbury Park: Sage, 1989.
6. Gudykunst, William. Communicating with strangers: An approach to intercultural communication [M]. New York: McGraw-Hill, 1992.
7. Gudykunst, William. Toward a theory of effective interpersonal and intergroup communication. In Richard L. Wiseman & Jolene Koester (Eds.), Intercultural communication competence. London: Sage, 1993: 33-71.
8. Gudykunst, William. Bridging differences: Effective intergroup communication [M] .2nd ed. Thousand Oaks, CA: Sage, 1994.
9. Hall, E. T. Beyond Culture [M]. Garden City, NY: Doubleday & Company, 1976.
10. Hall, E. T. The Dance of Life [M]. Garden City, NY: Doubleday/Anchor, 1984.
11. Hills, M. D. Kluckhohn and Strodtbeck's Values Orientation Theory. Online Readings in Psychology and Culture, 4(4). http://dx.doi.org/10.9707/2307-0919.1040. 2002.
12. Hills, M.D. Developing the Kluckhohn-Strodtbeck Values Orientation Instrument in New Zealand. Paper presented at the Biennial Conference of the International Association for

Cross-Cultural Psychology. Bellingham, WA, United States, 1998.

13. Hofstede, G. Culture's Consequences: International differences in work-related values [M]. Beverly Hills, Calif.: Sage, 1980.
14. Hofstede, G. Dimensions of national cultures in fifty countries and three regions. In J. Deregowski, S. Dzirawiec, & R. Annis (Eds.), Explications in Cross-Cultural Psychology Lisse, the Netherlands: Swets and Zeitlinger, 1983: 389-407.
15. Hofstede, G. Culture's Consequences: International Differences in Work-Related Values [M]. Beverly Hills, CA: Sage, 1984.
16. Hofstede, G. Cultures and organizations: Software of the mind. [M]. London: McGraw-Hill, 1991.
17. Hofstede, G. Foreword. Individualism and Collectivism: Theory, Method, and Applications. In U. Kim, H. C. Triandis, C. Kagitcibasi, S.-C. Choi, & G. Yoon, (Eds.). Thousand Oaks, CA: Sage, 1994: ix-xiv.
18. Hofstede G. A serious shortcoming of Trompenaars' data bank which no professional analysis can correct is its evident lack of content validity International Journal of Intercultural Relations, 20.(2). 1996: 189-198.
19. Hofstede, G. Culture's Consequences: Comparing values, behaviors, institutions and organizations across nations [M]. Beverly Hills, Calif.: Sage, 2001.
20. Kim, Young-Yun. Intercultural communication competence: A systems-theoretic view. In William Gudykunst & Young-Yun Kim (Eds.), Readings on communicating with strangers. An approach to intercultural communication. New York: McGraw Hill, 1992: 371-381.
21. Kluckhohn, C. K. Culture: A Critical Review of Concepts and definitions [M]. NY: Vintage Books, 1952.
22. Kluckhohn, C. K. Values and Value Orientations in the Theory of Action. In T. Parsons and E. A. Shils (Eds.), Toward a General Theory of Action. Cambridge, MA: Harvard University Press, 1951.
23. Kluckhohn, F.R. & Strodtbeck, F.L. Variations in Value Orientations [M]. Evanston, Ill.: Row, Peterson, 1961.
24. Kluckhohn Center. User's manual for the Value Orientation Method [M]. Kluckhohn Center for the Study of Values, Bellingham, WA, 1995.
25. Rokeach, M. Understanding Human Values: Individual and Societal [M]. New York: The Free Press, 1979.
26. Russo, K.W. (Ed). Finding the middle ground: Insights and applications of the Value

Orientations method [M]. Yarmouth, ME: Intercultural Press, 2000.

27. Samovar, Larry; Porter, Richard & Stefani, Lisa. Communication between cultures [M]. Belmont: Wadsworth Publishing Company, 1998.
28. Schwartz, S. H. and Bilsky, W. Toward a theory of the universal content and structure of values: Extensions and cross cultural replications [J]. *Journal of Personality and Social Psychology*, 58, 1990: 878-891.
29. Schwartz, S. H. Universals in the content and structure of values: Theory and empirical tests in 20 countries. In M. Zanna (Ed.), Advances in experimental social psychology (Vol. 25). New York: Academic Press, 1992: 1-65.
30. Schwartz, S. H. Value priorities and behavior: Applying of theory of integrated value systems. In C. Seligman, J. M. Olson, & M. P. Zanna (Eds.), The Psychology of Values: The Ontario Symposium, Vol. 8. Hillsdale, NJ: Erlbaum, 1996: 1-24.
31. Schwartz, S. H., Lehmann, A., and Roccas, S. Multimethod probes of basic human values, in: J. Adamopoulos and Y. Kashima, (eds.), Social Psychology and Culture Context: Essays in Honor of Harry C. Triandis. Newbury Park, CA: Sage, 1999.
32. Schwartz, S. H. and Bardi, A. Moral dialogue across cultures: An empirical perspective. In E. W. Lehman (Ed.), Autonomy and order: A communitarian anthology. Lanham, MD: Rowman & Littlefield, 2000.
33. Schwartz, S. H., Melech, G., Lehmann, A., Burgess, S., and Harris, M. Extending the cross-cultural validity of the theory of basic human values with a different method of measurement. *Journal of Cross Cultural Psychology*, 32, 2001: 519-542.
34. Schwartz, S. H. and Boehnke, K. Evaluating the structure of human values with confirmatory factor analysis. *Journal of Research in Personality,* 38, 2004: 230-255.
35. Schwartz, S. H. Value orientations: Measurement, antecedents and consequences across nations. In R. Jowell, C. Roberts, R. Fitzgerald, & G. Eva (Eds.), Measuring attitudes cross-nationally—lessons from the European Social Survey. London: Sage, 2006.
36. Singelis, T.M., Triandis, H.C., Bhawuk, D.P.S., & Gelfand, M.J. Horizontal and vertical aspects of individualism and collectivism: A theoretical and measurement refinement [J]. *Cross-Cultural Research*, 29, 1995: 240-275.
37. Ting-Toomey, Stella. Communicating across cultures [M]. New York: Guilford Press, 1999.
38. Triandis, H. C., Brislin, R., & Hui, C. H. Cross-cultural training across the individualism-collectivism divide [J]. *International Journal of Intercultural Relations*, 12, 1988: 269-289.

39. Triandis, H.C. Collectivism and individualism as cultural syndromes [J]. *Cross-Cultural Research*, 27, 1993: 155-180.
40. Triandis, H.C. Theoretical and methodological approaches to the study of collectivism and individualism. In U. Kim, H.C. Triandis, Ç. Kâgitçibasi, S. Choi & G. Yoon (Eds.), Individualism and collectivism. Thousand Oaks, CA: Sage, 1994: 41-51.
41. Triandis, H.C. Individualism and collectivism. Boulder, CO: Westview Press, 1995.
42. Triandis, H.C., Chen, X.P., & Chan, D.K.S. Scenarios for the measurement of collectivism and individualism [J]. *Journal of Cross-Cultural Psychology*, 29, 1998: 275-289.
43. Triandis, H.C., & Gelfand, M.J. Converging measurement of horizontal and vertical individualism and collectivism [J]. *Journal of Personality and Social Psychology*, 74, 1998: 118-128.
44. Triandis, H.C., McCusker, C., & Hui, C.H. Multimethod probes of individualism and collectivism [J]. *Journal of Personality and Social Psychology*, 59, 1990: 1006-1020.
45. Triandis, H. C., & Suh, E. M. Cultural influences on personality [J]. *Annual Review of Psychology*, 53, 2002: 133-160.
46. Trompenaars F and Hampden-Turner C. Riding the Waves of Culture: Understanding Diversity in Global Business [M]. NB Publishing, 1997.
47. Trompenaars F. and Peter Woolliams. Business Across Cultures (Culture for Business Series) [M]. Mankato: Capstone Publisher, 2004.
48. Trompenaars F. and Charles Hampden-Turner. Managing People Across Cultures (Culture for Business Series) [M]. Mankato: Capstone Publisher, 2004.
49. Trompenaars F. and Dumetz J. Cross-cultural management textbook: Lessons from the world leading experts in cross-cultural management [M]. CreateSpace Independent Publishing Platform, 2012.

Chapter 3

Intercultural Business Communication

"Despite popular beliefs to the contrary, the single greatest barrier to business success is the one erected by culture."

—Edward T. Hall and Mildred Reed Hall, Hidden Differences

"An ounce of prevention is worth a pound of cure."

—Ben Franklin

"We didn't all come over on the same ship, but we're all in the same boat."

—Bernard Baruch

"Seek to first understand, then seek to be understood."

—An Old Saying

1. Lead-in

1.1 Examples of Company Failure Due to Cultural Mistakes

LANGUAGE ISSUES

A brand name that conjures images of quality and reliability in one language may have serious negative connotations in another. An Iranian razor manufacturer used the brand name "Tiz," the Persian word for "sharp," to illustrate the quality of its product. When the company began exporting the razors to nearby Qatar, they learned that "tiz" was the Arabic slang word for "buttocks," which the Arabic-speaking residents of Qatar found highly offensive. Sales of the razors plummeted and the Iranian manufacturer lost money on the failed marketing campaign.

RESPECT AND HIERARCHY

Different cultures also have different contexts for displaying respect to superiors and receiving deference from subordinates. One American office manager took a similar position in an office in Seoul, South Korea. The manager expressed discomfort at the deference that his subordinates paid him, so he told them to treat him as an equal. The lack of deference led to a breakdown in discipline and professionalism, with employees wasting time in casual conversation. The office lost so much productivity that it was nearly shut down and the supervisor was reassigned.

RULE-CENTERED VS. RELATIONSHIP-CENTERED

Many Western nations use rule-centered approaches to building business agreements and settling disputes. In Eastern countries, entrepreneurs rely more on establishing individual relationships with their business partners, rather than depending on lengthy contracts and teams of attorneys. For example, when the leaders of one American firm met with a potential Japanese partner, the Americans presented a 50-page contract at the outset. Since the Japanese leaders felt that the Americans did not take the time to establish a relationship with them, they refused to read the contract and cut off the negotiations.

RELIGIOUS IMAGES

One of the most sensitive touchstones to any culture is its religion. The misuse of religious iconography can damage a company's image with those customers. During the 1994 World Cup, bottles of Heineken beer displayed the flags of all the participants in soccer's biggest tournament, including Saudi Arabia. The country's flag shows a verse from the Quran, Islam's holy book. The Quran forbids the use of alcohol, so thousands of Muslims registered complaints with the brewer for displaying the verse.

1.2 Examples of Cultural Differences in Business

As your business grows, you may develop a diverse group of employees. While diversity often enriches the workplace, it can bring a host of complications as well.

Different cultures have varying expectations about personal space and physical contact. Many Europeans and South Americans customarily kiss a business associate on both cheeks in greeting instead of shaking hands. While Americans are most comfortable at arms-length from business associates, other cultures have no problem standing shoulder-to-shoulder with their peers or placing themselves 12 or fewer inches away from the person to whom they are speaking. In Russia, according to the University of California, female colleagues often walk arm in arm, while the same behavior in other cultures may signify a more personal or sexual relationship.

CONTEXT

Different cultures communicate through various levels of context, according to the Tepper School of Business. Low-context cultures such as Canada, the United States, Australia, New Zealand and most of Europe, require little or no explanation of orders and requests. High-context cultures, which include most other Eastern and South American populations require and expect much more explanation about orders and directions. Businesses that operate with a low-context form of communication spell out the specifics in the message, while those from a high-context communication culture expect and supply more background with their messages.

CUES

Western and Eastern cues have substantially different meanings in business. The word "yes," for example, usually means agreement in Western cultures. In Eastern and high-context cultures however, the word "yes," more often than not means that the party understands the message, not necessarily that he agrees with it. A handshake in some cultures is as ironclad as an American contract. A period of silence during negotiations with an Eastern business associate may signify displeasure with your proposal. While frank openness may be desirable in Western cultures, Eastern cultures often place more value on saving face and avoiding disrespectful responses.

RELATIONSHIPS

While Western cultures proclaim to value relationship-based marketing and business practices, in Eastern and high-context cultures, a relationship involves longtime family ties or direct referrals from close friends. Judgments made in business often are based on familial ties, class and status in relationship-oriented cultures, while rule-oriented cultures believe that everyone in business deserves an equal opportunity to make their case. Judgments are made on universal qualities of fairness, honesty and getting the best deal, rather on formal introductions and background checks.

Cultural differences can interfere with productivity or cause conflict among employees.

Stereotypes and ignorance about different traditions and mannerisms can lead to disruptions and the inability of certain workers to work effectively as a team.

2. Main Text

2.1 Intercultural Business Communication

DEFINING INTERNATIONAL BUSINESS

International Business is only about selling your goods and services globally or is there more to it than this? International business is a term used to illustrate all commercial transactions that cross a national boundary at private, public or government level. It can be categorised into four sectors—foreign trade, trade in services, portfolio investments and direct investments.

Foreign trade includes importing and exporting tangible goods such as physical products; trade in services is about providing intangible services such as insurance etc. Portfolio investments are financial investments that only consider exchanging monetary value and nothing else, whereas direct investment involves taking control in invested firms. Thus, when you are trading internationally you have to think beyond just importing and exporting goods and services as there are many other aspects that are involved in making your business successful.

A key to being successful in business internationally is to understand the role of culture in international business. Whatever sector you are operating in, cultural differences will have a direct impact on your profitability. Improving your level of knowledge of international cultural difference in business can aid in building international competencies as well as enabling you to gain a competitive advantage. However, on the one hand where it is important to be aware of cultural differences of different countries, on the other, it is also hard to be aware of every single aspect of each country's organisational culture.

Appreciating the cultural differences and making a conscious effort to adapt to the ways of a country is necessary for any flourishing business. Even seemingly unimportant practices in some countries, might assume a great deal of significance in others. For instance, in some countries, taking too much interest in the personal affairs of the subordinates may be considered rude; whereas, in a few Asian countries, it is expected, and the employees might disapprove if the employer maintains a strictly formal relationship. Of course, one cannot hope to master the minutia of cultural differences, but can hope that a sincere apology will go a long way in smoothing the bumps along the path to cultural orientation.

There are three key issues in inter-cultural business communication. First, culture affects consumer behavior, by defining acceptable purchasing and product-use behavior for consumers and business. Secondly, culture affects the effectiveness of advertising. Advertising, for instance, is strongly influenced by language, which is one of the key elements of culture. Thirdly, business communication influences culture, contributing to cultural borrowing and change.

INTERNATIONAL BUSINESS ETIQUETTE

Business etiquette is about building relationships with other people. Etiquette is not about rules & regulations but is about providing basic social comfort and creating an environment where others feel comfortable and secure, which is possible through better communication. Business etiquette consists of two things. Firstly, thoughtful consideration of the interests and feelings of others and secondly, being able to minimise misunderstandings. These are influenced by individual behaviour & demeanour. Business etiquette instructs this behaviour.

Business etiquette differs from region to region and from country to country. This creates a complex situation for people as it is hard to balance the focus on both international business etiquette and other business activities at the same time. Business etiquette instructs on you how to present yourself professionally in different cultures. The keys for making a good impression are dressing appropriately, your body language, presenting your business cards, gift giving, conducting meetings and many other important elements. Therefore, a wise step is to focus on some key pillars of business etiquette. Here are some key business etiquette tips that mean real success to business:

"Thank You" Note: If you want to differentiate yourself from others then never forget to write a "Thank You" note to your job interviewer or your client. This will leave a good impression and also reflect well on your company.

Know the Names: Give others respect by knowing their names which will increase goodwill and communication. It is also worth management stepping back and acknowledging people individually for their good work as this will enhance their self esteem and increase motivation.

Observe the "Elevator Rule": Be mindful of saying appropriate things at a job interview or client meeting. Don't start discussing business with a client or interviewer as soon as you step out of the lift. By doing so, you avoid the risk of damaging your reputation.

Focus on the Face, Not the Screen: Never forget to switch off your phone and try not to use any other device just to prove you are a multitasking individual. In fact, in the world of business this is considered bad manners. Concentrate on the meeting and listen to what people are saying.

Don't Judge: Everyone is unique in their own way and uses a different approach to deal with situations. Therefore, if you disagree with another person's approach instead of criticising try to understand it from their point of view. By doing so, you create a friendly environment. Always remember you get respect by giving respect.

Character, Behaviour, Honesty: Your character reflects your individuality and your behaviour exhibits your personality. Business etiquette encourages revealing your positive qualities. This helps your reputation. Always be honest and remember that it takes a long time to develop trust and a good reputation and only one small mistake to lose it. Business etiquette provides a framework for stating the boundaries of terms & conditions, contracts and promises.

Sensitivity & Diplomacy: A key pillar of business etiquette is sensitivity, meaning giving careful thought to every business aspect before making a judgment. This gives a strong foundation to your business. Also, thoughtless words and actions lead to a negative outcome. Being aware of business etiquette encourages careful thought.

INTERCULTURAL BUSINESS COMMUNICATION

Intercultural business communication refers to the communication that arises during the course of business relationships with people from different cultures. Such an interaction is becoming more inevitable with the growth of globalization and the assurance that any sizable business can expect to encounter some form of intercultural business communication during its various transactions. This sort of business interaction can be viewed from several standpoints, including the influx of people from other cultures and the exportation of businesses to other cultures.

One of the major considerations in intercultural business communication is the application of sensitivity during such communications so as not to offend people of other cultures. The desire to be sensitive may be hampered by ignorance about other peoples' cultures and a basic understanding of their norms and values. This is due to the fact that no culture can be described as the best or the right culture in exclusion to others. Therefore, what makes sense in one culture might not make much sense in another. In intercultural business communication, behaving as one would normally do in his or her own culture might lead to incidences of unintentional offenses.

An example of this phenomenon can be seen in the cultural practice of shaking hands. While most cultures adopt this sort of greeting in their businesses, some might actually consider it offensive in various circumstance, especially when very young people try to shake the hands of elderly business men. In some African cultures, such a behavior is often considered extremely disrespectful, especially when the younger person initiates the handshake. An understanding of cultural etiquette would lead to the understanding that an elder must initiate the handshake. Younger people would win more business if they behave in a more deferential manner, especially when the company they represent is trying to obtain some kind of benefit from the other company.

The influx of immigrants into various countries across the world means that the typical company has a culturally diverse representation of employees. In this type of a situation, the company might institute a corporate culture where such people are integrated into the company, while still communicating with them in a knowledgeable and respectful manner about some salient aspects of their culture. The same applies during the process of intercultural business communication with people from other countries during the marketing process. A slogan that might be accepted in one country might be viewed differently in another. Also, an advertisement that might work in one country might be offensive in another, which is why a comprehensive market research regarding a particular culture must be included in the list of top priority.

Whether large corporations or small- and medium-sized businesses must adapt to communicating cross-culturally, which involves:

New Expectations: Technology has made it easier than ever to work with and sell to people who live and work thousands of miles away and who are members of diverse cultures. Therefore, your expectations about doing business as a business owner must change to meet new expectations. If you are a native English speaker you already have a distinct advantage, as English is quickly becoming the global language; however, this doesn't mean that you are immune from understanding the unique cultural experiences of those you're doing business with. Inter-culture communication in business is as much about understanding the norms and customs of another culture as it is about knowing the business terms or language requirements of your newly-found business prospects. In this light, inter-culture communication is concerned with how well you're able to make your contacts across the world feel comfortable, accepted as individuals and welcome in your business.

Cultural Diversity: Cultures, like people themselves, are ever-changing. As A.J. Schuler notes: "The pace of change is accelerated when cultures that reinforce different styles of communication, and which accent different binding customs and values, interact with each other." Embracing diversity is, therefore, an important part of inter-culture communication in small business. Businesses that have traditionally served one or a few particular demographics are now able to potentially reach customers around the world, but this requires that you are open to embracing diversity in all its forms, including language, community traditions, religious practices and gender and sexuality.

Developing Empathy: With the need to embrace diverse cultures and social practices, international business owners may find it helpful to develop a sense of empathy toward those they are working with and selling their products or services to. As a business owner looking to engage in inter-culture communication, you should remember that there is often more diversity within a given demographic than is at first readily apparent. You may perceive all customers within the United Kingdom, for instance, to be similar in buying patterns or social habits. It is important to remember, however, that each and every population is just as diverse within itself as it is between itself and another culture. People from the United Kingdom are just as racially, ethnically and socially diverse as people from the United States. Developing a sense of empathy or concern for people as individuals as opposed to thinking of them as members of a group helps you to meet people where they are and to make them feel comfortable doing business with you.

Combating Negative Attitudes: Closely related to developing empathy, it is important for businesses to combat negative attitudes in the workplace. This starts with you, the business owner. Evaluate your own attitudes toward diversity and inter-culture communication. Do you hold any racial insensitivity or unspoken gender norms? If so, you will need to work on overcoming these barriers before you can encourage your staff to be more open-minded and before you will truly be able to connect with customers and business partners in other parts of the world.

2.2 The Impact of Culture on an International Business

There are many things like culture, economy, politics, etc. that impact the working of international businesses in today's world. When the two aspects of human society, culture and business, interact with each other, it leads to the development of interesting conditions or scenarios. When different cultures converge at a common point with business as the platform, clashes are bound to take place. But most importantly, such a scenario helps us adapt to challenging situations. Many a business deal falls apart due to fundamental misunderstandings. The toughest aspect of understanding a people are their cultural values. Operating at very subtle level, individuals within a culture often do not clearly understand what those values are.

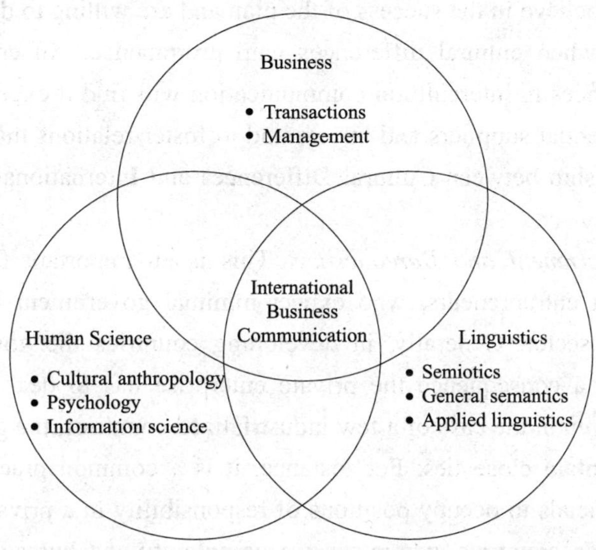

Figure 3.1 The Interdisciplinary Study of International Business Communication

It's like a fish trying to describe the nature of water or describing the components of air. The international business culture, as a whole, is a congregation of various business practices, cultural influences and the thought processes followed in different nations. What is the importance of understanding cultural value dimensions in businesses? Like other cultural systems, organizational culture controls the behavior, values, assumptions, and beliefs of organizational members. With today's businesses entering a "globalized" world, the interaction between different cultures is bound to happen. Merely learning different languages won't be enough. It is necessary for corporate houses to understand the social conditions of different countries, to successfully tap the respective markets. Being sensitive to the values and beliefs of different cultures of the world is necessary. International businesses are not only a way of making profits by the utilization of international talent, but also a bridge between different nations of the world. Tomorrow's world will rely more on a symbiotic relationship between international businesses and cultures as a whole.

Starting a business outside the geographical boundaries of a country requires assessing a number of factors. Drawing up a business plan, assessing demand and supply, applying for loans and grants, getting permits and licenses and deciding on the location of the business are important issues that preoccupy the entrepreneur. Very often, an entrepreneur focuses only on the technical aspects and ignores the cultural aspects of a business. A good business plan is useless, unless people believe in the success of the plan and are willing to do business with the entrepreneur. This is when cultural differences gain prominence. An entrepreneur who is unaware of the differences in intercultural communication will find it exceedingly difficult to communicate with potential suppliers and buyers and to foster relations that are necessary for any business. Relationship between Cultural Differences and International Business is listed below:

Role of the Government and Bureaucracy: This is an important factor that is often overlooked by foreign entrepreneurs, who expect minimal government intervention in the affairs of the private sector. Generally, in developing countries the government plays an important role and as a consequence the private enterprise has to deal with red tape and bureaucracy. In fact, even in the case of a few industrialized countries, the government and the private enterprise maintain close ties. For instance, it is a common practice in France, for retired government officials to occupy positions of responsibility in a private company. In the case of South American countries, administrative complexity and bureaucracy are common problems that are encountered by an entrepreneur.

Power Distance: Hierarchies and the delivery of respect based on position vary widely throughout the world. In some countries, like Japan, business practices and communication styles center heavily around a person's status and title in an organization. An employee speaks deferentially and formally to a manager, and is unlikely to object against or challenge a supervisor. In countries with less power distance, such as the United States, the relationship, and therefore communication, between an employee and employer may be more collegial and, in some company cultures, disagreement within limits is encouraged.

However, when cultures come into contact with each other, this can create friction. An American employee who addresses a Japanese executive too casually can create a tense situation. Similarly, a person who comes from a culture with a high degree of power distance may seem too aloof or subservient to their American co-workers. Managers must become aware of these differences and address them to create a successful outcome.

Directness: Some cultures are more direct than others. Some expect that when a person is asked a question, that person should respond with a full and complete answer. In other cultures, people respond more narrowly, and answer only what they are asked specifically.

For example, in an American or British workplace, a question regarding what time someone's flight arrives might earn a response that the flight was scheduled to land at 1:00, but, due to delays, it probably won't land until 2:00, meaning that the individual in question might not get to the office until 3:00. In other cultures, such as Turkey and Thailand, the answer may simply be that the person was scheduled to land at 1:00. However, it can work in other ways. In some cultures, such as Nepal and Thailand, asking a person's weight, income and even sexual orientation can be perfectly common, acceptable questions. However, in other cultures, such as in the United States, such personal questions would be considered to be intrusive and could inspire offense or discomfort.

Business Meetings: The duration of the business meetings is generally long in Asian and South American countries. Whereas, in the U.S., meetings are short and to the point. Most business decisions in Asian and South American countries are taken after a lot of deliberation. Despite this, strict schedule is rarely drawn and dispensed. In Japan, business ethics demand punctuality; while being well-prepared and getting the facts right is important in Germany. One should avoid setting up meetings well in advance, in South American countries, since there are frequent changes in schedule. Again, French business firms rely on long-term plans; while South American firms prefer short-term plans.

Communication: The way of communicating could be different in different cultures. The terms used by some might sound harsh to others. The way in which words are pronounced can impact the intercultural communication in the corporate houses. In fact, it is one of the major hindrance in the process of business communication.

In some countries, written communication is important; while others give preference to verbal communication. In Argentina and Brazil, verbal communication is very important. In France and Germany, written communication is desired. French lay great emphasis on grammatically correct communication; while Germans expect the business communication to be precise. Humor is often used in office communication in both Australia and the U.S., unlike Germany, Japan and China. In the U.S., excessive modesty is neither appreciated nor desired; but in Asian countries, modesty is essential. Diplomacy is the key to good communication in Britain.

Body Language: Much is communicated through bodily postures and facial expressions. However, even silently, we're not all speaking the same language. In some countries, like Nepal and parts of India, shaking one's head side to side signifies agreement or accord. This can be very confusing to the Western habit of shaking one's head up and down to agree. Similarly, in most Western countries, eye contact is a sign of listening, truth and understanding. In many Asian cultures, direct eye contact is considered rude and offensive. One person's attempt to communicate openly, honestly and with mutual understanding can have the exact opposite effect.

Time: People from Britain and Germany are keen on following the time-bound schedule. The different "time-cultures" might be the reason behind clashes between people from diverse cultures. The way in which the boardroom meetings are handled, is also a reason behind differences in opinions. Corporate houses from Western countries stick to the schedule during meetings. They get down to business in an outright manner. Other cultures may differ in this aspect of business.

Seniority, Meritocracy and Decision-Making: Seniority is given a great deal of importance in Asian countries; while meritocracy is important in countries like U.S., Australia and Germany. In France, a combination of seniority and meritocracy determines the promotions and importance of the individual in the organization. One should not assume that the senior-most person has the authority of making business decisions. This is especially true, in case of South American countries, where the decision-making rules are not strictly defined. Even in an industrialized country like Britain, many times, authority and responsibility may be unclear, since the job descriptions are not precise.

Gifts and Personal Favors: Gifts and favors are common in Asian and South American countries, unlike the U.S., where there are strict rules regarding exchanging favors within an organization. While Americans feel that gifts and favors affect impartial decision-making capacity, in Asian countries exchanging favors is a way of life.

2.3 The Importance of Cultural Sensitivity in Business Dealings

Companies often employ foreign workers and court foreign parties as their operations go global and they take advantage of new markets in other countries. This makes cultural sensitivity in business more important than ever. An ignorance of a country's cultural norms can offend important clients, alienate employees in other countries and even lead to a reduction of product or service sales.

One-on-One Cultural Sensitivity: Cultural sensitivity can play an important role on the personal level. Companies courting employees or executives from countries with other social norms or beliefs would do well to respect those beliefs. A failure to do so can lead to everything from personal offense taken to certain cultural insensitive moves (such as not taking into account a person's cultural dietary restrictions during a business lunch) to the failure to do business entirely if a company consistently offends the culture of a potential business partner.

Cultural Sensitivity and Products (Intercultural Marketing): Businesses that either market to, or negotiate with, foreign cultures should research cultural differences in order to avoid situations that could create conflict. Advertising to foreign culture should be carefully reviewed, especially if it is translated into another language.

Being sensitive to cultural considerations is also essential to selling products in other countries. Many firms have lost money when selling their products in other countries due to their failure to understand the culture. For instance, when debuting a film called "Hollywood Buddha," a film studio ran into serious trouble in Malaysia, Sri Lanka and Burma because the film lacked cultural sensitivity towards Buddhist symbols traditionally held in reverence in these countries.

Cultural Sensitivity and Negotiation (Intercultural Negotiation): Conflict in international negotiations can result from differences in language as well, but often, foreign cultures also have different attitudes about negotiating. For example, the intellectual property website *FPO* says some European countries don't have a culture of negotiation. In these cases, buyers or sellers who propose prices far off from what they are willing to accept in order to build room for negotiation are seen as untrustworthy.

When businesses need to sell products or negotiate deals in foreign countries, often these use the host country's own language. Being insensitive to the nuances of a foreign language can create real cultural relations problems for companies. Marketing efforts for an alcoholic beverage called "Irish Mist" ran astray in Germany because the company behind the product failed to notice that the word "Mist" in German means "manure."

Cultural Sensitivity and Employees (Intercultural HR): As globalization has companies frequently outsourcing work or recruiting global professionals from a range of countries, many firms have instituted cultural sensitivity training and expanded the range of languages into which their sales aids and brochures are translated. A failure to appreciate cultural differences like language and traditions can alienate foreign employees and, in the case of materials not translated into their language, actually prevent them from doing their jobs.

In business, intercultural communication plays a critical role in successfully carrying out business with teams and stakeholders in other areas of the globe. Even small businesses that don't trade overseas can be faced with cultural conflict issues. In some cases, cultural and ethnic diversity in the workplace can create conflict and affect employee morale if not managed properly. But through communication and leadership, small businesses can avoid these conflicts and reap the benefits that a workforce of diverse views and talents offers. When the communication is effective, everyone benefits from increased bandwidth, institutional knowledge, and competitive advantage. Ineffective communication however, can offend, confuse or send a misconstrued message which could lead to broken relations with customers, partners, vendors, and employees. Main intercultural communication barriers consist of:

Language Barriers: A common intercultural barrier in business communication is of course, language. Although English is regarded as the common international language of business, not every business globally uses English on a regular basis. Employees may have more difficulty when communicating in English, which can lead to misunderstandings when taking direction, understanding level of urgency and communicating issues or concerns. Never assume that you are perfectly understood because your instructions receive head nods. Check for real understanding by asking others to summarize what they have just heard.

Cultural Barriers: Every culture has a different set of values, business ethics, accepted behavior and decorum-even different facial expressions and gestures. It is important to understand these differences—to show genuine respect for other cultural mores—when communicating with professionals from other cultures. For example, in the United States it is common for the speaker to share personal anecdotes to build audience report, but in other countries this is considered tiresome. Humor can be especially tricky to employ; better to be straightforward rather than run the risk that your joke may inadvertently embarrass or insult the listener.

Presentation Style: Believe it or not, culture influences how people in different countries prefer to receive information. For example, how interactive you should make your presentation depends on the culture to which you present. In general, English speaking cultures like presentations to be lively and interactive. However, Eastern Europeans are accustomed to presentations that are formal, highly detailed and with few interruptions. Questions are answered at the end of presentation. Japanese audiences expect more technical information. Canadians, like Americans, enjoy a brisk pace; and Latin American audiences prefer a speech with a high level of emotional appeal. The key with any group of listeners from another culture is to do your homework, and don't rely on your personal frame of reference when addressing an audience of another culture. By focusing on their own frames of reference, you acknowledge their customs and perspective, which goes far towards winning them over.

2.4 Culture & Subculture in Business

Doing business abroad is a lucrative career option, especially when you know that a foreign economy is booming and there is demand for certain type of products and services, that you can provide. International business has become more dynamic than ever before and it is all about, "the survival of the fittest". Whether it is a part of your expansion plans or a new start-up, doing business overseas needs a plenty of skills and sensibility. When you move to a new cultural setting to conduct business, you need the perfect balance of risk-taking and cautiousness. Yet, you need to be aware of the challenges or obstacles of doing business overseas. For instance, you are to conduct a meeting with some businessmen from the Middle East and you show them a thumb up as a signal to close the deal. Things are going to plummet from there for you because you did not know that it is an offensive gesture in their country.

Every country has diverse cultural etiquette. Being unaware of them and committing a social faux pas can negatively affect your business dealings. Most businessmen admit to cultural differences being one of the biggest challenges of doing business overseas. It is very important to learn the cultural differences in international business because what may be acceptable in your country, could be regarded as being offensive in a foreign country. Also, it will help you to interact with your prospective clientage accordingly, as well as formulate a culturally sensitive tailor-made sales and marketing pitch.

Cultures and subcultures exist on national and internal levels of the business world. Globalization of business has caused these cultures to adapt to one another. Subcultures spring from overall, large cultures. Understanding a company's subculture and how it is derived from the larger business culture will help you avoid offending co-workers, clients and others.

Organizational culture is a term that defines specific patterns of behavior, including rituals, rules and identity within a professional environment. Culture specifically is a means of controlling behavior, providing stability within the organization and a sense of belonging. Individuals who disrupt normal behavioral patterns—or shun the cultural controls within their organization—might be deemed negative or deviant. Company leaders develop cultural controls to create social norms and a sense of shared values within the organization.

Unwritten Social Norms: Most large organizations espouse individuality but in reality create an environment of conformity. Most organizations, in fact, have expected levels of behavioral norms, whether they encourage individuality or conformity. Social norms are unwritten rules of behaviors that dictate how individuals react in specific situations. These are enforced by peers using social sanctions. For example, if your group has an unwritten rule of silence regarding unethical practices, an individual who speaks out against it may be shunned and excluded from future group activities.

Mission Statement: Every company has a mission statement, and most have it written in some form. The mission statement provides a direction for all members and employees to take in regards to actions, behavior and quality control. Culture within a business is not spontaneous. It is deliberately cultivated and created, and the mission statement is the starting point. For example, a mission statement that reads: "Our mission is to inspire and nurture the human spirit—one person, one cup, one neighborhood at a time," implies standards of high ethics, community activism and quality. It provides a base for company culture and how its employees should behave.

Rule and Regulations: That employee handbook you got on your first day on the job is good insight into your company's culture and methods of behavior control. Most company handbooks should include such things as nondisclosure agreements, anti-discrimination policies, expected work schedules, standards of conduct and general information. While many of these are included per national law, other company policies fall in line with the organization's structure and culture. Violating these policies could result in verbal or written reprimands by your superior or termination in extreme cases. Rules and regulations integrate into the company culture and sometimes become embedded in the shared values and social norms of the culture.

Deliberate Role Modeling: When you are a new hire, you receive training for a certain amount of time. This training period, in cultural terms, is deliberate role modeling. Your trainer or manager shows you how the organization works, what you are expected to do, and how you are expected to perform and act. This also applies to membership organizations. Deliberate role modeling continues throughout your membership or employment, as people look to leaders for reminders or clues about what is important. Leaders must act in a way that reflects the organization's values, otherwise, members and employees become cynical and resentful.

EUROPE

The overall business culture in Europe is formal. This trickles down to the subcultures when it comes to dress codes and attitudes. With business attire, Europeans are more formal than their American counterparts. Most business people in Europe dress in suits and ties. European business style is to address those in authority at the company using courtesy titles, not first names.

Etiquette in Europe is not uniform. Even the regions of Europe do not have common manners. For example, a Dane will prefer direct speech while a Finn will tend to prevaricate. Even within a single country there may be different customs, especially when there are different linguistic groups, as in Switzerland where there are French, German and Italian speakers.

Throughout Southern Europe, many people conduct ordinary conversations in a more lively manner than that to which other people, especially Northern Europeans, are accustomed. Loud volume, gesticulation for emphasis, interruptions and casual body contact that might seem rude or boisterous elsewhere are ordinary.

- **France**

The people of France observe some particular points of etiquette related to respect for and appreciation of wine. French manners were established by the ecclesiastical authorities in the Middle Ages, by the monarchy from the 15th to the 17th centuries, then by the aristocracies and political classes in the modern era.

Connections count heavily in this market. Trade shows and official trade promotion missions are good ways to make initial contact. The alternative is to arrange for a formal introduction to potential customers, distributors or partners. Ask your country's embassy to introduce you. Other useful intermediaries are chambers of commerce, trade associations and international banks, law and accounting firms. But don't overlook that golf buddy or neighbor of yours whose company has a big office in Paris! Your letter requesting a meeting should be in flawless business French. As in other hierarchical cultures, it is wise to start at the top. Address the letter to the President/Directeur General and if you are a senior person in your company request a meeting with him.

All business dealings in France are much more formal than in the United States. This extends to the use of names. In the US, business people quickly adopt the use of first names. In France, one remains "Mr. Jones" for years. Only if the French counterpart has been to the US and wants to show off how Americanized he has become would he use your first name quickly. It would be terribly bad manners, and it might lose you the contract or the sale, if you slap him on the back, smile broadly, and call him Francois (or Frank). When you greet your counterparts, you shake hands with everyone in the room. It is not acceptable to enter the room, wave, and say—hi folks! —You shake hands when you first meet and when you are saying good-bye at the end of the day. You do not shake hands when you meet for lunch or going back to the office for more meetings—you shake hands only twice in one day.

French management is more hierarchical and more rigid than American management. You don't want to go over your boss's head for any reason whatsoever. You've got to respect the hierarchy in both directions. As a manager, it is expected that you will maintain distance from your employees. You are not expected to be an equal or be friendly. You do not necessarily socialize with your employees outside of work. As a manager and as a leader, you maintain a certain image of formality. The French appreciate when they are asked for input. But there is no need to get consensus on decisions, though they do like to be consulted. In the end, the leader is expected to make decisions. If you are doing a good job, that's great, but you are not going to hear about it. You are expected to do a good job. French managers rarely give positive feedback. But they tend not to be shy about giving negative feedback. That sometimes sounds fairly harsh to Americans. It can be any kind of situation, such as missing a deadline or work done which does not meet expectations. It might sound personal, "I expected more from you" type of rebuke. The French are pretty thick skinned about these kinds of things.

- **The United Kingdom**

Introductions are very important. The polite greeting is "How do you do?" It is a rhetorical question—do not expect an answer. A woman should extend her hand first as a British male will not take a woman's hand unless she offers it. Do not rush to crush an individual's hand. The handshake should be firm but with a lighter pressure than most American handshakes. In business, it is best to be formally introduced by someone else. The exception to this rule is a large reception; one can properly introduce himself or herself in this environment. However, keep the conversation general, such as weather, hobbies, animals and gardens. Do not inquire about where someone lives, what school he or she attended or to which church he or she belongs. These topics are considered intrusive.

Brits usually want to chat with a new business contact at some length before getting down to business. Visitors are well advised to wait for their local counterpart to initiate the business part of the meeting. Asian, Latin and Arab negotiators find it quite normal that the English need to get to know their overseas counterparts a bit before talking business. In contrast, many Germans, Swiss, Danes and Americans become impatient and irritated with what they regard as unnecessarily long preliminary conversations.

The visitor is expected to be prompt. His host should receive him after a short wait. The British usually have separate offices for the majority of their executives. And the office proper has long functioned as a status symbol. Dark wood paneling, classic desks, fine rugs, paintings, and exquisite light fixtures are all prestigious. A private secretary, near whose desk one might wait a minute or two, is another indication of the executive's status. One greets a Briton with a firm handshake. Bowing is uncalled for. Often the secretary will introduce the visitor. If he or she does not, the foreigner should introduce himself. Many British have difficulty with foreign languages, and are apt to misunderstand a series of unfamiliar names.

- **Germany**

Formality makes it harder to reach a German. There is the model of the peach and the coconut, which illustrates the relationship-building styles of the two cultures. In America, you have the peach, where you can find out about someone very easily. The outer shell is very soft and simple to peel away, Americans will tell you all about their families, their backgrounds, and where they're from, all on a three-hour airplane ride. Afterwards they'll say, "oh, I've met a new friend here." In Germany, you find more of a coconut. It takes a long time to get through the outer shell, because it's a hard, tough shell to crack. Germans don't let you in so fast. Once you do get through, however, the inside is very soft, and you have made a friend for life and you share with one another very openly your deepest thoughts. But German formality makes for a much longer relationship-building process than is found in the US.

Americans often have difficulties with foreign business partners. They tend to "get right down to business" without taking the time to form the kind of personal relations that in many cultures are a prerequisite to initiating business relations. In the case of the American/German interface, Americans are in the opposite role. Personal relations play a smaller part in the German business world than they do in the US. Talks and meetings begin without preamble, and personal factors are rarely taken into account when considering business questions, even when the subject involves personnel or human resource issues. Colleagues rarely become friends, as Germans strongly separate their private life from their professional sphere.

They must understand that Germans are simply more formal. And the reason they are more formal is hierarchy. Sixty percent of top managers in German engineering and manufacturing companies have a doctorate degree. This cost them blood, sweat and tears. These are tough degrees to get, and they want you to know that. A wife of a German executive with doctorate is called "Frau Doctor." Age is also a rather important factor in the hierarchical business structure. The younger you are, the more you have to be conscious of formality. Germans shake hands more often than we do in the States. You shake hands when you meet someone, and you shake hands when you leave. The handshake should be firm, with good, strong eye contact. But that is about it for body contact. One should avoid grabbing someone's arm or slapping someone's back.

- **Russia**

In Russia, business meetings are serious and formal. Russian business culture retains many of the characteristics instilled during the Soviet era, most noticeably an autocratic management style that contrasts sharply to the more open and collaborative practices used by American businesses. When doing business in Russia or with Russian businesspeople, Americans should err on the side of formality and deference for those in positions of authority.

Corporate Structure: Russian companies follow a stricter, more clearly defined hierarchy than do American businesses. Many Russian businesses are led by a single, autocratic authority figure who makes the decisions and delegates tasks to middle managers and lower-level employees. Employees are expected to follow management's direction with little to no discussion. In American businesses, though, even lower-ranked employees often ask questions about duties assigned to them and collaborate with supervisors.

Communication Style: Russian businesspeople place greater emphasis on the spoken word than do professionals in the United States. While American businesspeople do much of their business via written communication such as email, letter or fax, Russian professionals prefer to hear things directly from people they trust. Face-to-face meetings are usually more productive than written correspondence because they allow participants to more fully discuss and explain issues. Russian businesspeople also demonstrate much less body language than American professionals, especially in meetings. They might listen silently without even nodding in agreement, confusing their American counterparts who rely on visual cues such as eye contact and posture.

Meetings and Teamwork: In Russia, meetings are formal, serious gatherings, and casual behavior is considered a sign of disrespect. Decisions are usually made in advance, either one on one or in small groups of decision-makers, with meetings held solely to share information and give direction. In contrast, in the United States meetings are slightly less formal, with participants interacting casually and frequently debating and discussing issues. Russian businesspeople value personal relationships and trust, and tend to be suspicious of strangers. As a result, they usually work in small teams where people know each other well. Instead of forming a new team for each project, these teams often work together regularly. By contrast, in America teams are often created on a project basis, and the participants frequently have not previously met.

Dress Code: Business attire in Russia is similar to that in the United States, with men usually opting for dark suits and women wearing business suits or skirts and blouses. Women in Russia wear slacks at work less frequently than American businesswomen. A major difference is the emphasis on designer labels. Russian professionals usually dress as expensively as their salaries permit, and clothing that is obviously expensive is a sign of credibility. While a tasteful wardrobe is also a status symbol in the United States, a designer label is less important. When doing business in Russia, though, American professionals should appear elegantly dressed to be perceived as equals.

Gender Roles: In theory, Russia's business culture advocates equality for women in the workplace, but in practice, the status of women is much lower than in America's corporate culture. While many Russian women work, few hold high-ranking positions, in contrast to the American workplace, where women frequently hold senior management and top governmental positions. American women doing business in Russia will often be treated politely and with old-fashioned courtesy but viewed as inferior to their male counterparts regardless of their position. They might have difficulty getting their voices heard in meetings, where men will likely be given preference.

- **The United States**

A primary component of the U.S. business culture is punctuality. Although other cultures don't watch the clock when it comes to meeting clients and co-workers, Americans believe punctuality is a sign of respect. Americans are as obsessed with time as many other cultures are with relationship-building. Famously monochronic, they treat time as a tangible asset which can be saved, spent, lost, found, invested and wasted. If U.S. business people have an appointment in someone's office at 9:00 they expect their counterpart to see them right on the dot. They regard a person who keeps them waiting for longer than ten minutes as either hopelessly undisciplined, intolerably rude or both. The importance of deadlines is also a subculture in U.S. business; they are strictly followed. Similarly, once the meeting starts Americans expect discussions to proceed to conclusion without interruption. When doing business in polychronic cultures they become easily upset when discussions are interrupted by phone calls, drop-in visitors or secretaries bringing in papers to be signed. This means that visiting negotiators should take care to be on time for all meetings in the USA and can expect an apology if they are kept waiting for more than a few minutes.

A visitor who is arriving in the United States as a member of a U.S. organization will usually have received an itinerary of his or her scheduled activities. This itinerary will include the name of the hotel and the time of first meetings at the office. It will mention by name the people who will take part in the opening discussions. Such a visitor need take no specific action before arrival. If he does not have a local office or agent, the visitor is well advised to arrange firm appointments with the people or companies he wishes to see. Such appointments are easy to make by mail. A letter is an acceptable substitute for personal contact in the United States, and if it contains a clear message, it will reach the appropriate person in the target organization. The visitor should insist that the subsequent appointment be with a specific individual. Otherwise he could waste much time searching for the appropriate contact.

The good foreign negotiator will be sensitive to signals that indicate areas of importance to the American. What does the U.S. counterpart hope to gain? Remember that, to the typical American, success related to personal accomplishment or organizational gains is the cornerstone to making a deal. This view encompasses a broad variety of potential advantages: making profits, earning more money, completing a job, advancing in the hierarchy, making new friends, introducing new products or data to the organization, and perhaps simply experiencing the prestige or excitement of opening a foreign connection. To strengthen his initial reception, the foreign visitor might well present some first-rate written material.

Casual relationships with regard to hierarchy is something the U.S. business culture enjoys that isn't seen in other business cultures. People are typically on a first-name basis at work, regardless of their respective positions. If you have a business appointment or interview with someone, you expect to have that person to yourself, and the business shouldn't take more than an hour or so.

If you're talking to someone, you get uncomfortable if they approach closer than about two feet. About the only things you expect to bargain for are houses, cars, and antiques. Haggling is largely a matter of finding the hidden point that's the buyer's minimum. Once you're past college, you very rarely simply show up at someone's place. People have to invite each other over—especially if a meal is involved. When you negotiate, you are polite, of course, but it's only good business to "play hardball". Some foreigners pay excessive attention to status, or don't say what they mean, and that's exasperating.

ASIA

Asian business culture is based on extreme politeness. For example, instead of saying no, business people have a hard time refusing requests. In some cases, they will just continue discussing it until the other party figures out the first party really doesn't want to fulfill the request and withdraws it. In addition, the Asian business subculture values gift giving as a sign of respect. Buying presents for the spouses of clients is a typical Asian business practice.

◆ Chinese Business Culture. Chinese business practices, culture and etiquette can be challenging for Westerners to navigate.

"Giving Face" and "Losing Face": Be aware of seniority in your interactions, as well as in introductions, seating during business meetings and social functions, and in conversation. Giving due respect by honoring titles, age and length of service (aka "giving face") is important to the Chinese and a critical part of the culture. Equally, the Chinese hate to suffer any loss of respect (aka "losing face"), which happens when titles, age and length of service are ignored, purposefully or otherwise. The importance of this cannot be overstated.

Business Meetings: As is the case in many societies outside the United States, Chinese business culture is geared toward formal presentation. Conservative business attire; dark, tailored suits, pants and skirts are all appropriate. Stick with classic styles and clean lines. Avoid anything overly flashy or casual. Interpersonal communication is also formal, with the use of titles important during all introductions. Bowing as a greeting is common courtesy. Your Chinese counterpart may extend a hand for a handshake as well, which you should accept. Avoid overly demonstrative hand gestures or pointing, as this can be perceived as threatening. Give and receive business cards, brochures and marketing collateral with two hands. Ensure that all items are distributed with the idea of "giving face" and handed out to face the receiving party. Punctuality is very important to the Chinese, so avoid being late.

Gifts: Giving gifts to your Chinese host is appreciated. You should also expect to receive gifts in return. This custom often plays an important role in your future business relationship because trust and allegiance are often equated with the size and variety of the gift. Also, senior executives and associates should receive gifts of a higher value (real or perceived) than their subordinates. File this recommendation under "giving face." Avoid giving straw sandals, handkerchiefs or anything wrapped in black, white or blue, as these all have connotations of death and funerals. Finally, avoid gifting clocks of any kind, as the Chinese word for clock is pronounced the same as the word for "end."

Lunch, Dinner and Post-Dining Entertainment: Business talk often happens at a formal Chinese business meal, usually at dinner. A pre-business meal at lunchtime is also common, with most Chinese executives dodging any business discussions beforehand. Expect a complicated seating arrangement (by seniority—more "giving face") for any Chinese business meal, hosted in a private room at a restaurant chosen by the host. Formal business dinners in China can be lengthy with unique customs. These include lively social discussions, karaoke, "drinking contests" and (in some rare instances) retiring to a night club or sauna. Be prepared for several hours of communal activity to accompany your meal.

◆ Japanese Business Culture. Many a businessman transplanted to the Land of the Rising Sun has come back with tales of culture shock and bewilderment. To people in the West, Japanese culture remains a mystery wrapped in an enigma.

Meeting and Greeting: There is heightened sense of formality in Japanese interaction. When doing business in Japan, your suitability in respect to conducting business will be assessed during a first meeting, so always maintain a sense of professionalism. The bow is an integral part of Japanese society. It is used when meeting, getting attention, to show gratitude, to express sympathy or as an apology. Whilst doing business in Japan as a Westerner, you would not be expected to bow. You will most likely to be greeted with a handshake combined with a slight nod of the head. Introduce yourself with your full name followed by your company name. It is important to use proper titles when addressing someone, so always establish the position of the other person. The exchanging of business cards when doing business in Japan involves a degree of ceremony. The card is seen to represent the individual, so should be treated with respect. Before travelling to Japan, ensure you have ample cards and have one side translated into Japanese. Include your position within the company on it. Invest in a carry case to store cards and keep this in the inside pocket of a suit jacket.

Building Relationships: When doing business in Japan a successful relationship with a Japanese colleague or client is based on three factors: sincerity, compatibility and trustworthiness. Sincerity means that you are compromising, understanding and you want to conduct business on a personal level. Compatibility is established when you are seen to be concerned about the personal relationship, the well being of the company and not just focused on financial gain. Trustworthiness relates to the faith put in you to protect from losing face.

Communication: The emphasis in Japanese culture on maintaining harmony has developed in such a way as to allow very vague forms of expression. The cultural logic behind this is that by avoiding direct or explicit statements one has a better chance of not causing offense. When doing business in Japan clarify meanings and dig deeper for more information. The Japanese are implicit communicators. An explicit communicator assumes the listener is unaware of background information or related issues to the topic of discussion and provides it themselves. The Japanese however assume the listener is well informed on the subject and minimises information relayed on the premise that listener will understand from implication. Thus the saying, "Say one, understand ten," i.e. you will be expected to understand nine additional points to every one made.

Meetings and Negotiations: At a meeting you will always deal with a team as opposed to an individual. Each attendee will be there with a particular expertise so either bring assistance or be sure you are confident enough to handle all the questions you will receive. You will greet the most senior employee first and then others in descending order. The senior employee will be there as a ceremonial representative of the company. The lesser ranking attendees will usually do the talking or negotiating. Meetings usually take place for only one of three reasons: to build rapport, exchange information or confirm previously made decisions. Decisions are rarely made in a meeting. If rapport has yet to be established then this is your priority. It is important not only to build relationships with all the senior figures but all lower ranked ones too. Remember group consensus is important so the opinions of all staff will be taken into account when coming to a decision on any proposal. The Japanese are very detail orientated. Expect lots of questions and lots of questions repeated in different ways. Be sure to have the answers as the failure to do so will look unprofessional. Be sure to bring as much information as possible, in writing, on your company, service, product or proposal.

The Japanese like dealing with quiet, sincere and compromising individuals. Extroverts are seen as brash and arrogant. Early on in negotiations remain humble, indirect and non-threatening. Do not disagree openly, do not put people on the spot and always employ diplomatic language when doing business. Be sure to hold off concessions till the end of proceedings. If made early your integrity will be questioned. Silence is considered a virtue. If things go quiet when doing business in a meeting then do not panic. Reflection is taking place. Silence may be also be accompanied by the closing of the eyes. Never interrupt or break the silence.

LATIN AMERICA

Latin Americans like to do business with people they know, including their family and friends. Establishing and maintaining an informal network of close partners is a normal practice, without some negative connotations it would have in the US, Canada or Europe. You can expect loyalty and gratefulness for doing somebody a favor. The same can be expected of you when somebody helps you. From Argentina to Venezuela, it is customary to ask friends and partners for assistance, which is a powerful relationship-forming force. Latin Americans do show due respect to those in authority.

Latin Americans are often seen as more passionate than Americans or Europeans. They do prefer face-to-face contact to formal correspondence or even communication by phone. This reflects their willingness to interact directly and include body language or gestures into the process. It is part of business etiquette in Latin America to maintain contact with your business colleague. How you present yourself and your message can be as important as information itself.

Latin Americans are sensitive to double meaning so you might want to double check if you understood the key details correctly to avoid misunderstanding. Should you find yourself in a confrontational situation, it is best to step back and not escalate it.

Attitude to appearance is varied throughout the region, but it is safe that while doing business in Latin America you are expected to wear formal and stylish attire. Argentina has a reputation for high fashion sense, Brazil seems to be the most laid-back in this respect. Handshakes are relatively firm and brief.

Strict punctuality is not a standard in the region, although some countries (Chile, Bolivia) consider it a priority. You might have to wait longer for people with authority. Regardless of that, it is best to arrange the meeting a week or two in advance and arrive on time in order to show deference and the right attitude. Engaging in some small talk at the start of the meeting is welcome. Meetings tend not to end with a final decision or agreement.

Respecting social and business hierarchy while arranging and conducting negotiations is necessary. Decision-makers will expect to talk to their peers at your organization.

Final decisions take time to materialize and in larger organizations they involve contribution from multiple stakeholders.

2.5 How to Overcome Intercultural Communication Barriers in Business

In global companies, effective intercultural communication enables businesses to run more smoothly. By acknowledging the potential problems that can occur and taking proactive steps to minimize conflict, you can help your employees work together better. Adjusting behavior takes time, so be sure to provide opportunities for your employees to learn about each others' cultures and habits before problems arise. Set expectations throughout your company that additional effort might be required to understand each other. Foster engagement in thoughtful consideration instead of jumping to hasty conclusions that lead to volatile, unproductive conflicts.

STEPS RECOMMENDED TO OVERCOME INTERCULTURAL BUSINESS COMMUNICATION BARRIERS

Step 1: Run meetings to expose your employees to other cultures. Introducing employees who will be working together in a non-threatening environment enables a good working relationship long term. Learning about another culture's language, rules and norms for acceptable behavior helps prepare your employees to deal with situations as they arise. Changing preconceptions can lead to more conducive working relationships.

Step 2: Conduct activities to demonstrate how dependent we are on language. For example, dedicate a day to being silent. Have each employee develop a contract stating what they hope to learn, how long they will remain silent (what exceptions can be made) and how they plan to cope without speaking all day. After experiencing a day with limited communication, participants can typically relate to being in a foreign environment more easily.

Step 3: Provide workshops, tips and techniques for communicating effectively in intercultural work environments. People act according to the values of their own culture. Others from another culture might interpret behavior differently. Practicing such strategies as active listening (paraphrasing what is said to ensure understanding can be achieved) and using multiple forms of communication, such as written, audio and visual, can enhance employee involvement in assuring that conflicts do not arise because of cultural misunderstandings due to lack of awareness.

Step 4: Coach employees to mediate conflicts related to cultural misunderstandings. Provide opportunities for employees to respond to situations from viewpoints different than their own. Divide a group of people into pairs to conduct role-playing exercises that allow participants to acknowledge culture difference exist. Encourage each pair to think about a conflict they have experienced recently due to cultural differences. Have each participant describe what they might find offensive or unusual. Let each participant suggest how the problem would be handled in their own culture. Together, have the participants develop a resolution to the problem. Have each pair report to the larger group on their experiences.

SOME TECHNIQUES IN INTERCULTURAL BUSINESS COMMUNICATION

Awareness: Just the simple act of being aware of your surroundings before you enter business negotiations in another country can help you succeed. Study the culture of the country to which you're traveling before you arrive. Learn what insults them and determine the cultural norms in situations like dining out and meeting new people, both of which are common in business dealings. Americans and Japanese view business negotiations very differently, for example. Americans view original contracts as being very important, while Japanese view them as a starting point for future negotiations.

Do as the Romans Do: When you're in another country, try to act as the locals do whenever possible. No amount of pre-trip studying of a culture can prepare you for every social situation, but paying attention to those around you can help you work your way through business and social dealings. For example, British business culture allows for discussion and criticism of ideas in a business meeting, but in many hierarchical cultures, business meetings are the forum to inform employees of decisions already made. There is no room for criticism or questioning.

English: Although English is the world's language of business communication, remember that many people learn English as a second language. The figures of speech you use on a regular basis may not be understood by someone whose native language is not English. This can be the case even in two English-speaking countries. Speak clearly and simply. Don't speak louder, or so slow as to insult the person with whom you're speaking, however. Get a reliable interpreter if necessary to ensure clear communication.

Presentations: Again, study the culture before you make your presentation. If the culture is more relaxed than yours, you may have to start your presentation later than you originally anticipated. Allow for networking and talking time before your presentation in these cultures. Be ready to present your material using the technology available in the country. You may have to use an overhead projector or a blackboard instead of a computer and projector. People in some cultures do not like visual aids in presentations, but would rather witness your oratory skills.

3. Exercises

I. Analysis of Four Cases in the Intercultural Offices

1) A case study on project deadlines…

Rebecca works with United Technologies, a Chicago based company. She is talking on the phone to Abhinav, the manager of one of United Technologies vendors for customer service outsourcing.

Rebecca: *We really need to get all of the customer service representatives trained on our new process in the next two weeks. Can you get this done?*

Abhinav: *That timeline is pretty aggressive. Do you think it's possible?*

Rebecca: *I think it will require some creativity and hard work, but I think we can get it done with two or three days to spare.*

Abhinav: *Ok.*

Rebecca: *Now that our business is settled, how is everything else?*

Abhinav: *All's well, although the heavy monsoons this year are causing a lot of delays getting around the city.*

Two weeks later…

Abhinav: *We've pulled all of our resources and I'm happy to say that 60% of the customer service representatives are now trained in the new process. The remaining 40% will complete the training in the next two weeks.*

Rebecca: *Only 60%? I thought we agreed that they all would be trained by now!*

Abhinav: *Yes. The monsoon is now over so the rest of the training should go quickly.*

Rebecca: *This training is critical to our results. Please get it done as soon as possible.*

Abhinav: *I am certain that it will be done in the next two weeks.*

2) A case study on virtual teams and hierarchy…

Based in Cleveland, Ohio, Jim has been managing a software development team in Pune for the past two years. He has been working closely with Aruna, the Indian team leader, to develop a new networking program. While Jim has over 25 years of experience in software development, Aruna knows the program inside and out. While reviewing his work from the previous week, Jim discovers that he made a mistake in the programming code. He notices that Aruna corrected his error, but wonders why Aruna did not bring it to his attention so that he could avoid delays and keep from making the same mistake in the future.

3) A case study on miscommunication in multicultural teams…

Sandeep has just joined the Banglore office of a New York based MNC. As part of his training he will be spending 3 months in the U.S., but has already been assigned to a team with members in New York, Tokyo and Banglore. Sarah, the New York based project manager, has scheduled a teleconference meeting for Tuesday. Sandeep will be traveling to Delhi to get his U.S. visa over the meeting time. Here's their conversation…

Sarah: *Can we do the teleconference tomorrow, 7 p.m. for you, or should we wait until you get back?*

Sandeep: *Better if we can wait, but I can do it if you like—if it's necessary.*

Sarah: *Do you want to postpone it? Tell me, yes or no?*

4) A case study on cultural conflict and the values of status and community…

Mayank has been working as an Information Officer at a foreign consulate in New Delhi for several years. His boss, Hendrick, wants to reward Mayank for his hard work and offers him a promotion and pay raise to become an Information Clerk. Mayank politely declines the offer, leaving Hendrick confused.

II. Group Discussion

Topic 1

Carrefour China: A Local Market

Source: linkshop.com.cn

Several years ago, the typical Chinese consumer purchased his vegetables and groceries at open-air markets. Supermarkets were out of his league; they were uncompetitive and overpriced. This has changed. In recent years, shopping in China has become easier and cheaper as the number of supermarkets and retail stores in major cities has rapidly mushroomed. Foreign retailers continue to steadily flow into the country as China gradually opens its retail market to overseas investment. And with over a billion mouths to feed, the opportunities for food retailers are huge indeed.

Carrefour, the French retail giant, has foreseen China's potential. It is the largest retailer in Europe and second largest worldwide (the first being American retailer Wal-Mart). Though Carrefour Group's Asia operations accounts only for 11 percent of its business (over 50 percent of its business is in Europe), and revenues from China were just 3 percent of total 2004 Carrefour Group profits, China's retail market is one of its top priorities. Since 1995, Carrefour has opened 59 Carrefour supermarkets, 8 Champion hypermarkets, and over 150 DIA hard discount stores throughout China.

BOOMING BUSINESS

At the end of the 1980s, Carrefour considered Asia as the next market for its future development, and arrived in China's Taiwan in 1989. "At that time, the goal was to build a hypermarket of 10,000 square meters on multiple levels, similar to stores in France," says Eric Deliers, Regional Manager of Carrefour China, North Region. "But it did not work. Carrefour could not just transfer their French concepts, even though it has been done in other countries." The Chinese concept of retail and operations were significantly different.

In order to set up their stores on the island, Carrefour needed first to completely revise its concept to adapt to the specifics of the local environment. This included changes in management structure, products carried and even store design. The company had to operate in high density urban areas with stores built inside of preexisting buildings, not on flat, open, undeveloped land as had been done elsewhere. Carrefour has since opened 34 outlets on the island and is China's Taiwan's largest hypermarket chain in terms of current sales. "Our Taiwanese experience was very important," adds Deliers. "It was Carrefour's laboratory not only for China but for all Asia."

After China's Taiwan, Carrefour expanded first into Malaysia and then to the Chinese mainland, where it built its first hypermarket in Beijing in 1995. Over the next five years, Carrefour established 27 chain stores in 15 Chinese cities, with revenues that reached more than US$1 billion in 2000. This figure rose to US$1.2 billion in 2002 and to US$1.6 billion the following year. In 2004 alone, with an eye on major cities with populations of more than 2 million, the French retailer opened more than 12 stores, and revenues reached US$1.9 billion.

Overall, in less than ten years of operation in China, Carrefour has doubled its revenues and the number of stores in the country. The French company is currently the fifth largest retailer in the country and the third in its category.

LOCATION AND LOCALIZATION

Carrefour's strategy is to create and expand retail stores best suited to the local market, setting up hypermarket, supermarket and hard discount stores. Each of these three formats is linked and work together. "We need to have, overall, a large number of supermarkets (and hypermarkets) for the concept [of hard discount stores] to be viable," explains Deliers. "Thus, we would like to create 300 to 500 hard discount DIA stores across China at a rate of 20 DIA stores per month".

Carrefour China's approach is to pull in Chinese consumers with low prices and large supermarkets. The two main Carrefour principles are best location and strong localization. Before opening a store, in-depth research of store location is conducted, followed by research of the local culture and traditions, and local consumer purchasing habits. "The total investment for launching a new store runs from US$650 to US$1,040 million, depending on the city and locations," explains Deliers.

To further increase effectiveness and answer local needs, Carrefour has decentralized its management. Each store manager has autonomy in decision-making and store operation. A Carrefour China Institute in Asia was also created to train its staff so as to engender the "Carrefour Spirit".

The success of Carrefour China has shown that the combination of the concepts of "localization management" and "low price and high quality" has worked in the Chinese world. The French retailer has developed its own labeling to guarantee high quality products and hygiene. It has provided more than 400 commodities of its own brand covering four varieties (food, grocery, daily necessities, and clothes), which account for 2 to 4 percent of its total goods and are 20 to 40 percent cheaper than market prices.

"China does not have an easy market," comments Carrefour China President, Jean-Luc

Chereau. “The country is more like a continent where the variety of cultures and traditions set up challenges for us in how to adapt our concept to each area. We have to deal with strong differences between cities and provinces, and with different institutional levels in the country. However, it is a fantastic challenge to adapt our concept to each area of the country.” Being able to shape itself to local habits has allowed the French retailer to be at the top of its game. But how long will it last?

NOT ABOVE THE LAW

In the beginning of 2002, Carrefour lost its smile when the company had to abruptly stop its aggressive expansion in China. During the following two consecutive years it was unable to expand its business because of violations of Chinese regulations.

In dealing only with local regional authorities, the French retailer had ignored stipulations that foreign retailers had to register with the State Economic and Trade Commission (SETC) to get permission before building stores in China. In addition, Chinese law required foreign retailers to operate through joint ventures. Thus, Carrefour China had to reorganize its Chinese operations and rapidly transfer 35 percent of its ownership to three local stores and two trading firms. The French retailer has since created 31 joint ventures and now has 32 Chinese partners.

At the same time, China’s entrance into the World Trade Organization (WTO) led to the lifting of all restrictions for foreign investments in retail business on December 11, 2004. As a result, entry and expansion of foreign retail business anywhere in the country is unrestricted and foreign companies can, for the first time, wholly own stores.

This change of events has thus further opened the door to Carrefour and other retail groups to continue their expansion and strengthen their positions in China. Foreign supermarkets in China represent both a threat and an opportunity. They are a threat to the small-scale local retailer, but at the same time they are an opportunity for their Chinese partners, who benefit by learning from the knowledge and experience of their foreign partners.

Already ranked the third largest in the world, China’s retail market is expected to maintain an annual growth rate of 8 to 10 percent from 2005 to 2010, according to statistics from the China Economic Information Network. Carrefour seems ready to take a lion’s share of this and plans to expand into several regions in China.

Very confident in China’s economy, Carrefour China President Chereau feels that the country has a unique market. He says that over the near future the company plans to open one store per month in China in major cities, and it has strong ambitions for Beijing and Shanghai.

Carrefour's next commercial offensive is to add another 40 stores over the next five years, investing some US$780 million in its Chinese operations, and to double the number of its hypermarkets that increasingly offer non-food products. For 2005, the company plans to increase its market share in Taiwan to 50 percent and hopes to add 12 stores each in Shanghai, Beijing, Shenzhen and Guangzhou by the end of the year. Added to this, it signed a new joint venture between its DIA stores and domestic chain Shanghai Lianghua to open 300 discount outlet stores in the residential areas of Shanghai.

While the secret of Carrefour China's success is to find the best location and then localizing its operations, this requires knowing the rules of the game. As Deliers puts it, "This is not a chess game, where you kill the king at the end. Rather, it is like the game of Go, where you have continuously to develop a new strategy to expand on the map." So far, Carrefour has learned how to play well.

Topic 2

METRO's Marketing Policy in China

Source: http://english.ppdljm.com/news/disp_news.asp?id=18&Class=1

BACKGROUND INFORMATION

Since 1990s, numbers of international retail chain enterprises expanded into Chinese market one after another. METRO, the founder of warehouse type supermarket with headquarter in Germany, introduced this internationally influential new format into China. It not only impacted China's circulation industry, but also brought in new strategy and concept to China's commerce. It benefited the development of Chinese retail industry.

METRO was established in 1964. It ranked in the Top 50 among the world's top 500 and NO. 3 among the world's commercial enterprises. METRO was the world's No. 1 Cash & Carry system business. METRO came to China in 1995 in cooperation with the famous Jinjiang Group, establishing METRO Jinjiang Cash & Carry Co., Ltd. In 1996, METRO opened its first Cash & Carry and member system store in Shanghai.

METRO Jinjiang Cash & Carry Co., Ltd had opened 15 stores, among which Shanghai alone had 4 stores. There were over 110, 000 members in each store. The turnover ranked No. 9 in the national top 100 chain stores and sales reached 4.94 billion Yuan.

METRO'S CHARACTERISTICS

1) Business Type

METRO's warehouse type business combines the function of supermarket and warehouse. It can fill the sold-out goods rapidly and guarantee low cost and high efficiency by omitting the traditional independent warehouse and delivery center. Warehouse type supermarket is fundamentally different from normal supermarket in overall design.

2) Site selection

METRO is usually located near highways or main roads on outskirts in big cities. In this way, it avoids traffic congestion in downtown area and reduces investment risk with the relatively low price of land on outskirts. Moreover, exploring outskirts area is in tune with the trend of integration of urban and rural areas and takes up the advantageous region earlier than others. And the business range normally covers 50 km in radius.

3) Architecture design

METRO looks like a big modern warehouse from outside. It covers a business area of 15,000 to 20,000 square meters. The parking place is almost as large as the business area. With simple interior structure, it usually uses 4.5-meter high industrial shelves. On the lower part of the shelves, like normal supermarkets, goods are displayed, while the higher part functions as a warehouse, on which the same goods are stored. In this way, sales and storage are integrated. Forklift truck is easy to go between the shelves to fill the goods vacancy in time with big space between the shelves.

GOOD ASSORTMENT

The stores offer a full range of goods up to 20,000 items, which can meet the customer's one-stop shop requirement. Food takes up 40% of all the goods, with relatively stable varieties, while 60% are nonfood. Particularly strong are the fresh food offer, comprising fruits/vegetables, fresh fish, meat and dairy products. Nonfood segment is regularly adjusted according to the season and customer's needs. It ranges from daily items, official items to small machine tools. Most of the goods are sold in bulk packaging or boxes. Single items are seldom displayed except household and mechanical appliances.

MARKETING POLICY

Warehouse type supermarket does wholesale by the means of retailing. The store is the center for both service and wholesale & delivery. This kind of market position enables METRO becomes the super warehouse for professional buyers.

1) Limited target customers.

Normal supermarkets usually serve all ordinary consumers. Though ordinary buyers often do repeat purchasing in a short time, their purchasing is happened at random and with a small volume. Warehouse type supermarket focuses on limited customers and offers membership only to operators in industrial and commercial areas and group buyers. The members must be enterprises or other organizations with corporate capacity.

2) Mailing ad promotion

METRO usually does the promotion through mailing ads instead of mass media. They mail to members "METRO POST" every two weeks. The post, a colorful detailed catalogue covering the latest prices, newly added merchandise and recent promotional goods, tells members the latest goods information, helps enterprises cut purchasing costs efficiently and improve the fairness and openness in purchasing.

3) Particular commodities

Along with the low price policy, METRO attracts customers with sole and particular commodities and commodities with its own brand name since greater competition is rising in the retail industry. Particular imported goods such as cheese, butter, coffee, curry powder and interregional goods are offered in each store, e.g. Qingdao METRO is the first supermarket who sells southern style foods like dried salted ducks, lotus with glutinous rice. Moreover, commodities with its own brand name cover metal tools besides daily items.

4) Unit service for enterprises

METRO wins customer's favor and confidence through "Customer Festival", on which it shows its regard to small industrial and commercial enterprises by reiterating its service concept in which customers are business partner and the store and the customers should seek progress jointly. On the Customer Festival in April 2000, Shanghai METRO presented ten professional unit services for industrial and commercial enterprises. It enabled them to purchase the most comprehensive goods with the lowest payment possible by helping them select the most suitable goods. The unit services include suggested goods list for small decorating teams, tableware for small restaurant and suggested welfare goods list for enterprises and organization, to name just a few.

5) Sales format

METRO Group has other retail format like department store, discount store besides cash & carry store. Based on six-year Chinese market research and analysis, METRO only opened cash & carry store in China. The cash & carry store is self-service wholesale: customers pick their own orders, pay in cash and take away the goods themselves. This format meets the requirements of rapid and efficient sales and substantially cuts the store's cost.

SALES MANAGEMENT

The success of METRO's C&C marketing system in China attributes to its complete and highly informationized internal management system. METRO realized the informationization by creating a set of management system of goods and members information of its own.

1) Customer management

At first, the staff input the information on Registration Card filled out by members to create a member database. Member Information Management System put down automatically the purchasing record of each member, which allows METRO to make quick response to customer's needs by looking at the purchasing frequency figures, consumption pattern and analyzing the dynamic developing trend of their needs.

METRO divides customers into "ABC" three groups according to their sizes and purchasing volume. The "Customer Consultant Group" provides customers, especially small and medium-sized enterprises with special consultant services after a careful analysis on customer's pattern of consumption. At the same time, they communicate with major customers and present buying advice to them to help them cut costs. Through offering comprehensive services, METRO establishes stable relations with a large number of customers and gets updated with the variable market trend in time, so that they improve their initiativeness and flexibility in commodity management.

2) Commodity management

METRO makes centralized purchasing, i.e. all purchasing is made by the headquarter and the regional stores cannot purchase by their own. The headquarter determines the distribution according to sales situation of each store and makes uniform distribution. Uniform bulk purchasing strengthens headquarters' control over purchasing and reduces costs. METRO controls all information about buying, selling and goods in stock by using Goods Information System; computer does everything including goods selecting, ordering, reordering, receiving, selling and checking out. The System prospects the sales, makes purchasing plan and generates order lists automatically according to the recorded information to limit the stock goods within a reasonable range.

3) Supplier management

As a multinational franchise retail group, METRO is demanding on suppliers' goods quality and supplying stability. They acquire quality goods and guarantee reliable supply in compliance with the established comprehensive trading stipulation and a set of systematic procedure instead of signing a traditional trade contract with the supplier.

METRO made a special "METRO Supplier's Manual" with contents covering each step of offering certificate, filling out information form, making orders, supplying, adjusting price, managing and paying bills, as well as trade rules and working system which should be observed by both parties. A long-term cooperation relationship is established between METRO and suppliers with an agreement from both parties; and they don't have to sign contract for every single trade. METRO involves suppliers into its own management system and turns suppliers' transport system into its own goods delivery system by standardizing purchasing process, thereby realizing cost-efficient running.

To maintain the partner relationship with the supplier, METRO often assists them in selecting the most economic delivery rout, receiving orders through Internet to cut order-disposing cost and provides them with market demands in time.

4) Sales plan management

Different from ordinary retail companies, in order to unify selling and purchasing, the sales plan is carried out by the Purchasing Department. To make sales plan is to work out programs in accordance with the promotional activities. In order to leave enough time for overall arrangement, one should be considerably far sighted when making the sales plan. The key to success is to make sales plan consistent with purchasing plan and combine purchasing-selling plan with suppliers' promotion plan vigorously.

5) Finance management

METRO makes centralized and uniform control over finance by applying R/3 system provided by German SAP Company, the world's largest supplier of company management software. The sales data of each store in China are delivered to the headquarter in Shanghai for them to do accounting. Purchasing payment is also controlled by the Shanghai headquarter. The finance personnel in each store shall only collect the daily sales amount and apply for daily expenditure reimbursement within the impest fund set by the headquarter. This managing pattern makes the finance management open to a high degree and maintain the financial cost to a comparatively low level.

Topic 3

IKEA's Path To Success in China

Source: http://www.franchiseek.com/feeds/NewsDetails.asp?NewsID=48&News=ikea-china-success

SIMPLICITY IS BEAUTY

The concept "Simplicity is beauty" is popular in artistic circles, while it becomes impracticable when the art of business management is concerned. For these international enterprises that have to seek global expansion, they are facing rising business management costs and decreasing growth rate due to the global market diversity which results in enlargement of products varieties, longer circulation terms, clog of information delivery and horsy institutions. However, we will find that IKEA is perfect in every aspect when we are getting to know it. IKEA's beauty originates from its simplicity. IKEA turns complicated enterprise management into simple principles: to design products according to consumption demand, spare no efforts in reducing costs to create significant low price, create smooth global supply chain and experiencing-style sales terminal. Probably, with its home on a Peninsula in northern Europe, Sweden-based IKEA obtains its particular qualities from the national characteristics which seek simplicity and perfect.

IKEA'S ACHIEVEMENT

Brand name value—According to a brand survey conducted by American Business Weekly, IKEA ranks forty-three on the list of the fifty world's most famous brands with a brand value of 56 billion crown (US$ 7 billion). Another Sweden company Ericsson ranks eighty.

Sales performance—IKEA has 76,000 employees and runs business in 43 countries. Its sales reached Euro € 11.3 billion in the financial year 2003.

Design, Purchase, Distribution and Sales—IKEA is the only enterprise in the world which succeeds in both channel and products operation. Swedwood, the industrial group within IKEA, manufactures wooden furniture and accessories. Swedwood owns 32 industrial departments in 9 countries. Ãlmhult-based IKEA of Sweden is in charge of developing IKEA line of products covering 10,000 varieties. IKEA boasts 43 trade companies (TSO) in 33 countries and 1,600 suppliers in 55 countries. IKEA stores are supplied by 27 distribution centers in 16 countries. Currently, there are 186 IKEA stores in 31 countries and regions, among which 165 stores are company-owned in 22 countries and the other 21 stores are operated by franchisees in 14 countries and regions. It's said that there were 310 million visitors to IKEA stores globally last year.

CHARM OF IKEA

IKEA entered Chinese market in 1998. It has brought tremendous influence despite it has opened only two stores in China, which is located in Shanghai and Beijing. Chinese customers' traditional concept of household goods purchasing was strongly challenged. It's considered a fashion to go shopping in IKEA, even if for people living in cities other than Beijing and Shanghai.

Now let's experience the shopping journey to IKEA. The store boasts: simple appearance but with strong contrast, spacious retail space, innovative and various sample rooms with nice color blend, vivid and cozy children's playground, Sweden style restaurant to take a rest in, the secure feeling of fetching goods directly from warehouse and most important, products with practical and delicate design. They use wood to make most of the products, other materials including clay, metal, glass and paper. The distasteful feeling of industrial products is removed with IKEA's people-oriented products, which have nice shape and rich color making you feel warm at home.

The products are various but not pretentious, simple but not coarse. Surrounded by the simple and romantic North European music, buyers' mind gets calmed and feel as if they have returned to nature.

IKEA'S TROUBLE

The first trouble is price. IKEA household goods get prevailed in European market by the low price, but not in China. A small wooden table costs several hundred yuan and a paper lampshade costs about a hundred. IKEA is still only the choice of some middle-class people in China despite its lower and lower price year by year. Most of the visitors are to buy small household goods or just to experience the atmosphere. This is the reason why Chinese IKEA is small in sales and just regarded as a potential market.

IKEA's purchase volume in China accounts for 18% of the global amount and exceeds all the other countries. The transport and producing costs are decreasing. However, the price still can't beat that of domestic products in a short term. So it's not the low price that attracts Chinese consumers. Of course it would be better if the price were lower.

The second is design. The design is simple, delicate and special in IKEA. When the Beijing and Shanghai stores were opened, you could hear such voices like "Fantastic! I will buy all the furnishing things from IKEA for my new house", "Well, what's this? Is it used to contain flavor?" or "The corner of this cabinet is well-designed." etc. But now we can hear another voice: "I will only buy some small daily household goods in IKEA instead of furniture. There are dozens of and hundreds of same things in IKEA. There is nothing special if everyone else buys the same furniture." The products of IKEA are regarded as short-term consumer commodities in European market, but as durable commodities which can be used for a long term in China. Chinese consumer wants to buy special designs from IKEA and is willing to pay higher price for this special design. But with too many people purchasing the same thing, it's no more special.

The third is service. Chinese customers, who used to inquiring, usually can't find service staff in IKEA store. There are always some customers walking here and there to look for the promotional shoe shelf or vase. Moreover, customarily IKEA doesn't make delivery and do the installation. The service is cut down to reduce costs. IKEA's price in China is the lowest among its stores all over the world, but still considered to be higher than that of domestic products, in which delivery and installation fee is included.

These are the troubles, resulted from global market differences, faced by the perfect-pursuit IKEA. Among IKEA's global retail network, most stores are company-owned, which are mainly located in markets like Europe. Franchising format is applied in markets which are pole apart from European market. It's a wise policy since by franchising, it can explore an unfamiliar market rapidly and without many troubles.

However, IKEA owns the store by itself in China, the most strange and complicated market. During the years of business in China, IKEA "makes compromise" again and again by setting the price to the lowest point, extending the goods return time limit to 60 days and locating the Shanghai store on Xujiahui area, where the land is extremely expensive. We might say that if IKEA managed well its stores in China, then it would be able to get rid of all the disturbances created by regional differences and expanded globally further.

IKEA COULD HAVE DONE BETTER

When we look back on IKEA's business in China over the past years, we would say IKEA could have done better. IKEA impressed customers as innovative, fashionable, and expensive on its entry of Chinese market, which decided that its target customers were those high-end customers such as white-collar, entrepreneur and foreigner. If it employed membership system at that time to fully exploit those customers' favor of innovative and fashionable things and concentrated promotion on those potential families, it could be able to stimulate customer's purchasing desire and save costs as well. During that period, IKEA should display some classic designs in the two stores and go with the membership system. After getting familiar with the characteristic of Chinese regional market, it can decrease the purchase and sales price and cancel membership system to release its sales potential to a full degree, so as to fulfill its ideal of serving common customers.

By looking ahead, IKEA will inevitably encounter various challenges on its exploring of Chinese market. IKEA has refined products and fine purchasing environment. We will wait to see its future in China.

4. References

1. Bronitsky G. Creating Spaces Where Things Happen: The Life Story of a Business Anthropologist [J]. *Int. J. Bus.* Anthropol., 1(1), 2010: 115-121.
2. Ferraro G. P. The Cultural Dimension of International Business [M]. 4th Edition. Upper Saddle River, NJ: Prentice Hall, 2002.
3. Gesteland R. R. Cross-Cultural Business Behavior: Marketing, Negotiating, and Managing Across Cultures [M]. 2d Ed. Copenhagen, Copenhagen Business School Press, 1999.
4. Harris P. R. & Moran R. T. Managing Cultural Differences [M]. 2nd ed. Houston: Gulf., 1987.
5. Hofstede G. Cultures and Organizations: Software of the Mind [M]. London: McGraw-Hill Book Company, 1991.
6. Jordan A. T. Business Anthropology [M]. Prospect Heights, Illinois: Waveland Press Inc, 2003.
7. Jordan A. T. The Importance of Business Anthropology: Its Unique Contributions [J]. *Int. J. Bus.* Anthropol., 1(1), 2010: 15-25.
8. Lillis M. & Tian R. Cultural Issues in the Business World: An Anthropological Perspective [J]. *J. Social Sci.*, 6(1), 2010: 99-112.
9. Lowe S., Purchase S. & Veludo M. Proceedings from 18th IMP Conference: Business relationships: cross-cultural analysis. Perth, Australia, 2002.
10. Michel Walter Pharand. Bernard Shaw and the French [M]. University Press of Florida. 2001: 113.
11. Rhodes D., Emery C. & Tian R. A Cross-cultural Comparison of Leader Ethics [M]. Academy of Organizational Culture: Communications and Conflict, 2005 (Spring.): 8-15.
12. Tian R. G. The Implications of Rights to Culture in Trans-national Marketing: An Anthropological Perspective [M]. High Plains Appl. Anthropol., 20(2), (2000b): 135-145.

13. Tian R. G. Canadian Chinese, Chinese Canadians: Coping and Adapting in North America. Lewiston [M], NY: The Edwin Mellen Press. 2(2), 1999: 273-279.
14. Trompenaars F. and Peter Woolliams. Business Across Cultures (Culture for Business Series) [M]. Mankato: Capstone Publisher, 2004.
15. Trompenaars F. and Peter Prud'homme. Managing Change Across Corporate Cultures [M]. Mankato: Capstone Publisher, 2005.
16. Trompenaars F. and Charles Hampden-Turner. Managing People Across Cultures (Culture for Business Series) [M]. Mankato: Capstone Publisher, 2004.
17. Tu Y.T. & Chih H. C. An Analysis on Negotiation Styles by Religious Beliefs [J]. *J. Int. Bus. Res.*, 4(3), 2011: 243-253.
18. Weber Y., Belkin T. & Tarba S. Y. Negotiation, Cultural Differences, and Planning in Mergers and Acquisitions [J] *J. Transnatl. Manag.*, 16(2), 2011: 107-115.
19. Zandpour F. Chang C. & Catalano J. Stories, Symbols, and Straight Talk: A Comparative Analysis of French, Taiwanese and U.S. TV Commercials [M]. J. Advert. Res., 32(January/February), 1992: 25-38.

Chapter 4

Intercultural Business Negotiation

"In all negotiations of difficulty, a man may not look to sow and reap at once; but must prepare business, and so ripen it by degrees".

—Francis Bacon (1561-1626) "Of Negotiating"

"In many cultures, negotiation is ritualized, especially in its early stages".

—Andrew Rosenbaum

"When nations have existed for a long and glorious time, they cannot break with their past, whatever they do; they are influenced by it at the very moment when they work to destroy it; in the midst of the most glaring transformation they remain fundamentally in character and destiny such as their history has formed them."

—Guizot, F

"The Chinese think in terms of process that has no culmination. Americans think in terms of concrete solutions to specific problems.... The Chinese approach is impersonal, patient and aloof... To Americans, Chinese leaders seem polite but aloof and condescending. To the Chinese, Americans appear erratic and somewhat frivolous."

—Henry Kissinger,Newsweek, May, 2001

"The software of negotiation—that is, the nature and the appearance of the relationship between the people pursuing common goals—need to be carefully addressed in the negotiation process."

—Tse, Francis, and Walls

1. Lead-in

CASE 1: Negotiating a Cooperative Agreement

At the end of 1999, the "F" District Council of Beijing sent a delegation to visit their sister town of "S" in Australia. F and S had already established a sound relationship. The delegation, headed by the deputy governor, consisted of eight people, including four government officials and three businessmen. Following is a description of the meeting, broken down into processes.

Process 1: When the Chinese delegation arrived at the seminar, more than fifteen business people from S were waiting for them. John, head of the Australian delegation, and Mr Wang, head of the Chinese delegation, greeted each other:

John: *"How do you do?"*

Mr Wang: *"How do you do?"*

John: *"Welcome to S."*

Mr Wang: *"We are so glad to meet so many business people from S at this meeting, thank you for your hospitality."*

Process 2: Business began soon after they greeted each other. At the meeting, five Australians from different business areas introduced their products and services to the Chinese in detail. For example, Tom, a double-rider bicycle producer, brought a sample to the seminar and explained the functions of his product in detail for the Chinese delegation.

Process 3: Tom said to the Chinese delegation: "I know China has long been called the 'bicycle kingdom,' so I am sure most Chinese people, especially young people, will like this double-rider bicycle, because it looks smart and is of very high quality. If you introduce it to the Chinese market, it must be very popular."

A clear pause occurred after Tom's presentation. Tom seemed to be waiting for responses and questions from the Chinese; the Chinese group, however, responded by nodding and smiling.

Interlude: Now it was the turn of the Chinese delegation. The following was the conversation among the three Chinese businessmen when they felt pressed to make a speech:

Mr Lin: *"I don't know what to say. You two can represent me."*

Mr Ma: *"I prefer to be the audience too. You two just feel free to talk."*

Mr Liu: *"I am not good at talking at all, you two are much better than me, why do both of you ask me to talk?"*

Process 4: Since the three didn't reach an agreement, Mr Wang, head of the delegation, announced: "I order Xiao Lin and Xiao Ma to make a speech immediately, and not to hesitate any more." Obeying this order, Mr Lin and Mr Ma talked respectively without any sign of reluctance. They said they were very grateful to the F District Council because the government had offered them long-term support, and they could not succeed in their business without this support. Concerning their own businesses, they provided the audience with very brief introductions.

The seminar then ended abruptly without any agreements or even cooperative initiative mentioned. Worse, no further contact ensued between the F and S groups after the F delegation returned to China.

CASE 2: Negotiating a Joint-venture

An American company planned to collaborate with a local Chinese company to set up a joint venture company. The American company would like to provide capital and technology support, and the Chinese company will provide the land, the warehouse and the sales channel. The negotiation processed very smoothly until the parties encountered the issue of Valuation Adjustment Mechanism proposed by the American company. The original intention of the American company was just to set up some kind of incentive mechanism for its Chinese partner for mutual parties' benefits. As long as the joint venture reached the pre-set sales target, the American company shall be obligatory to buy certain amount of shares with a high premium from the Chinese company. Otherwise, the Chinese Company should make the relevant compensation for the American company' investment. Through this way, it was deemed by the American company that both parties shall have the motive to run the business successfully. However, the Chinese party was reluctant to accept this arrangement on the ground that they could not promise the performance of the joint venture in future, although it was obvious that the joint venture could reach the pre-set sales target without any difficulties. The reaction of the Chinese party caused the American company to doubt the good faith of the Chinese party because it was a common practice to set up this kind of mechanism in a joint venture company, and finally both parties could not make the deal.

The real reason for the Chinese company not to accept this mechanism is that it is a state-owned company. If the mechanism works out positively, it is the duty that the leaders of the Chinese company should fulfill; otherwise, if the mechanism works out negatively and the Chinese company should compensate the American company, the leaders of the Chinese company shall probably bear the personal responsibility for the compensation. Thus, the leaders of the Chinese company will not take any tiny risk of compensation, although, technically speaking, such mechanism was invented for the mutual benefits and there would be no problem to meet the pre-set sale target. Through this case, we can see that it is not sufficient to just set up the mutual benefit. Sometimes, negotiator should think more about the counter party's situation, especially the personal concern, and avoid some potential risk for the counter party.

CASE 3: Negotiating Salary and Payment

When a student in Japan has an interview for his future career, it is common sense that his salary and other fringe benefits not be discussed in the first interview. In the first interview, the Japanese company representative is interested in learning his background, the kind of job he can do well, his specialty, and the like. After the company has decided whether or not they can utilize the student's services, and after getting the hiring process approved by the personnel, the company makes offers. Discussing his salary normally comes at the very end of the interview process. If the candidate talks about salary before the company is ready to, his manners and motivations are considered questionable. His concern with salary implies that he is more interested in money than in his service to the company. Bringing up salary considerations is not the prerogative of the candidate. Japanese business people are more sensitive about discussing salary and money because of their historical and cultural backgrounds. The kind of service offered plays a major role in terms of contracts if it is related to services and technology transfer.

When an American consultant wishes to offer his services as a translator, an interpreter, or a negotiator to a Japanese firm, the Japanese firm becomes the client. In this situation, it would be rude for the consultant to speak of the service fee such as "We charge $50 an hour if the job requires a day but if it takes two, we will charge $40," and so on. The right time to speak of the service charge is determined by the client, after finding out whether or not the client can utilize the service. The first step is for the Japanese to determine the value of the service. When the client feels a necessity to ask for a service, he will usually inquire about the service charge. The American consultant may feel that discussing the charge may be a consideration for the Japanese client in accepting the services. However, to many Japanese, it is a topic for the client to bring up. If the American firm starts talking about the service charge, the first impression the Japanese may have is, "How dare you speak of the charge before we decide to accept your services!" The Japanese company clearly knows that the consulting service fee will be assessed based on their service. They know that "there is no free lunch." The consultant should wait until the client starts talking about the fee.

When a Japanese company wishes to obtain the technology for the manufacture and sale of a product from an American company, the issues for the Japanese negotiating team are the reliability of the technology and whether or not other companies have developed similar products utilizing this technology. Unless the Japanese finds it worthwhile to have the technology, negotiations on the royalty and/or transfer fee should not be dealt with. To many Americans prices are a part of the entire negotiation agenda, however, price and/or royalty for the transfer for the Japanese is a second stage in the negotiations. A Japanese negotiator would rarely discuss the price in the first stage. This should be dealt with as a separate entity to be initiated by the buyer. In the American's mind, costs are always a consideration, but this is not necessarily true with the Japanese. As has been pointed out, the first goal of the Japanese team will be determining the quality of the technology and the potential advantage of possessing it. The content of the two stages are entirely separate in the minds of the Japanese.

2. Main Text

2.1 Intercultural Negotiation

INTRODUCTION

In the Camp David negotiations that led to a peace treaty between Egypt and Israel, the Israeli preference for direct forms of communication and the Egyptian tendency to favor indirect forms sometimes exacerbated relations between the two sides. The Egyptians interpreted Israeli directness as aggressiveness and, therefore, an insult. The Israelis viewed Egyptian indirectness with impatience and suspected them of insincerity, of not saying what they meant.

Henry in Los Angeles and Hiroshi in Tokyo both like Armani suits, baseball, Mozart, and good Bordeaux. But Henry recently spoke for days with Hiroshi, his potential business partner, and yet the barriers between them were never broached—and the deal didn't get inked. The problem had to do with different conceptions of the negotiation process itself and misinterpretations of the other's behavior. For Henry, negotiation is about pushing through a deal, period. When Henry didn't think their discussion was moving forward as quickly as he thought it should, his arguments became increasingly forceful. Because Hiroshi read this as disrespect, the negotiation essentially ended days before their talks did.

There are two negotiators dealing with the same potential client in the Middle East. Both have identical proposals and packages. One ignores the importance of cross cultural negotiation training, believing the proposal will speak for itself. The other undertakes some cross cultural training. He/she learns about the culture, values, beliefs, etiquette and approaches to business, meetings and negotiations. Nine times out of ten the latter will succeed over the rival. This is because 1) it is likely they would have endeared themselves more to the host negotiation team and 2) they would be able to tailor their approach to the negotiations in a way that maximises the potential of a positive outcome.

There is one case that received significant media attention in the mid-1990's, a long-term electricity supply contract between an Enron subsidiary, the Dabhol Power Company, and the Maharashtra state government in India, was subject to significant challenge and was ultimately cancelled on the grounds that it was concluded in "unseemly haste" and had been subject to "fast track procedures" that circumvented established practice for developing such projects in the past. Important segments of the Indian public automatically assumed that the government had failed to protect the public interest because the negotiations were so quick. In the company's defense, Rebecca Mark, chairman and CEO of Enron International, pointed out to the press: "We were extremely concerned with time, because time is money for us." In fact, the loss of the contract underlines the important role that cultural differences play in international negotiation. For one country's negotiators, time is money; for another's, the slower the negotiations, the better and more trust in the other side.

(Enron's Rebecca Mark: "You Have to be Pushy and Aggressive" BusinessWeek, February 24, 1997, http://www.businessweek.com/1997/08/b351586.htm.)

Negotiation is always a delicate business, requiring determination and diplomacy in equal measure. But finessing a cross-cultural negotiation is a particular challenge. The impact of international business in domestic markets compels us to ask a question: "How can we survive in this global playing field, and what can we do to run our businesses more effectively?" The diverse makeup of many societies and global nature of business today make cross-cultural negotiation a regular part of life. Unfortunately, many major disputes in need of resolution also cross ethnic and cultural lines. Communication and negotiation etiquette varies widely across cultures. In France, it is rude to talk money over dinner while in Brazil the American "OK" gesture (thumb and forefinger forming a circle) can be a major insult. Understanding when, where, how and with whom it is appropriate to negotiate any given issue is extremely important to working across cultures. The international negotiator must not allow cultural stereotypes to influence his or her relations with local businesspersons.

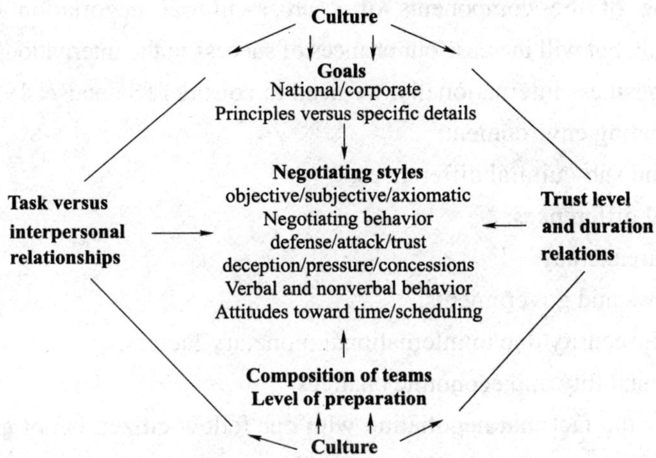

Figure 4.1 Negotiating Across Cultures

Culture influences negotiation in three ways:

1) by determining one's perception of reality;

2) by dismissing information inconsistent or unfamiliar with culturally accepted notions;

3) by projecting meaning onto the other party's words and actions.

Cultures are not the same in regard to information sharing. Negotiators from separate cultures differ as to what information they deem important and they also differ in the processes and methods used to share information. Some cultures use a direct approach when sharing information about interest and priorities, while other cultures. use an indirect approach and some do not share information at all. Culture is the most important variable affecting international negotiations and the values and norms that are encompassed by culture can affect negotiations. Cultural values establish what members perceive as important, while cultural norms outline what is considered proper and improper behavior. Together, cultural values and norms influence how one perceives situations and how one reacts to the behavior of others. The cultural values of individualism versus collectivism, egalitarianism versus hierarchy and direct versus indirect communications are relevant to norms and negotiation strategies.

Nowadays, businesses of all sizes search for suppliers and customers on a global level. International competition, foreign clients and suppliers may pose a challenge, but they may also create huge opportunities to develop one's business. The increasingly global business environment requires managers to approach the negotiation process from an global perspective. This approach includes aspects which are usually unimportant in domestic negotiations. Some of the components of a cross-cultural negotiation process are more complex and difficult, but will increase our chances of success in the international business arena.

When doing business internationally, we need to consider (Salacuse, 1991):

1) The negotiating environment;

2) Cultural and sub-cultural differences;

3) Ideological differences;

4) Foreign bureaucracy;

5) Foreign laws and governments;

6) Financial insecurity due to international monetary factors;

7) Political instability and economic changes.

If we consider the fact that negotiating with our fellow citizen is not an easy task due to many individual differences, it would be reasonable to suggest that negotiating with foreigners may be even more difficult. The way we perceive and create our own reality may be completely different to our counterpart's way of thinking, behaving and feeling. Unfortunately, knowledge of any foreign language is not enough to face and solve the problem. Language is a cluster of codes used in communication which, if not shared effectively, can act as a barrier to establish credibility and trust. We need more effective tools, and the most important is knowledge of all factors that can influence the proceedings. Nations tend to have a national character that influences the type of goals and process the society pursues in negotiations. This is why specifying and understanding cultural differences is vital in order to perform successfully in intercultural communication. As we understand that our partners may see things differently, we will be less likely to make negative assumptions and more likely to make progress when negotiating.

MAIN FACTORS IN INTERCULTURAL NEGOTIATION

1) Basic conception of the negotiation process can be competitive, cooperative, or mixed. How is the negotiation being seen? Is mutual satisfaction the real purpose of the meeting? Do we have to compete? Do they want to win? Different cultures stress different aspects of negotiation. The goal of business negotiation may be regarded as a substantive outcome or a long-lasting relationship, depending on culture.

2) Negotiator selection criteria include experience, status, personal characteristics, product knowledge, etc.

3) Types of negotiation issues include contract terms; relationship; procedural; personal.

4) The concern for negotiation protocol can be formal or informal. There are as many kinds of business etiquette as there are nations in the world. Protocol factors that should be considered are dress codes, number of negotiators, entertainment, degree of formality, gift giving, meeting and greeting, etc.

5) Communication styles in negotiation can be direct verbal or nonverbal. Verbal and non-verbal communication is a key factor of persuasion. The way we express our needs and feelings using body language and tone of voice can determine the way the other side perceives us, and in fact positively or negatively contributes to our credibility. Another aspect of communication relevant to negotiation is the direct or indirect approach to exchanging information. Is the meaning of what is said exactly in the words themselves? Does "it's impossible" really mean impossible or just difficult to realise? Always use questions to identify the other side's needs, otherwise assumptions may result in you never finding common interests.

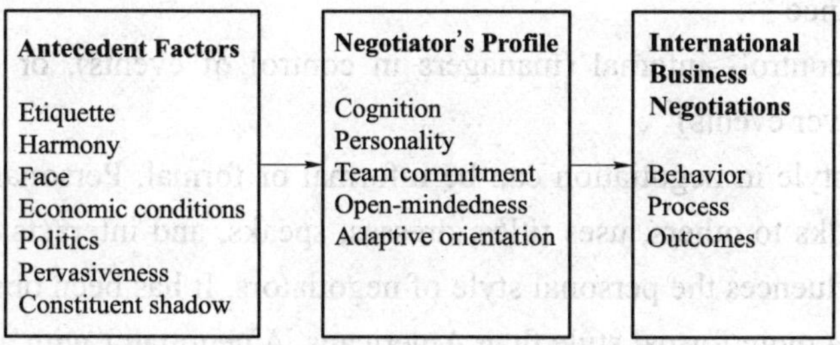

Figure 4.2 Factors in Negotiating

6) Negotiation persuasive arguments & style can be rational, ideological, emotional, or experiential.

7) Goals or aspirations in negotiation are catergorized as individual or company / country.

8) Basis of trust in negotiation comes from past dealings or intuition.

9) Risk-taking tendency in negotiation can be low or high. There is always risk involved in negotiations. The final outcome is unknown when the negotiations commence. The most common dilemma is related to personal relations between counterparts: Should we trust them? Will they trust us? Certain cultures are more risk averse than others, e.g. Japan. It means that less innovative and creative alternatives are available to pursue during the negotiation, unless there is a strong trust-based relationship between the counterparts.

10) View of time in negotiation is limited or plentiful. In some cultures time is money

and something to be used wisely. Punctuality and agenda may be an important aspect of negotiation. In countries such as China or Japan, being late would be taken as an insult. Consider investing more time in the negotiating process in Japan. The main goal when negotiating with an oriental counterpart is to establish a firm relationship, which takes time. Another dimension of time relevant to negotiation is the focus on past, present or future. Sometimes the past or the distant future may be seen as part of the present, especially in Latin American countries.

11) Decision-making system in negotiation can center on one person or consensus. The way members of the other negotiating team reach a decision may give us a hint: who we shall focus on when providing our presentation. When negotiating with a team, it's crucial to identify who is the leader and who has the authority to make a decision.

Cultural Variables Affecting Decision Making

◇ Objective (basing decisions on rationality) versus subjective (basing decisions on emotions) approach

◇ Risk tolerance

◇ Locus of control—internal (managers in control of events), or external (managers have little control over events)

12) Personal style in negotiation can be informal or formal. Personal style concerns the way a negotiator talks to others, uses titles, dresses, speaks, and interacts with other persons. Culture strongly influences the personal style of negotiators. It has been observed, for example, that Germans have a more formal style than Americans. A negotiator with a formal style insists on addressing counterparts by their titles, avoids personal anecdotes, and refrains from questions touching on the private or family life of members of the other negotiating team. A negotiator with an informal style tries to start the discussion on a first-name basis, quickly seeks to develop a personal, friendly relationship with the other team, and may take off his jacket and roll up his sleeves when deal making begins in earnest. Each culture has its own formalities with their own special meanings. They are another means of communication among the persons sharing that culture, another form of adhesive that binds them together as a community. For an American, calling someone by the first name is an act of friendship and therefore a good thing. For a Japanese, the use of the first name at a first meeting is an act of disrespect and therefore bad. Negotiators in foreign cultures must respect appropriate formalities. As a general rule, it is always safer to adopt a formal posture and move to an informal stance, if the situation warrants it, than to assume an informal style

too quickly.

13) Form of agreement in negotiation can be detailed or general, specific points or basic principles, oral or written. In most cultures, only written agreements stamp a deal. It seems to be the best way to secure our interests in case of any unexpected circumstances. The "deal" may be the contract itself or the relationship between the parties. In this case, if any unexpected circumstances arise, parties prefer to focus on the relationship than the contract to solve the problem.

14) The buy-seller relationship in negotiation can be equal.

Range of Cultural Responses

Negotiation Factors			
Goal	Contract	←——→	Relationship
Attitudes	Win/Lose	←——→	Win/Win
Personal Styles	Informal	←——→	Formal
Communications	Direct	←——→	Indirect
Time Sensitivity	High	←——→	Low
Emotionalism	High	←——→	Low
Agreement Form	Specific	←——→	General
Agreement Building	Bottom Up	←——→	Top Down
Team Organization	One Leader	←——→	Consensus
Risk Taking	High	←——→	Low

Figure 4.3 The Impact of Culture on Negotiation

STRATEGIES IN INTERCULTURAL NEGOTIATION

Chris Moore and Peter Woodrow have identified five strategies based on the variables regarding your willingness or ability to adapt to the counterpart's culture and his/her willingness or ability to adapt to yours. The five resulting choices are: adhering, avoiding-contending, adapting, adopting, and advancing. Ability in this discussion describes a negotiator's power, capacity and/or competency to adapt to another culture. Willingness relates to a negotiator's inclination to adapt. In a situation where both parties are somewhat knowledgeable about each other's cultures and fairly compliant towards each other, you may arrive at a strategy of adapting. Each person compromises a bit, probably adhering in some areas and adopting the counterpart's ways in other matters, resulting in a mixed set of procedures. If you are willing to adapt to the other culture and know more about it, a different set of choices presents itself. If your counterpart demonstrates unwillingness or inability to move toward your way of doing things, while you are more flexible, you will end up adopting the cultural norms of your counterpart. This is the analogue of the adhering strategy with the roles reversed. An intriguing fifth option is also available. If you and your counterpart both know each other's cultural norms pretty well and both exhibit real willingness to adapt to another way of doing things, you can move into the advancing mode. In this mode you and your counterpart invent a third way that is based neither wholly in your culture nor in his/hers. This shares some attributes with the adapting model, but goes beyond a series of compromises to advance shared norms for interaction that are completely comfortable for both parties.

Working across cultures can be frustrating and fascinating. Once you have decided upon a strategy, try it out. Observe the responses of the other party. See if your strategy is effective. If not, try another strategy or go back to your analysis and see if another interpretation of the situation or the difficulty might be more accurate. If so, develop new strategies and try to

◇ use a trial and error process to develop strategies or responses that help achieve your desired ends;

◇ be flexible and consider using multiple possible responses;

◇ remain open to doing it their way if it will achieve the results you want, and it does not go beyond your comfort level.

In today's global society and economy, cross-cultural negotiation strategies ensure communications with people of other cultures are fruitful and beneficial to all parties. According to Rosenbaum's "How to Steer Clear of Pitfalls in Cross-Cultural Negotiation," a problem-solving rather than a contentious approach works best when negotiating across cultures. The contentious negotiator avoids making concessions and appears to be less effective in cross-cultural negotiations. In contrast, the problem-solving approach focuses on reaching a shared agreement and avoiding deal-breakers.

● **Speech**

When negotiating across cultures, communicators should recognize and avoid verbal expressions with which the other party may be unfamiliar. Negotiators should refrain from using slang terms, acronyms—even those associated with the particular business or industry—and figures of speech. The negotiator should pause periodically for questions rather than delivering the entire message at once.

- **Context**

Negotiators should conduct research to discover whether the audience prefers communication to be direct or indirect. High-context cultures, such as those in Asian countries, prefer indirect communication, and like to establish relationships or reinforce existing ones before negotiating. Arabian and Mediterranean cultures also share these high-context preferences for indirect communication. In contrast, the U.S., Switzerland and Germany exhibit low-context behaviors and prefer direct communication.

- **Active Listening**

In cross-cultural negotiations, participants should employ active listening techniques in conversations. The process of active listening involves restating or summarizing the content of another person's verbal message. These responses ensure immediate feedback on whether the message has been interpreted correctly. Active listeners also facilitate deeper communication with probing questions. Active listening increases the likelihood of better understanding among negotiators.

- **Time**

Negotiators should consider the concept of time as an important variable in cross-cultural negotiation strategies. According to "The Intrapersonal and Interpersonal Effects of Anger on Negotiation Strategies: A Cross Cultural Investigation", Chinese cultures take more time for negotiations than their Western counterparts. Having patience and operating under fewer time constraints can ease potential tensions during negotiations.

- **Organization**

Organization style influences people's negotiation and communication methods, as well. Monochronic cultures, such as the U.S., Germany, Scandinavia, Switzerland and England, prefer tackling tasks and processing information in a sequential and discrete manner. They prefer to complete tasks and trains of thought one at a time. Polychronic cultures, in areas such as the Middle East, Africa and Latin America, tend to think in terms of the entire problem or situation rather than breaking it down into separate parts.

- **Mediators**

While mediators can assist in relaying information, they sometimes intensify tensions in cross-cultural negotiation. Groups and individuals in negotiations sometimes detect bias if the mediator has the same cultural background as one of the negotiating parties.

- **Appreciation**

When building business relationships abroad, it is important to recognize the foreign associate's business and cultural practices. Avoid talking negatively about the business partner's country, principles, religion, or business practices. Instead, talk of the advantages of the country and their positive cultural customs and beliefs. Your appreciation of a country will make up for any etiquette mistakes you make during a meeting or conversation.

- **Time of Year**

Depending upon the country in which you are meeting, you should determine the best time to hold an important business meeting. For instance, in Scandinavia, it is inconsiderate to hold important business meetings in July or August as many companies close for extended periods during these months for holiday purposes. Just about every country has a particular time in the year when business transactions should not be conducted.

- **Formalities**

In some countries, formalities are extremely important. Proper greetings are expected, and asking about family and personal well-being can be crucial. In some areas, etiquette requires a proper handshake, while others prefer no handshake or touching at all. Others believe a handshake is too formal and impersonal and prefer an embrace or other personal greeting. In some areas it is important to address a person by his title, while in others it is a sign of arrogance. Determine the best greeting practices by speaking with people from that country, if possible. Most international business people meet with a handshake. In some countries this is not appropriate between opposite genders. Some may view a weak handshake as sign of weakness whereas others would perceive a firm handshake as aggressive. How should people be addressed? Is it by first name, surname or title? Is small talk part of the proceedings or not? All these should be taken into consideration in negotiation.

- **Gift-giving**

In Japan and China gift-giving is an integral part of business protocol; however in the U.S. or U.K., it has negative connotations. Where gifts are exchanged, should one give lavish gifts? Are they always reciprocated? Should they be wrapped? Are there numbers or colours that should be avoided? All the above in one way or another will impact cross cultural negotiation and can only be learnt through cross cultural training. Doing or saying the wrong thing at the wrong time, poor communication and cross cultural misunderstandings can all have harmful consequences. Cross cultural negotiation training builds its foundations upon understanding etiquettes and approaches to business abroad before focusing on cross cultural differences in negotiation styles and techniques.

- **Non-verbal Communication**

Body language and communication will also vary in different countries. Although the entire conversation may be conducted in English there may still be communication differences. For instance, in some countries the physical communication is done at a much closer proximity than you may be used to, and pulling back from a person may be seen as an insult. In some countries a "yes" answer may only be an acknowledgement of a conversation, but not an authorization of a transaction. In other areas a shaking of the head from side to side (as Americans do to indicate "no"), may indicate agreement or acknowledgment. In these cases it is best to simply address the cultural difference and explain your conclusion of the conversation. Always apologize for your misunderstanding, and make it clear that it is a misunderstanding. The foreigner is more likely to help you understand when you have expressed your lack of cultural knowledge.

Eye Contact: In the US, UK and much of northern Europe, strong, direct eye contact conveys confidence and sincerity. In South America it is a sign of trustworthiness. However, in some cultures such as the Japanese, prolonged eye contact is considered rude and is generally avoided.

Personal Space & Touch: In Europe and North America, business people will usually leave a certain amount of distance between themselves when interacting. Touching only takes place between friends. In South America or the Middle East, business people are tactile and like to get up close. In Japan or China, it is not uncommon for people to leave a gap of four feet when conversing. Touching only takes place between close friends and family members.

2.2 Negotiations of Different Cultural Styles

Different cultural systems can produce divergent negotiating styles—styles are shaped by each nation's culture, geography, history, and political system. Unless you see the world through the other's eyes (no matter how similar they appear to you), you may not be seeing nor hearing the same. No one can avoid bringing along his cultural assumptions, images, and prejudices or other attitudinal baggage into any negotiating situation. It is difficult to track the myriad starting points used by negotiators from different national settings, especially as cultures are in constant flux, and context influences behavior in multiple ways. Another complication is that much of the cross-cultural negotiation literature comes from the organizational area. While it cannot be applied wholesale to the realm of intractable conflicts, it may provide some hints about approaches to negotiation in various national settings. Dr.

Nancy Adler compares key indicators of success as reported by negotiators from four national backgrounds. Her table is reproduced here, ranking characteristics of negotiators in order of importance as reported by managers in each national setting:

Table 4.1 Negotiation Styles of Four Cultures

AMERICAN NEGOTIATORS	JAPANESE NEGOTIATORS	CHINESE (TAIWAN) NEGOTIATORS	BRAZILIAN NEGOTIATORS
Preparation and planning skill	Dedication to job	Persistence and determination	Preparation and planning skill
Thinking under pressure	Perceive and exploit power	Win respect and confidence	Thinking under pressure
Judgment and intelligence	Win respect and confidence	Preparation and planning skill	Judgment and intelligence
Verbal expressiveness	Integrity	Product knowledge	Verbal expressiveness
Product knowledge	Demonstrate listening skill	Interesting	Product knowledge
Perceive and exploit power	Broad perspective	Judgment and intelligence	Perceive and exploit power
Integrity	Verbal expressiveness		Competitiveness

(**Source:** http://www.beyondintractability.org/essay/culture-negotiation)

Brazilians and Americans are almost identical in the characteristics they identified, except for the final category. The Japanese tend to emphasize an interpersonal negotiating style, stressing verbal express iveness, and listening ability, while their American and Brazilian counterparts focus more on verbal ability, planning, and judgment. To the Chinese in Taiwan, it is important that the negotiator be a person who shows persistence and determination.

Negotiators also vary in the styles of persuasion they rely upon and their comfort with emotionality. In American settings, appeals tend to be made to logic, relying on "objective" facts. Emotional sensitivity is not highly valued, and dealings may seem straightforward and impersonal. Japanese negotiators value emotional sensitivity highly, and tend to hide emotions behind calm exteriors. Latin American negotiators tend to share the Japanese appreciation of emotional sensitivity, and express themselves passionately about their points of view. Arab negotiators may appeal to emotions and subjective feelings in an effort to persuade others. Russians, in contrast, tend to appeal to ideals, drawing everyone's attention to overarching principles.

Many other cultural differences have been identified by negotiation scholars. Some of these differences are discussed in the other Beyond Intractability essays regarding culture and conflict resolution. As with all cultural patterns, these generalizations do not apply to every circumstance or individual. They are general patterns that will shift as cultures and contexts shift.

AMERICAN APPROACHES TO NEGOTIATION

American negotiators tend to rely on individualist values, imagining self and other as autonomous, independent, and self-reliant. This does not mean that they don't consult, but the tendency to see self as separate rather than as a member of a web or network means that more independent initiative may be taken. Looking through the eyes of the Japanese negotiator who wrote "Negotiating With Americans", American negotiators tend to:

◇ be competitive in their approach to negotiations, including coming to the table with a fall-back position but beginning with an unrealistic offer;

◇ be energetic, confident, and persistent; they enjoy arguing their positions, and see things universally—i.e., they like to talk about broad applications of ideas;

◇ concentrate on one problem at a time;

◇ focus on areas of disagreement, not areas of commonality or agreement;

◇ like closure and certainty rather than open-endedness or fuzziness.

Do these generalizations ring true? Clearly, it depends which Americans you are talking about, which sector they represent, and the context surrounding the negotiations. Is this a family matter or a commercial one? Is it about community issues, national policy, or a large public conflict? Strategies change according to context and many other factors.

● **Key Skills for Successful Negotiation with Americans**

ESTABLISHING CREDIBILITY

◇ Use a firm, crisp handshake (not too long);

◇ Make it a two-way conversation (offer information, ask questions);

◇ Maintain eye contact;

◇ Clarify; check comprehension;

◇ Project self-confidence (don't hesitate to be assertive).

PRESENTING AND PERSUADING

◇ Present with confidence—(no need to apologize unless there is something to apologize for);

◇ Use a direct style of logic (put main point first, followed by rationale and supporting data, and a conclusion that returns to the main point. Not too much detail.);

◇ Emphasize business opportunity (link your proposal to concrete business results);

◇ Be prepared for questions (either ask the audience to hold their questions until you are finished or being ready to handle questions as they come up);

◇ Offer solutions and action steps (have plan for going forward with concrete recommendations about what to do about the problem. Be pro-active. Offer solutions and next steps.)

● **Profile of a Successful American Negotiator**

◇ Knows when to compromise

◇ Takes a firm stand at the beginning of the negotiation

◇ Refuses to make concessions beforehand

◇ Keeps his or her cards close to his or her chest

◇ Accepts compromises only when the negotiation is deadlocked

◇ Sets up the general principles and delegates the detail work to associates

◇ Keeps a maximum of options open before negotiation

◇ Operates in good faith

◇ Respects the "opponents"

◇ States his or her position as clearly as possible

◇ Knows when he or she wishes a negotiation to move on

◇ Is fully briefed about the negotiated issues

◇ Has a good sense of timing and is consistent

◇ Makes the other party reveal his or her position while keeping his or her own position hidden as long as possible

◇ Lets the other negotiator come forward first and looks for the best deal

EUROPEAN STYLES OF NEGOTIATION

European styles of negotiation vary according to region, nationality, language spoken, and many other contextual factors. One study found the French to be very aggressive negotiators, using threats, warnings, and interruptions to achieve their goals. German and British negotiators were rated as moderately aggressive in the same study.

● **Profile of a Successful Swedish Negotiator**

◆ Very quiet and thoughtful;

◆ Punctual (concerned with time);

◆ Extremely polite;

- ◆ Straightforward (they get straight down to business);
- ◆ Eager to be productive and efficient;
- ◆ Heavy-going;
- ◆ Down-to-earth and overcautious;
- ◆ Rather flexible;
- ◆ Able to and quite good at holding emotions and feelings;
- ◆ Slow at reacting to new (unexpected) proposals;
- ◆ Informal and familiar;
- ◆ Perfectionist;
- ◆ Afraid of confrontations;
- ◆ Very private.

- **Profile of a Successful Italian Negotiator**

◇ Has a sense of drama (acting is a main part of the culture).

◇ Does not hide his or her emotions (which are partly sincere and partly feigned).

◇ Reads facial expressions and gestures very well.

◇ Has a feeling for history.

◇ Does not trust anybody.

◇ Is concerned about the bella figura, or the "good impression," he or she can create among those who watch his or her behavior.

◇ Believes in the individual's initiatives, not so much in teamwork.

◇ Is good at being obliging and simpatico at all times.

◇ Is always on the qui vive, the "lookout".

◇ Never embraces definite opinions.

◇ Is able to come up with new ways to immobilize and eventually destroy his or her opponents.

◇ Handles confrontation of power with subtlety and tact.

◇ Has a flair for intrigue.

◇ Knows how to use flattery.

◇ Can involve other negotiators in complex combinations.

- **Russian Styles of Negotiation**

Negotiating is very serious business for a Russian because just about everything requires negotiation. Most Russians are simply born to negotiate. That may help to explain why negotiation is still rather conservative business. There is a lot of theatre in any negotiation—and Russians are a truly artistic bunch.

Understanding against whom you are negotiating is a critical part of the negotiator's brief—and this requires attention to the relationship factor. In short—who is really calling the shots? These phrases indicate that interrelationships and networks of obligations, formal and informal, are vital parts of the structure of the Russian political economy.

They also show that the results of any negotiation have to be approved by the real power—so your task as a negotiator is to be sure of who that real power actually is. Sometimes, what seem to be very small negotiations can be referred to a power that is very, very high up in the Russian political and economic systems. Finding out where power lies in any given situation is a key task.

If you manage to connect with the Russians as they hope you will, it is almost guaranteed that the vodka will be brought out before any contracts are signed. Here is where your pre-negotiation practice really comes in. If you fail to down at least three shots, your new friends aren't going to want to know. Not only do you need to work your way steadily through those three shots (vomiting will automatically send you back to the airport), but also you have to know how to correctly toast your new business partners. Russians don't want to drink to world peace or generic things such as good health. You need to keep things personal when you raise a glass. Drink to your new friendship, or to their great country, and always make a point of mentioning women. It may be quite a rarity to see a female in the boardroom in Russia but they are still highly respectful and appreciative of the finer sex, especially when drinking!

One thing that is incredibly easy to forget when negotiating in Russia is that if nothing is signed at the end of your meeting then you may as well not have had the negotiations in the first place. This minor detail can be often overlooked in an age where contracts and the finer details are often thrashed out after negotiations are done by the emailing or faxing of documents, but in Russia paper is still king. Drink for drink with your hosts on the vodka, but always remember that all you are doing is getting drunk if you've not managed to get their signature down before the singing starts.

American and Russian people are not similar; their ethical attitudes do not coincide and they evaluate behavior differently. What an American may consider normative, positive behavior (negotiating and reaching a compromise with an enemy), a Russian perceives as showing cowardice, weakness, and unworthiness; the word "deal" has a strong negative connotation, even today in contemporary Russia. Similarly, for Russians, compromise has negative connotation; principles are supposed to be inviolable and compromise is a matter of integrity. When the Americans thought they had an understanding, the Russians said it was a procedural matter, meaning they had agreed to a process for conducting the negotiation.

Table 4.2 Comparison of American and Russian Negotiation

	U.S.A	Russia
Primary Style	Factual: Appeals to logic	Axiomatic: Appeals to ideals
Conflict: Countered with…	Objective facts	Asserted ideals
Making Concessions	Small, early on	Few, if any, made
Response to Other's Concessions	Reciprocate concession	Viewed as weakness, rarely reciprocated
Relationship	Short term	No continuity
Authority	Broad	Limited
Initial Position	Moderate	Extreme
Deadline	Very important	Ignored

So, key to successful negotiations in Russia:

◇ Be sensitive, but not overly so, to past political issues

◇ Dress conservatively

◇ Be prepared to offer authentic gifts

◇ Slow the pace of negotiations, and treat time loosely:
Have patience; Have a good interpreter

◇ Display group unity

◇ Be confident in your demands

◇ Don't ignore relationship after signing

ASIAN STYLES OF NEGOTIATION

- **Chinese Styles of Negotiation**

When the Chinese engage with Westerners, a number of Chinese values will always be reflected in their behavior.

Confucianism: Confucianism emphasises the responsibilities of individuals toward one another within five important human relationships: those between ruler and subject, husband and wife, father and son, brother and brother, and friend and friend. Confucianism also advocates a social order that values duty, loyalty, honour, filial piety, respect for age and seniority, and sincerity.

Guanxi: The first and maybe most underestimated pillar of Chinese business culture is Guanxi. Guanxi can be literally translated as "relationships". To Chinese, Guanxi is the most important part before the actual phase of business, as it builds the framework for a good relationship (=Guanxi) between two or more business partners. Chinese people opt to do business with someone they trust and know.

Face: The Chinese are preoccupied with the concept of face and are very sensitive to having and maintaining face in all aspects of social and business life. Having face means having high status and prestige in the eyes of one's peers. To the Chinese, face can be compared with a prized commodity, something that can be given, earned, taken away, or lost. The concept of face goes hand in hand with the previous pillar, Guanxi. Face is another term for reputation and plays a very important role in the everyday lives of the Chinese.

Harmony: The level of harmony before the actual phase of doing business indicates the emergence of a solid business relationship. Americans tend to rush into business, even before really knowing the business partner. The only thing that matters to them is to settle a deal, without taking into account the harmony or environment in which the deal takes place. This is a tactic that would never work for the Chinese. The Chinese will not be doing business before the creation of a solid harmony. The Chinese cannot simply operate outside a caring environment, in association with harmonious actions that eases the way of doing business. Patience is also a core concept in this matter, as rushing business would have a negative influence on their business harmony.

Collectivism: The collective feeling can be understood as being part of a larger group than the individual. To the Chinese it is not important what you can achieve on a personal level for your own personal interest. The importance is much rather focused on the contribution that you are capable of offering to the whole. It shows us the balance that has to be reached between your personal and collective goals. The "mission" in Chinese business is to see your own goals and the goal of the collectives as one.

Humility: Acting modestly is a very important aspect of Chinese behavior, not only in daily life, but also certainly in business culture. By showing humility and thus being humble, you show complete respect towards the work of someone else. Putting your trust and knowledge entirely in the hands of Chinese experts will prove your willingness to learn and complete the gaps in your knowledge.

Hierarchy: Confucius formulated hierarchy as a "tool" whose function is to maintain social stability. In order to maintain this stability, it's necessary to live in a social system with respect for the dominant figure in the situation concerned. The main idea is that the absence of hierarchy would cause frictions because of the fact that people find themselves on the same level. Possible consequences would be competition, conflict, rivalry or even dispute. It's true that through the last few years, due to, for example, globalization, some aspects of Chinese business changed. However, hierarchy in Chinese remained strongly present. Hierarchy is something that will never completely disappear and should be respected by Westerners.

China represents a vast emerging market for foreign businesses and entrepreneurs. Effective business communication in China has more barriers, however, than mere language. To be successful closing deals in China, foreign business people must learn some important cultural differences. They also must remain sensitive to the importance of business customs that may seem quite the opposite of the casual and somewhat bold approach to business learned at home.

- **Japanese Styles of Negotiation**

There is a great deal of writing about Japanese approaches to negotiation, and collisions between American and Japanese approaches are legendary. The following values tend to influence Japanese communication: focus on group goals, interdependence, and a hierarchical orientation. In negotiations, these values manifest themselves in awareness of group needs and goals, and deference to those of higher status. Japanese negotiators are known for their politeness, their emphasis on establishing relationships, and their indirect use of power. Japanese concern with face and face-saving is one reason that politeness is so important and confrontation is avoided. They tend to use power in muted, indirect ways consistent with their preference for harmony and calm. In comparative studies, Japanese negotiators were found to disclose considerably less about themselves and their goals than French or American counterparts.

A primary bargaining strategy of the Japanese is to ask questions to put the opponent on the defensive. Many times the initial meeting is merely used to gather information, which is then fed back to their superiors and peers for deliberation and a carefully prepared response. The Japanese strongly believe it is folly to make an offer until one knows what the other side wants. This explains the slow start, lack of initial proposal, the emphasis on information gathering, and the long drawn out preliminary ground work that is usually encountered when negotiating in Japan. The Japanese need detailed information to build the foundation for whatever decision they intend to put forward. Should the venture fail, no one can be rebuked or blamed. On the other hand, in Latin America questions are not valued as in the Orient; in fact, there they are often interpreted as prying and inappropriately nosy.

Japanese negotiators tend to put less emphasis on the literal meanings of words used in negotiation and more emphasis on the relationships established before negotiating begins. They are also less likely than their U.S. counterparts to make procedural suggestions.

- **Profile of a Successful Indian Negotiator**

◇ Looks for and says the truth;

◇ Is not afraid of speaking up and has no fears;

◇ Exercises self-control;

◇ Seeks solutions that will please all the parties involved;

◇ Respects the other party;

◇ Uses neither violence nor insults;

◇ Is ready to change his or her mind and differ with himself or herself at the risk of being seen as inconsistent and unpredictable;

◇ Puts things into perspective and switches easily from the small picture to the big one;

◇ Is humble and trusts the opponent;

◇ Is able to withdraw, use silence, and learn from within;

◇ Relies on himself or herself, his or her own resources and strengths;

◇ Appeals to the other party's spiritual identity;

◇ Is tenacious, patient, and persistent;

◇ Learns from the opponent and avoids the use of secrets;

◇ Goes beyond logical reasoning and trusts his or her instinct as well as faith.

- **Profile of a Successful Arab Negotiator**

◇ Protects all the parties' honor, self-respect, and dignity;

◇ Avoids direct confrontation between opponents;

◇ Is respected and trusted by all;

◇ Does not put the parties involved in a situation where they have to show weakness or admit defeat;

◇ Has the necessary prestige to be listened to;

◇ Is creative enough to come up with honorable solutions for all parties;

◇ Is impartial and can understand the positions of the various parties without leaning toward one or the other;

◇ Is able to resist any kind of pressure that the opponents could try to exercise on him;

◇ Uses references to people who are highly respected by the opponents to persuade them to change their minds on some issues;

◇ Can keep secrets and in so doing gains the confidence of the negotiating parties;

◇ Controls his temper and emotions;

◇ Can use conference as mediating devices;

◇ Knows that the opponent will have problems in carrying out the decisions made during the negotiation;

◇ Is able to cope with the Arab disregard for a time.

LATIN AMERICAN APPROCHES TO NEGOTIATION

Role expectations influence negotiation in Latin American contexts. Responsibility to others is generally considered more important than schedules and task accomplishment. Their negotiation approach relates to the polychronic orientation to time and patterns of high-context communication and communitarianism described earlier. Lederach reports that a common term for conflict in Central America is *enredo*, meaning "entangled" or "caught in a net." He explains that *enredo* signifies the way conflict is part of an intimate net of relations in Guatemala and elsewhere in Central America. Thus, negotiation is done within networks, relationships are emphasized, and open ruptures are avoided.

In Central America, people think about and respond to conflict holistically. Lederach contrasts his natural (American) inclination to "make a list, to break [a] story down into parts such as issues and concerns" with his Central American experience, where people tended to respond to requests for naming issues to be negotiated with "yet another story." They preferred a storied, holistic approach to conflict and negotiation, rather than a linear, analytical one. When Central Americans needed help with negotiations, they tended to look to insider partials rather than outsider neutrals, preferring the trust and confidence of established relationships and cultural insight to other credentials or expertise. They referred to the concept of *confianza* to explain this preference. *Confianza* means "trustworthiness," that "they know us" and "we know them" and they will "keep our confidences."

Latin Americans expect their manager to tell them what they can and cannot do, to provide authority and to give detailed instructions. They would not think of contradicting a superior and to make a suggestion that the superior had not already, in some fashion, suggested. Americans, thus, often view Latins as lazy, slow, and not motivated while Latins see the Americans as irresponsible, immature, informal, disrespectful, and insensitive to the needs of the people they are depending on.

- **Brazilian Styles of Negotiation**

Brazil is a vast country that offers a lot of cultural diversity from north to south, east to west. Therefore, depending on one's negotiating counterpart, the pace of an agreement can differ tremendously (Acuff, 2008).

Higher positions: Decision making tends to stay within the high executive positions. Consequently, tailoring your approach to the correct authority will ensure little time is lost. It is important to keep in mind that middle subordinates, who will assuredly be present when negotiations are taking place, do not have any power to influence final decisions. With this in mind, it is beneficial if you want the negotiation process to be run smoothly, to maintain a good relationship with these intermediaries, and it is crucial for your success; pairing them up with the foreign negotiation team will strengthen understanding toward technical objectives held (Khen-Group, 2013).

Bargaining: Brazilians are known to be fond bargainers, but any sense of invasion or haggling will not be looked upon kindly. Concessions are best used in a strategic manner throughout negotiation, with an expectation to receive one back, again one should always remain calm and collected and watch out for use of deceptive means for "competitive advantage" (Katz, 2005).

Techniques: Pressure techniques may include making final offers and refusing to change an idea on a particular objective, to name a few. It is useful to also keep in mind that in Brazil status and power can be more valued than any financial gain. Any inclination that one is not trustworthy, which can be showed through opening with best offer or using pressure tactics, will produce signs of unwillingness towards building a long term relationship. Silence instead may be the best way to show rejection of an offer just made.

Verbal communication: It is vastly used and can be seen (from a non-expressive culture) as over theatrical and emotive. This is because it is believed that if you feel a certain way, you should express it using facial, verbal and body expressions; one should not be negatively affected by this as it is a sign of passion and belief. Opening up to reinforce trust and rapport along with using emotion to communicate one's goals, having a positive attitude and learning how to manage conflict will be considerable skills when working with a Brazilian professional.

Contracts: Contracts can often be changed as they are viewed as fluid and open to adjustment. Assuming a fatalistic view of future, in that one cannot predict what may occur Brazilians approach contracts with an understanding that things may not always go to plan and it may be necessary to deal with situations cleverly as they arise. When forming a contract in Brazil it is crucial to have with you a national lawyer and it would be seen as unpleasant if a foreign attorney was present.

AFRICAN APPROACHES TO NEGOTIATION

Many African nations have indigenous systems of conflict resolution that have endured into the present, sometimes quite intact and sometimes fragmented by rapid social change. These systems rely on particular approaches to negotiation that respect kinship ties and the elder's roles, and the structures of local society generally. In Nigeria, for example, people are organized in extended families (*nnu'*), village (*idu' or obio*), lineage (*'duk*), and lineage groups (*iman*). A belief in the continuing ability of ancestors to affect people's lives maintains social control, and makes the need to have formal laws or regulations minimal. Negotiation happens within social networks, following prescribed roles. Women in conflict with husbands, for example, are to defer and apologize, preparing a ritual meal to symbolize the restoration of harmony.

In the Nigerian Ibibio context, the goal of restoring social networks is paramount, and individual differences are expected to be subsumed in the interest of the group. To ensure that progress or an agreement in a negotiation is preserved, parties must promise not to invoke the power of ancestors to bewitch or curse the other in the future. The aim of any process, formal or informal, is to affect a positive outcome without a "residue of bitterness or resentment." Elders have substantial power, and when they intervene in a conflict or a negotiation, their words are respected. This is partly because certain elders are believed to have access to supernatural powers that can remove protective shields at best and cause personal disaster at worst. In other African contexts, a range of indigenous processes exist in which relationships and hierarchies tend to be emphasized.

- **South African Styles of Negotiation**

South Africa has a nickname as "Rainbow Culture" as it is indeed one of the most multi-cultural nations on earth. Its culture is quite heterogeneous. There are also vast differences in business styles between urban and rural areas in South Africa. This great diversity makes preparing for specific business interactions difficult.

Attitudes and Styles: Negotiation approaches in South Africa may depend on your counterparts' cultural background. With Afrikaners, the primary approach to negotiating is often to employ distributive and contingency bargaining. They can be quite competitive and may be unwilling to agree with compromises unless it is their only option to keep the negotiation from getting stuck. In contrast, Black and British South African, may view negotiating as a joint problem-solving process, who are often willing to compromise as necessary to reach an agreement.

Sharing of Information: South African negotiators may spend considerable time gathering information and discussing details before the bargaining stage of a negotiation can begin. Most of them believe in information sharing as a way to build trust. This does not mean that they will readily reveal everything you might want to know.

Pace of Negotiation: How long your negotiation in South Africa may take can be hard to predict. Traditional companies may be very slow, spending considerable time gathering information, bargaining, and making decisions. Attempts to accelerate the process may be counterproductive. On the other hand, South Africans can be decisive and quick on their feet once you have managed to win their trust.

Bargaining: Cultural influences play a big role in the bargaining stage to a negotiation in South Africa. British South Africans view bargaining as a necessary element of the process to find a compromise between the parties, but often dislike haggling. They can be tough negotiators but will strive to play a "fair game". While Afrikaners are not overly fond of bargaining and dislike haggling, they can be quite good at both. Blacks may be most fond of both bargaining and haggling.

Decision-making: South African companies are often very hierarchical, and people expect to work within clearly established lines of authority. The decision maker is usually a senior executive. If decisions are made at lower levels, they often require top management approval. Black mangers often consult with others and carefully consider their inputs. It can be time and patience consuming. It is very important to learn about the company structure and win the support of people at all organizational levels involved in the negotiation, rather than focusing on upper management only.

INTERNATIONAL STYLE OF NEGOTIATION

The proficient international negotiator understands the national negotiating style of those on the other side of the table, accepts and respects their cultural beliefs, and is conscious of his or her own mannerisms and how they may be viewed by the other side. Even as different approaches to negotiation across national cultures are identified, change is constant. International business culture tends to privilege Western approaches to negotiation, centered in problem-solving and linear communication, as do many settings. As Western norms are balanced with Eastern and Southern values, and local traditions are balanced with regional and national approaches, negotiation practices continue their global evolution.

Making assumptions can create distrust and barriers that can jeopardize both your and the other side's needs, positions and goals. The way we view other people tends to be reserved and cautious. We usually expect people to take advantage of a situation, and during the negotiations the other side probably thinks the same way, especially when there is a lack of trust between counterparts. Instead of generalising, we should make an effort to treat everyone as individuals. Find the other side's values and beliefs independently of values and beliefs characteristic of the culture or group being represented by your counterpart.

KEY FACTORS IN NEGOTIATING SUCCESSFULLY IN INTERCULTURAL SITUATIONS

Intercultural negotiations have begun to take on an increasing importance to the globalizing firm. Differences in culture between business executives—for example, between a Chinese public sector plant manager in Shanghai and a Canadian division head of a family company in Toronto—can create barriers that impede or completely stymie the negotiating process.

- **Expectation**

Negotiators from different cultures may tend to view the purpose of a negotiation differently. Contract or Relationship? For deal makers from some cultures, the goal of a business negotiation, first and foremost, is a signed contract between the parties. Other cultures tend to consider that the goal of a negotiation is not a signed contract but rather the creation of a relationship between the two sides. Although the written contract expresses the relationship, the essence of the deal is the relationship itself. In *The Global Negotiator*, it is found that whereas 74 percent of the Spanish respondents claimed their goal in a negotiation was a contract, only 33 percent of the Indian executives had a similar view. The difference in approach may explain why certain Asian negotiators, whose negotiating goal is often the creation of a relationship, tend to give more time and effort to negotiation preliminaries, while North Americans often want to rush through this first phase of deal making. The preliminaries of negotiation, in which the parties seek to get to know one another thoroughly, are a crucial foundation for a good business relationship. They may seem less important when the goal is merely a contract.

It is therefore important to determine how your counterparts view the purpose of your negotiation. If relationship negotiators sit on the other side of the table, merely convincing them of your ability to deliver on a low-cost contract may not be enough to land you the deal. You may also have to persuade them, from the very first meeting, that your two organizations have the potential to build a rewarding relationship over the long term. On the other hand, if the other side is basically a contract deal maker, trying to build a relationship may be a waste of time and energy.

- **Rationale**

The line of reasoning method most persuasive to most Americans may not work at all in other cultures. Americans are usually swayed by expert opinion and hard evidence and usually want to concentrate on the facts available; others prefer to spend what to the Americans are inordinate amounts of time on principles. Mexican and Russian negotiators habitually start with the most general aspects and purpose of a negotiation session by defining major and minor issues, categorizing them, and then deciding on the main points to be solved. The Chinese seek agreement on general principles; they expect the other party to reveal their interests first while the Chinese mask their own interests and priorities. Especially in the Far East, the negotiating session is less a forum for working out issues than a formal and public expression of what has already been worked out beforehand.

The concept of discussing problems in a systematic, sequential and orderly manner, is promoted by Americans while the Japanese prefer haragei, to talk around a subject in order to get a holistic view. Only after this is accomplished will they go into details. The Japanese prefer avoiding any area in which an agreement cannot be easily reached. Instead they tend to move to another topic in its place. To Americans, this often appears as if the Japanese are trying to elude the issue. To an American, an unsolved issue is a point of contention. This, not any general principle, must be first dealt with before the agreement as a whole can be considered. Many cultures are holistic, especially cultures in the Far East; all issues are discussed at once and no decisions are made until the end.

Many who come from a non-Western tradition have to learn the value of "give and take" as well as the confrontational aspects of Western style negotiation. In a host of cultures, especially those from East Asia, people depend more upon feelings and personal relationships than intellectual confrontations. In numerous cultures, conflict avoidance is central and paramount in any negotiations. In these cultures, mediators, go-betweens, facilitators, brokers, and middlemen are used to assist in smoothing the negotiation process. In the Middle East, the Bedouin model is often used: intermediaries who enjoy trust of both sides play an important part; honor of both is regarded uppermost important; face saving is crucial; and gestures of generosity and reciprocation must be adhered to. On the other hand, the authoritarian traditions of the Latins often spurn use of mediators or third parties.

- **Language**

Even the discussion of negotiation, compromise, and agreement have different meanings to different cultures. Both the U.S. and Korean meanings for the word "corruption" are negative; however in the U.S., the word connotes being morally wrong while for the Koreans it implies being socially unfortunate. The Mexican will not compromise as a matter of honor, dignity and integrity. The Arab fears loss of manliness if he compromises. In Russia, compromise has negative connotation; principles are supposed to be inviolable and compromise is a matter of integrity. For Russians, a negotiation is treated as a whole without concessions. At the SALT talks, the Americans thought they had an "agreement" (meaning conclusive commitment) while the Russians said it was an "understanding" (meaning an expression of mutual viewpoint or attitude). When the Americans thought they had an "understanding," the Russians said it was a "procedural matter," meaning they had agreed to a process for conducting the negotiation. In the American culture, those who refuse to bargain are viewed as cold, having secret agendas, and not really being serious about business. The Dutch are not hagglers; you should make your offer fairly close to your true asking price; if you start making large concessions you will lose their confidence. The Swedes have a reputation as tough negotiators, not hagglers; they are methodical, detailed individuals who are slow to change positions. Bargaining is not highly valued in Swedish culture; those who bargain, who attempt to negotiate by offering a higher price in order to concede to a lower price, can be viewed as untrustworthy, inefficient, or perhaps out for personal gain at the expense of others. The English (and American) notion of "fair play" seems to have no exact equivalent in any other language.

The linguistic framework can be based on three factors: topic allocation, verbal immediacy of speaker and listener references, and topic progression. Topic allocation refers to the individual's need for personal autonomy concerning such aspects as independence, self determination and privacy; speakers can refer explicitly to the speaker, the listener, to both, or to neither. Verbal immediacy refers to how closely speakers associate themselves verbally with the interaction, with the topics they communicate about, and with their listeners' or own utterances; this can range from "remote" to "intimate". Topic progression refers to the sequencing and structure inherent in a dialogue.

For example, Spanish negotiators were found to be more person-oriented and preferred to establish a high degree of immediacy to the here-and-now of conversation; they are not inclined to separate the task from the person but prefer to bring their persons into the center of the interaction and allow the other party to penetrate much further into their own personal territory. The Danish negotiators were considered more task-oriented and preferred to use strategies in which the topic of conversation does not explicitly concern persons, and in which topics and persons are separated from each other; when they want to address topics within the opposite party's domain, they proceed by asking implicit questions, seldom commenting on each other's behavior. They prefer a low degree of immediacy, proceeding in a tentative and coordinated fashion. As a result of differences between the two groups, the Spanish negotiators would interpret Danish negotiators as emotionally uninvolved and impersonal and afraid of intimacy and too concerned with doing business. Danish negotiators would interpret Spanish negotiators as self-assertive, confrontational and uncooperative, consuming more time and energy in the negotiations than necessary.

Argumentation in global negotiations involves a blend of logic, emotion and dogma. Negotiators who use logic try to persuade their counterparts with substantive proof, that is, empirical (statistics, analyses, financial statements) or factual evidence. Negotiators who use emotional proof try to persuade their counterparts with motivational proofs by providing evidence from historical and cultural tradition. Negotiators who use dogma try to persuade the other side with authoritative proofs by providing a statement of opinion from an expert. Dogmatic bargainers make fewer concessions, achieve fewer agreements, take longer to reach an agreement and are more prone to view compromise as a defeat. Emotion and drama carry more weight than logic for Mexicans. Latin Americans place a high value on verbal agility and have a tendency to respond quickly; they may even answer a point once they have understood it even though the other side has not finished.

- **Forming and Building an Agreement**

Whether a negotiator's goal is a contract or a relationship, the negotiated transaction in almost all cases will be encapsulated in some sort of written agreement. Cultural factors influence the form of the written agreement that the parties make. Generally, Americans prefer very detailed contracts that attempt to anticipate all possible circumstances and eventualities, no matter how unlikely. Why? Because the deal is the contract itself, and one must refer to the contract to handle new situations that may arise. Other cultures, such as the Chinese, prefer a contract in the form of general principles rather than detailed rules. Why? Because, it is claimed, that the essence of the deal is the relationship between the parties. If unexpected circumstances arise, the parties should look primarily to their relationship, not the contract, to solve the problem. So, in some cases, a Chinese negotiator may interpret the American drive to stipulate all contingencies as evidence of a lack of confidence in the stability of the underlying relationship.

Related to the form of the agreement is the question of whether negotiating a business deal is an inductive or a deductive process. Does it start from an agreement on general principles and proceed to specific items, or does it begin with an agreement on specifics, such as price, delivery date, and product quality? Different cultures tend to emphasize one approach over the other. Some observers believe that the French prefer to begin with agreement on general principles, while Americans tend to seek agreement first on specifics. For Americans, negotiating a deal is basically making a series of compromises and trade-offs on a long list of particulars. For the French, the essence is to agree on basic principles that will guide and indeed determine the negotiation process afterward. The agreed-upon general principles become the framework, the skeleton, upon which the contract is built.

- **Decision Making**

In any negotiation, it is important to know how the other side is organized, who has the authority to make commitments, and how decisions are made. Culture is one important factor that affects how executives organize themselves to negotiate a deal. Some cultures emphasize the individual while others stress the group. These values may influence the organization of each side in a negotiation. In international negotiations one must also take into account the nuances in other culture's decision processes, that is, the way officials and executives reach decisions and instruct their negotiators, as well as personal styles of decision-making behavior. American managers usually make decisions by themselves, while Japanese managers tend to make decisions by consensus, a practice that can add time to the negotiation process. Americans place a high value on flexibility, whereas once a Japanese manager has reached a decision, he believes it is shameful to change it. Understanding these underlying attitudes helps you see what your potential partner's priorities are, and you can then adapt your strategy accordingly.

The accomplished international negotiator prepares for his negotiation by understanding the decision-making pattern of the specific culture, learning what the limitations of the delegates authority are and who within the nation or company will make the final decision, and readies himself for culture-based power plays that may occur within the negotiation.

- **Personal Relationships**

To most Orientals and Latins good personal relationships and feelings are all that really matter in a long-term agreement. After all, the written word is of lesser importance than personal ties. Once personal trust has been established, cooperation increases. The social contacts developed between the parties are often far more significant than the technical specifications and the price. The Chinese word "guanxi" signifies that personal connections require significant personal obligations. In many countries, the major point of the negotiations is getting to know the people involved. Brazilians and many Latin Americans can not depend on their own legal system to iron out conflicts so they must depend on personal relationships. Relations are important because of the need to have contracts. Contacts can help you determine who to approach in order to get the business moving; government is very much involved in business. Social competence is paramount. Relationships are important for Latin Americans; in many cases, the people they do business with are more important than the company; the quality of the personal relationship plays a vital role in the business relationship. No one rushes into business but rather spends time in pleasantries which assist in the creation of a suitable climate for interaction. The goal is to nurture a mutual confidence, engage in informal discussions and seek solutions to problems. Therefore personal rapport, preliminary meetings, telephone conversations, social activities are necessary when dealing with business people of these culture.

Americans negotiate a contract, the Japanese a relationship. In many cultures, the written word is primarily used to satisfy legalities. In their eyes, emotion and personal relations are more important than cold facts in business relations. The key issue is: Can I get along with these men and their company and do I want to sell (or buy) their products rather than can I make money on this deal? They are particularly interested in the sincerity of those they are negotiating with. The Japanese are especially unwilling to do business with someone they think may prove to be arrogant or unpleasant: "I do not do business with a man who does not like us!" Japanese do not separate personal feelings from business relationships. The effective negotiator should therefore display cultural empathy, be polite and honest, go out of his way to be good natured, practical, social, frank, responsible and efficient—to appreciate Japanese and most other Orientals value.

- **Status and Protocol**

American egalitarianism can also present a problem in cross-cultural negotiations. Friendliness for Americans is merely an expression of egalitarianism, a way to emphasize similarities, to clear the decks to enable Americans to get to the business at hand. While Americans want relationships built on equality and similarity, Europeans expect to build relationships based on the acknowledgment of differences, on respect for status, and on deference to title. In less egalitarian cultures, ascribed criteria are more important than achieved ones with some being more critical than others.

Most Westerners expect a prompt answer when they make a statement or ask a question. In a culture that values directness (German) you can expect to receive clear and definite response to questions and proposals. Western cultures tend to believe that human relations cannot stand still and they must be continuously reinforced to progress towards greater intimacy. The Chinese accept that relations can remain on the same level for an indefinite period of time. What they want is a sense of reliability, not warmth.

Women in business have a complete set of different protocol rules. Men may shake hands with women, but not in Arab countries. Women may kiss women but not men in Latin America. At the end of business in Latin America, men may embrace other men but not women. An appreciation, understanding, and respect of national protocols, rituals or special status symbols is in the best interest of the successful negotiator. The competent global negotiator subordinates his or her own preferences to that of his hosts or guests.

- **Social Aspects of Negotiations**

The function of entertainment and other social activity related to negotiation varies markedly from culture to culture. The unbelievably high level of entertainment expenses incurred by the Japanese is seen to be part of the preliminary stage of establishing interpersonal relationships; eating has long been established as a rapport-building activity. Americans feel comfortable in a relaxed social setting to conduct business; negotiators in other cultures may feel awkward in such settings and may even see this as a breach of etiquette towards one's guests. Americans eat in public and bath in private, the Japanese vice-versa. Japanese rarely bring spouses or family members to a business gathering. The French, likewise, believe the home is for more intimate relationships, not for conducting business. The bazaar model of bargaining through a series of formal sequential steps is found in Egypt and in many parts of the Middle East. It starts with a preliminary period of discussing issues that go well beyond the transaction that is contemplated; the negotiators subsequently focuses on establishing a personal relationship often with endless rounds of coffee and tea; finally the actual bargaining aimed at a compromise position commences. The parties engage in the fine art of haggling, sometimes simply for the fun of it. No step must be passed over. Patience is the key to success.

Different values and different priorities are clearly given to the social aspects and business considerations by different cultures. In many cultures, especially the Orient, giving a gift creates an obligation between parties; a reciprocal gift is required if you are being given a gift. To an American, ceremonies as part of the negotiating process are time-consuming, useless and an unnecessary expense.

● **Interpreters, Translators and Bicultural Brokers**

To augment his or her own capabilities, a business negotiator can employ cultural experts, translators, outside attorneys, financial advisors, or technical experts who have at least moderate and preferably high familiarity with both the counterpart's and the negotiator's cultures. These experts serve two distinguishable roles, as "agents" who replace the negotiator at the negotiating table or as "advisers" who provide information and recommend sources of action to the negotiator. The use of go-betweens, middlemen, brokers, and other intermediaries is a common practice within many cultures and represents a potentially effective approach to cross-cultural negotiation as well.

Using their language greatly improves communication and trust. For example, when their satellites met in space, the Americans spoke Russian and the Russians spoke English. Both sides knew that speaking the other's language reduced communications problems and increased trust. The same principles apply to many business negotiations. As a general rule, however, you should not negotiate in a foreign language unless you know it extremely well. Otherwise you will be focusing your attention on the language rather than on the substance of the deal. To be truly efficient, one should not only know both languages but both cultures and how to do business in both cultures. It is often advisable to have another bilingual person available to serve as a back-up listener and who can provide additional insight to the conversation.

● **Management Implications**

Let's assume that you have passed successfully through the initial stages of the negotiation and that you have agreed upon common ground with your prospective partner. The game of tactics now broadens. It is at this stage, in which the actual issues go back and forth between participants, that your awareness of negotiating behavior typical to your potential partner's culture can be put to use.

Italian negotiators, for example, will often try to push through this stage quite quickly, repeatedly insisting on their terms to tire out their opponents. Knowing this, a foreign negotiator may find a good tactic is to display no great hurry. Most Europeans won't break off discussions unless they are deeply offended, but Asian negotiators are often happy to drop the project if they are uncomfortable with some aspect of the negotiations. If this happens, try to backtrack and fix the problem.

Now the real work can begin. You'll need to choose which of the two classic negotiating styles you'll adopt: contentious or problem-solving. The contentious negotiator, a tough, demanding guy who makes few compromises, can be a great success given the right conditions. He either wins or loses, but never comes to a conditional agreement. The problem-solving negotiator takes a broader view, attempting to get as much as he/she can without handing out a deal breaker. He/she establishes common ground wherever he/she can find it and approaches negotiations on a step-by-step basis.

It is obviously important to learn these negotiating rituals for a given culture, even if your foreign partner turns out not to require them. Germans, for example, often need to spend a large part of the initial negotiations in number crunching. All the facts and figures must be agreed upon, and woe betides the negotiator who makes a mistake! This German trait is not really about number crunching; however, it is a confidence-building ritual in which two potential partners run through a series of routine checks just to display trustworthiness.

3. Exercises

I. Quiz

1. Although the steps involved in the negotiation process do vary somewhat according to cultural norms, which step generally follows persuasion?

   A. Preparation B. Relationship building

   C. Exchange of task-related information D. Concessions and agreement

2. Which step would least likely be part of the preparation phase of a negotiation meeting?

   A. Engage in general, polite conversations and informal communication

   B. Assess the kinds of demands that might be made

   C. Determine the composition of the other parties involved in the negotiation

   D. Evaluate the relative authority of the members of the other parties involved in the negotiation

3. Which variable in the negotiation process would involve determining the importance of procedures and social behaviors in the negotiation process?

   A. Complexity of communicative context B. Decision-making system

   C. Concern with protocol D. Significance of type of issues

4. Which phase in the general negotiation process usually involves social events, tours, and ceremonies?

A. Concession and agreement B. Persuasion
C. Preparation D. Relationship building

5. Based on research conducted on bargaining behaviors between different countries, compared to Americans, Which behavior are South Americans more likely to use?
A. Self-disclosure B. Question the purpose of the negotiation
C. Use commands D. Use misleading or false information
6. As to negotiation strategies, which two countries are most likely to act similarly?
A. Japanese and Americans B. Japanese and Brazilians
C. Americans and Russians D. None of these countries act similarly
7. What would be considered the primary purpose underlying all stages of the negotiation process?
A. Concession and agreement B. Persuasion
C. Exchange of task-related information D. Relationship building
8. Based on research examining negotiation styles in Japanese, North American and Latin American cultures, which behavior would be most consistent with a Japanese culture?
A. Being argumentative when one is right or wrong, but impersonal
B. Being argumentative when one is right or wrong and passionate
C. Being not argumentative and quiet when one is right
D. Being not argumentative, vocal when one is right
9. In order to succeed in intercultural negotiations, a manager has to:
A. Gain specific knowledge of the parties in the upcoming meeting
B. Be prepared to adjust to and control the situation
C. Be innovative
D. All of these factors are important for successful intercultural negotiations
10. In following the rational decision-making model, which step usually comes first?
A. Gathering and analyzing relevant data
B. Defining the problem
C. Determining who should be involved in the decision-making process
D. Considering alternative solutions
11. Loss of control is least likely to impact which step in the decision-making process?
A. Data gathering B. Consideration of alternative solutions
C. Decision making D. Implementation
13. A futuristic orientation is most likely to impact which aspect of the decision-making

process?

A. Problem definition B. Data gathering

C. Consideration of alternative solutions D. Implementation

Decide whether the following statements are true or false.

14. The negotiation process outside the U.S. typically involves getting to know one's contacts in the host country and building mutual trust before embarking on business discussions and transactions.

O True O False

15. The negotiation process is comprised of five steps beginning with preparation and ending with persuasion.

O True O False

16. When examining the negotiating behavior of various countries, the behaviors of Japanese and Brazilian managers are very similar.

O True O False

17. When negotiating, rough tactics would include putting opposing negotiators in stressful situations so that they may become more pliant.

O True O False

18. Research indicates that in order to maximize negotiation results in the U.S., it is best to start with extreme positions.

O True O False

19. In general, for Arabs, negotiations are businesslike and their factual appeals are based on what they believe is objective information, presented with the assumption that it is understood by the other side on a logical basis.

O True O False

20. In general, Russians are tough negotiators that stall for time until they unnerve Western negotiators by continuously delaying and haggling.

O True O False

21. Modern technological improvements have, in effect, eliminated the need for the face-to-face elements previously required in most negotiations.

O True O False

22. In high-context cultures, the approach to conflict could typically be considered expressive-oriented.

O True O False

23. Negotiation can be seen as a series of explicit and implicit decisions.

O True O False

24. In general, countries with an objective approach would be more likely to base their decisions on rationality.

O True O False

II. Case Analysis

Case 1: Jayant J., representing an Indian software company, waited impatiently for a local manufacturer in Sao Paulo, Brazil to clinch a business deal. After waiting almost one-and-a-half hours, Jayant finally welcomed the relaxed Brazilian, who barged into the lounge without even apology and started the conversation with a joke. The Brazilian's habit of communication by standing very close and touching Jayant frequently made Jayant, stickler for etiquette, very uncomfortable and irritated. At the close of the deal, the Brazilian's reply for a firm commitment, "si Deus quizer" ("if God wishes"), was the final straw for Jayant, who thought the Brazilian was being vague. The meeting was a failure and they never met again. (*Mishra and Sinha 1999*)

Case 2: A Japanese manager wanted to study a multimillion-dollar business proposal before he gave his American counterpart an answer. "Give me five minutes," he said. The American smiled back and waited. A few seconds later, the American's mouth twitched. Then he fidgeted a bit more. A whole 18 seconds later, the American interrupted the silence, startling the Japanese businessman, who was much more accustomed to the silence. (*Iwata 1995*)

4. References

1. Adler, N.J., T. S. Gehrke & J. L. Graham. Business Negotiations in Canada, Mexico, and the United States [J], *Journal of Business Research*, 15,1987: 411-430.
2. Adler, N. J. & J. L. Graham. Cross Cultural Interaction: The International Comparison Fallacy [J], *The Journal of International Business Studies,* 20 (3), 1989: 515-537.
3. Casse, P. & S. Deal. Managing Intercultural Negotiations [M]. Washington D.C.: Sietar International, 1985.
4. Cohen, Raymond. Negotiating Across Cultures [M]. Washington, D.C.: United States Institute of Peace, 1997.
5. Fang, T. Chinese business negotiating style [M]. Thousand Oaks, CA: Sage Publications, 1999.
6. Graham, J. L. The influence of culture on the process of business negotiations: An

exploratory study [J], *Journal of International Business Studies*, 1985a : 81-96.

7. Griffin, T. J.& W. R. Daggatt . The Global Negotiator [M]. NY: Harper, 1990.
8. Grindsted, A. The impact of cultural styles on negotiation: a case study of Spaniards and Danes [J]. Professional Communication, IEEE Transactions on (Volume: 37, Issue: 1), 1994.
9. Hank, Dan. "Working Across Cultural Barriers: A Critical Senior Leader Skill." Lecture. Air War College, Maxwell AFB, AL. 31 Aug 2006.
10. Herbig, P. A. & H. E. Kramer. The Dos and Don'ts of Cross-Cultural Negotiations [J], *Industrial Marketing Management,* 1992.
11. Herbig, P. A. & H. E. Kramer. The Role of Cross Cultural Negotiations in International marketing, *Marketing Intelligence and Planning*, 10/2, 1992: 10-13.
12. Lederach, John Paul. *Preparing for Peace*. Syracuse, NY: Syracuse University Press, p. 43. <http://www.beyondintractability.org/citations/8297>. 1995.
13. L. J. Brahm. When Yes Means No: How to Negotiate a Deal in China [J]. Boston: Tuttle Publishing, 2003.
14. Liu. Meina. The Intrapersonal and Interpersonal Effects of Anger on Negotiation Strategies: A Cross-Cultural Investigation [J], *Human Communication Research*, v35 n1, 2009: 148-169.
15. Luo, Y. Guanxi and Business—Guanxi Versus Western Networks. Vol 1. NJ: World Scientific Publishing Company, 2000.
16. Moore, Chris and Peter Woodrow, "Mapping Cultures—Strategies for Effective Intercultural Negotiations" (March 2004). http://www.mediate.com/articles/cdr1.cfm# (Accessed on 24 Jan 2007) Negotiation Center of Excellence, Air War College. Enrichment Seminar on Negotiations. Executive Workshop, 16—18 October 2006.
17. Moran, R. T. & W. G. Stripp. Successful International Business Negotiations [M], Houston: Gulf Publishing Company, 1991.
18. Ott U.The Influence of Cultural Activity Types on Buyer-Seller Negotiations: A Game Theoretical Framework for Intercultural Negotiations [J]. *J. Int. Negotiation*, 16(3), 2011: 427-450.
19. S. D. Seligman. Chinese Business Etiquette: A Guide to Protocol, Manners, and Culture in the People's Republic of China [M]. New York: Warner Books, 1999.
20. Salacuse, J. W. Making Global Deals: Negotiating in the International Marketplace [M], Boston: Houghton Mifflin, 1991.

21. Salacuse, J. W. The Global Negotiator: Making, Managing and Mending Deals Around the World in the Twenty-First Century [M], 1 edition. Palgrave Macmillan, 2003.
22. Thompson, L.L, & Hastie, R. Social perception in negotiation [J]. *Organizational Behavior and Human Decision Process,* Volume 47 Issue 1, 1990: 98-123.
23. T. Fang. Chinese Business Negotiation Style [M]. Thousand Oaks, CA: Sage Publications, 1999.
24. Triandis, H. Culture and Conflict [J]. *International Journal of Psychology,* 2000: 145-151.

Chapter 5

Intercultural Marketing

"Marketing communication or promotion is one of the elements of the marketing mix and is responsible for putting the marketing offer to the target market. It is the planned and integrated communication activity that communicates with an organization's stakeholders."

—Chris Fill

Globalization is the reason for the revival of local cultural identities in different parts of the world.

—British sociologist Anthony Giddens

When a passenger of foot heave in sight, tootle the horn. Trumpet him melodiously at first, but if he still obstacles your passage tootle him with vigor."

—from a brochure at a Tokyo car rental firm

"Effective and clear communication with the consumer is a must as it determines the success for your product."

—Gerbe, K, Intercultural Communication as a Strategy of Global Marketing. Germany: Grin. 2007

1. Lead-in

BLUNDERS IN INTERCULTURAL MARKETING

The marketing executives sent for international assignments, are bound to face problems in dealing with the corporate cultures of that particular country. Understanding a foreign market and formulating the company policies to cater to the need of international clients is a challenging job. Skilled professionals possessing the quality called "empathy" are able to deliver the goods in such cases. Many of you may have heard of these infamous errors made by multinational corporations when translating brands or slogans abroad.

Language is one of the main barriers to Intercultural Marketing, both oral and written. Oral communication usually presents more problems than written communication, such as in the pronunciation of vowels, in the use of voices and tones, and in the use of idiomatic expressions. For example, English, as the international language used not only by its native speakers but also by so many nonnative speakers all over the world, has many varieties. We may distinguish the American English from British English, but besides those two countries, when we communicate with people from other English speaking countries, such as Ireland, Australia, you will find the so-called English they are speaking is so strange. Their pronunciation is different from the Standard English and so is their usage of English. Also, people use their voices and tones in different ways, which can lead listeners to misunderstand their intentions. Russian speakers, for example, speak in flat, level tones in their native tongue. When they speak English, they maintain this pattern, and non-Russian listeners may assume that the speakers are bored or rude. Middle Easterners tend to speak more loudly than Westerners and may therefore mistakenly be considered more emotional. On the other hand, the Japanese are soft-spoken, a characteristic that implies politeness or humility to western listeners. Idiomatic expressions are another source of confusion. For instance, suppose you are dining with a German woman who speaks English quite well. You inquire, "More bread?" she says, "thank you," so you will pass the bread. But she will look confused. Because in German thank you (danke) can also be used as a polite refusal. If the woman had wanted more bread, she would have used the word please (bitte in German).

Marketing activities need correct oral communications between staff and managers as well as consumers and companies. Language shapes our worldview, dictating our perception of the universe. People of different languages will undoubtedly think differently, so the potential for misunderstanding in intercultural interaction is great. Even the way in which information is approached and processed can differ greatly between various cultures. For example, an English speaker feels responsible for transmitting the meaning of a message, but a Chinese speaker is more likely to expect the receiver to discover the meaning in a message that uses indirectness and metaphor. Further, an English speaker often places sentences in a chronological sequence to establish a cause-and-effect pattern. However, a Chinese speaker often begins by creating a context with generalizations that forms a web to receive and support a given topic. Language difference can trap the business up even when a U.S. executive is doing business in an English-speaking country. A U.S. paper products manufacturer learned this the hard way while trying to crack the English market for paper napkins by using its usual advertising slogan: "There is no finer paper napkin for the dinner table." Unfortunately for the English people, napkin is the British term for diaper. Also likely are misunderstandings involving vocabulary, pronunciation, or usage when business people come from different language environments deal with each other.

- **In Language**

When releasing their car the Pinto in Brazil, Ford apparently presumed that they didn't need to localize the name. After all, it has a vaguely "Spanish-sounding" ring to it, and Brazilians speak Spanish, right? Wrong. While *pinto* can have a number of different meanings in Spanish (the verb "to paint," for example), in Portuguese—the language spoken in Brazil—*pinto* is a slang word for "tiny male genitalia." After sales for the Pinto flopped, Ford changed the car's name to Corcel (horse). In the English langnage, the meaning of *pinto* is more associated with men who drive big cars in general.

"Two nations divided by a common language" was how George Bernard Shaw (or possibly Oscar Wilde—history isn't clear) described the relationship between Britain and the USA. Accordingly, this example goes some way towards showing how localization can be a tricky procedure even when occurring between (what we in the localization industry would call) EN (UK) and EN (US). The vacuum cleaner manufacturer Electrolux had a big hit with their British advertising campaign "Nothing sucks like Electrolux." However, when transferred across the ocean, the meaning changed from a simple, rhyming slogan into a declaration of inferior quality. In America, "sucks" is a slang term applied to something awful or useless, while in the original market, the slogan doesn't have any negative connotations.

As one of America's leading suppliers of chicken, Perdue Farms CEO Frank Perdue was one of the first CEOs to appear in advertisements promoting products. Perdue's famous slogan was "It takes a tough man to make a tender chicken," which commonly featured on advertising billboards with an accompanying photo of Frank Perdue himself clutching a rooster. This odd slogan sounds funny enough in English, but when translated into Spanish, it came out as "It takes a hard man to make a chicken aroused." Whoops.

Chinese translation also proved difficult for Coke, which took two tries to get it right. They first tried Ke-kou-ke-la because when pronounced it sounded roughly like Coca-Cola. It wasn't until after thousands of signs had been printed that they discovered that the phrase means "bite the wax tadpole" or "female horse stuffed with wax", depending on the dialect. Second time around things worked out much better. After researching 40,000 Chinese characters, Coke came up with "ko-kou-ko-le" which translates roughly to the much more appropriate "happiness in the mouth".

The Japanese company Matsushita Electric was promoting a new Japanese PC for Internet users. Panasonic created the new web browser and had received license to use the cartoon character Woody Woodpecker as an interactive internet guide. The day before the huge marketing campaign, Panasonic realised its error and pulled the plug. Why? The ads for the new product featured the following slogan: "*Touch Woody—The Internet Pecker.*" The company only realised its cross cultural blunder when an embarrassed American explain what "touch Woody's pecker" could be interpreted as!

The Swedish furniture giant IKEA somehow agreed upon the name "FARTFULL" for one of its new desks. Enough said.

In the late 1970s, Wang, the American computer company could not understand why its British branches were refusing to use its latest motto "Wang Cares". Of course, to British ears this sounds too close to "Wankers" which would not really give a very positive image to any company.

There are several examples of companies getting tangled up with bad translations of products due to the word "mist". We had "Irish Mist" (an alcoholic drink), "Mist Stick" (a curling iron from Clairol) and "Silver Mist" (Rolls Royce car) all flopping as "mist" in German means dung/manure. Fancy a glass of Irish dung?

"Traficante" and Italian mineral water found a great reception in Spain's underworld. In Spanish it translates as "drug dealer".

In 2002,Umbro the UK sports manufacturer had to withdraw its new trainers (sneakers) called the Zyklon. The firm received complaints from many organisations and individuals as it was the name of the gas used by the Nazi regime to murder millions of Jews in concentration camps.

Sharwoods, a UK food manufacturer, spent £6 million on a campaign to launch its new "Bundh" sauces. It received calls from numerous Punjabi speakers telling them that "bundh" sounded just like the Punjabi word for "arse".

In Italy, a campaign for "Schweppes Tonic Water" translated the name into the much less thirst quenching "Schweppes Toilet Water".

The American slogan for Salem cigarettes, "Salem—Feeling Free," got translated in the Japanese market into "When smoking Salem, you feel so refreshed that your mind seems to be free and empty."

General Motors had a perplexing problem when they introduced the Chevy Nova in South America. Despite their best efforts, they weren't selling many cars. They finally realized that in Spanish, "nova" means "it won't go". Sales improved dramatically after the car was renamed the "Caribe."

Sometimes it's one word of a slogan that changes the whole meaning. When Parker Pen marketed a ballpoint pen in Mexico, its ads were supposed to say "It won't leak in your pocket and embarrass you." However, the company mistakenly thought the Spanish word "embarazar" meant embarrass. Instead the ads said "It won't leak in your pocket and make you pregnant".

- **In Traditions and Customs**

If we're lucky our cross cultural marketing blunders will only cause great hilarity. When we're not, they can cause offence and cost us money. Here are a few of the blunders of the latter type. With all their marketing budgets they can still get things wrong. Cross cultural communication runs deep so it is important to research carefully the cultural codes for specific products or brands and do some well-undertaken market research.

Procter & Gamble may need to consider doing a bit more cultural research before forming an advertising campaign for a new product abroad. This article describes how they made assumptions about gender themes and portrayal of women in Japan while creating a soap commercial. The campaign's pitch was making women more attractive to men, so the ad showed a Japanese man walking into the bathroom while his wife sat in the tub. Japanese women were offended because it is considered bad manners for a husband to break his wife's privacy while she is bathing (Wooten). In this case, P&G needed to better understand local attitudes to avoid being offensive and to increase likelihood of targeting the correct market.

United Airlines unknowingly got off on the wrong foot during its initial flights from Hong Kong. To commemorate the occasion, they handed out white carnations to the passengers. When they learned that to many Asians white flowers represent bad luck and even death, they changed to red carnations.

A US telephone company tried to market its products and services to Latinos by showing a commercial in which a Latino wife tells her husband to call a friend, telling her they would be late for dinner. The commercial bombed since Latino women do not order their husbands around and their use of time would not require a call about lateness.

Pepsodent tried to sell its toothpaste in Southeast Asia by emphasizing that it "whitens your teeth." They found out that the local natives chew betel nuts to blacken their teeth which they find attractive.

A company advertised eyeglasses in Thailand by featuring a variety of cute animals wearing glasses. The ad was a poor choice since animals are considered to be a form of low life and no self respecting Thai would wear anything worn by animals.

A soft drink was introduced into Arab countries with an attractive label that had stars on it—six-pointed stars. The Arabs interpreted this as pro-Israeli and refused to buy it. Another label was printed in ten languages, one of which was Hebrew—again the Arabs did not buy it.

EXAMPLES OF SUCCESSFUL INTERCULTURAL MARKETING

- **Samsung**

Despite gaining a later entry into the French market than competitors such as Sony, Philips, and Nokia, Samsung has outperformed the rest, owing to deliberate localization efforts from the beginning. While Samsung may be a Korean company, they have not marketed themselves as such, at least not in France. Appealing to the local desire for artistic design, in 2010 Samsung hosted an art exhibition, displaying works of art in high definition on their 3D TV sets. Held at the Petit Palais, the exhibition saw 600,000 visitors in its first month. In addition to public campaigns such as this, Samsung paid special attention to the French mobile phone market when launching its own operating system, "bada." By determining the most downloaded apps for the local market, like the Yellow Pages and applications for navigating art museums, Samsung released localized "bada" optimizations, which were hugely successful. In a matter of six months the operating system went from practically zero to 2,000 local apps. Rounding out a comprehensive localization initiative, Samsung has not only marketed and produced locally, they have hired locally as well, giving the brand much more authenticity and even a sense of French ownership.

- **Apple**

Several years ago, Apple created a successful advertising campaign in America, designed to highlight the differences between Macs and PCs. The adverts featured a cool, laid-back hipster-type representing the Mac, and a staid, nerdy-looking actor to represent PCs. The two bickered over features in a series of commercials that emphasized how much "cooler" Macs were than PCs. When it came time to expand this campaign to Japan, Apple sensibly examined the cultural mores of Japanese society and correctly concluded that these ads repeated verbatim would not attract customers to Apple. In Japan, directly criticizing ones rivals/competitors is seen as decidedly low class, which was certainly not the message Apple wanted to convey. The Japanese version of these ads employed a duo from the established Japanese comedy troupe, Rahmens, who focused on the idea that Macs were more for personal, weekend use, while PCs were primarily for office use. The message taken, Apple reaped in the rewards with its localized advertising strategy in the Japanese market.

2. Main Text

2.1 Defining Intercultural Marketing

Intercultural marketing is defined as the strategic process of marketing among consumers whose culture differs from that of the marketer's own culture at least in one of the fundamental cultural aspects, such as language, religion, social norms and values, education, and the living style. The most significant part of this definition is "more than one nation". If transaction occurs inside the territory then it is known as domestic or native marketing. The last and final part is for profit. If transaction occurs without profit then it may be known as donation or grants. But to be international marketing transaction must be occurred for profit.

Intercultural marketing combines culture and marketing together and concentrate on the optimal use of cultural elements in the marketing activities aiming to help consumers understand a certain culture so as to enable them to develop a sense of belonging in the consuming world. Thus they would identify the products and are more likely to buy the products. The traditional ways of marketing which are full of exaggerations and flirtations have obviously been out of date. Consumers would be more likely to choose products that comply with their culture, not the opposite, even when the latter is more competitive in quality and price. Thus a successful international marketer should be fully aware of cultural elements.

In order to match marketing with consumer preferences, purchasing behavior, and product-use patterns, marketers should understand the target market's cultural environment. Business firms should not focus on cultural differences merely to adjust marketing communication programs to make them acceptable to consumers. This is to suggest that firms should also identify cultural similarities in order to identify opportunities and modify standard marketing strategies based on marketing communication theory informed with cultural information. Working skillfully with these cultural similarities and differences in the worldwide marketplace is an important marketing task for businesses.

Communication among people from the same culture is often difficult enough. Therefore, communication between people from different cultures from the point of view of language, values, customers, and ways of thinking, will be far more difficult, with a degree of miscommunication being almost inevitable (Ferraro, 2006). Problems in marketing communication conducted cross-culturally often arise when participants from one culture are unable to understand culturally determined differences in communication practices, traditions, and thought-processing in another cultural context.

Marketing communication literature focused on advertising supports the hypothesis that advertising content differs between countries. International advertising research has confirmed differences in advertising content between countries. The premise upon which these studies are predicated indicates that advertisements, in part, reflect individual countries' social systems (Emery and Tian, 2003; McLeod and Kunita, 1994; Mueller, 1992; Ramaprasad and Hasegawa, 1992; Zandpour, Chang, and Catalano, 1992). Values, norms, and characteristics embedded in advertising messages appear in various cultures to a greater or lesser degree (Emery and Tian, 2003; Mueller, 1993). Therefore understanding the importance of cultural values in advertising has great practical value in marketing communication. Recognizing differences in cultural values should guide the formulation of international marketing communication strategies (Munson and McIntyre, 1979). Ignoring the cultural meaning embedded in advertising could lead to a misinterpretation of the firm's intended message (McCracken, 1987). Such miscommunication is mainly responsible for businesses failing in international marketing.

Cross-cultural marketing communication demands that firms be aware of and sensitive to cultural differences. To respect the right to culture by the consumers in various cultures and marketplaces, marketers should understand that their customers have a right to maintain, practice, and identify with their own culture. Marketing abroad involves expanding corporate activities in a complex multicultural environment. More specifically, international marketers must manage two different sources of cultural diversity: external diversity and internal diversity.

External diversity: marketing managers are faced with numerous obvious and less obvious effects of cultural determinants on buying and consumption processes (who buys? what? where? how? why?), as well as with the cultural traits characteristic of doing business with foreign partners (negotiation and relationship management with suppliers, distributors, and others) in a variety of entry strategy contexts (greenfield, mergers-acquisitions, international joint-ventures…);

Internal diversity: marketing managers working in the different subsidiaries of multinational companies have to cooperate with teams operating in different countries on key issues ranging from strategic marketing decision making to the implementation and execution of specific marketing programs. Departments are increasingly multicultural, especially in Europe, but also more generally in world companies located in emerging economies. Organizational issues are numerous (management styles, corporate identity, information systems, HRM…) and are reinforced by market forces concentration in most sectors, in most countries.

The globalization of the economic world has made it important for marketing managers to understand how to do business in different cultures. Within this managerial context, knowledge of cultural variations in management can make international managers more effective when dealing with customers, suppliers, subordinates, colleagues and negotiation partners in foreign countries. It may also help decision makers react better to any ethical, political, social or economic issues that arise in the international operations of their companies.

The ability of marketers and consumers to communicate cross-culturally is critical for success. Marketing communication is a two-way interactive communication. Marketers deliver information to the market they gather, collecting, interpreting, and putting this information to use. If the marketers want to succeed in intercultural marketing, they must work in a way that respects the consumer's values and their right to cultural ties. For example, for Western marketers to communicate in a business setting, it is important for them to respect the Chinese government's claim for *guoqing*. Marketing communication is not an independent behavior, but is related to all other business or market behaviors. From the anthropological perspective, then, all market behaviors are culture-bound. Buying and selling take place within the culture itself.

Failure to do so may lead to a loss of business. One classic case discussion about the successful marketing of color TV sets in the China market by Japanese marketers can be used to support this argument. In the late 1980s and 1990s, Japanese-made color TV sets dominated the imported TV set market in China. In the early 1980s, Japanese and European TV manufacturers made comprehensive studies of the Chinese market. Based on their research, European marketers decided not to market their products in China. They concluded that, given the low GDP per capita in China, it was unlikely that the Chinese people would be willing to buy luxuries like color TV sets. The Japanese TV set marketers decided otherwise, based on their research and observations that the Chinese have a cultural tradition of savings being handed down from generation to generation. In addition, the Chinese save money for future consumption, unlike Western culture where people spend future money for present consumption. Almost every family in China had been saving for two to three years to realize the dream of owning a color TV set. Moreover, the Japanese research revealed that, although Chinese companies manufactured color TV sets, Chinese consumers had more confidence in imported products. Accordingly, the Japanese marketers concluded that Chinese families would buy high quality Japanese color TV sets. As a result, Japanese color TV marketers profited greatly in China because they understood a facet of Chinese culture that their European competitors did not.

2.2 Key Issues in Intercultural Marketing

Intercultural marketing communication requires that firms discover if markets are viable by including in its business and marketing planning the study of the culture in which the company intends to do business. This involves identifying cultural factors that can be employed to support marketing communication in the proposed markets. To succeed, the business uses pre-existing factors and creates new ones that suit the situation. Since culture dictates customers' behaviors including buying goods, it becomes crucial for today's companies to understand the impact of intercultural differences on business, trade and internal company organization. The success or failure of a company, venture, merger or acquisition is essentially in the hands of its people. If these people are not interculturally aware then misunderstandings, offense and major break-down in communication can occur. In intercultural marketing, companies need to realize the following:

◇ Differences in consumer needs, responses, wants and usage of the product;

◇ Differences in product placements, legal environment and infrastructures;

◇ To determine the cultural viability of a certain market means that the marketers should positively identify cultural factors that can be used to facilitate the marketing program in the targeted market since most human behaviors, including market behaviors, take place within a cultural context.

Classic anthropological theory claims that while all human behaviors, including market behaviors, take place within a cultural context, people are able to influence and even change, through their behaviors, the cultural context within which their behaviors take place (Hall, 1976; Hamilton, 1987; Harris and Moran, 1987). For instance, Geely might face some challenges in the development of the Volvo purchase and Welch (2010) questions whether this endeavor will be successful given previous failures with the automaker's acquisitions such as the Daimler-Chrysler case. The Chinese luxury market is booming and still has room for some other players to come in and build a brand. The brand is upscale and Chinese consumers might even see Geely's ownership as a preferable outcome. So in the opinion of Welch's interviewee Jim Hall, principal of 2,953 Analytics in Birmingham, Michigan, the company can grow sales and get fatter margins in China. Bloomberg (2007) publishes that the advertising in China is Westernized, from huge billboards to tiny screens in taxicabs. Every day, many events are sponsored by companies, many of them Western, looking to connect with local customers. On the other hand, the Google.cn withdrawal from China serves as an example that it is important to understand all the intricacies of the country that one is trying to do business with. As Levy (2011) states, the Chinese logged onto Google.cn and typed in a vulgar term for breasts. Google Suggest offered links that displayed raw nudity, and more. The official typed in the word meaning "son," and one of the Google Suggest terms was "love affair between son and mother." The links to this term yielded explicit pornography. The woman serving tea in the conference room almost fainted at the spectacle. The lack of intercultural communication is evident in this case.

Accordingly, culture influences marketing communication, just as marketing communication, in turn, influences culture. Firms can be agents of change within a culture. The interactions between marketing communication and culture can be examined from three perspectives.

1) Culture defines acceptable purchasing and product-use behavior for consumers and business. Based on their analysis of data collected in Denmark, Great Britain, France, and Germany, Brunso and Grunet (1998) found that intercultural factors impact people's food shopping. Using business gifts as an example, in cultures such as Japan where a business gift is expected, a host who is not presented with a gift will feel insulted. However, an important feature of marketing communication may work to the detriment of the company seeking business in other cultures where offering a business gift could be interpreted as a bribe or inappropriate gesture, and would offend the recipient (Arunthanes, Tansuhaj and Lemak, 1994).

2) Where culture is at the center of all social interaction, it is expected that the impact of culture on marketing communication per se would be easier to identify than any other business variable. Advertising, for instance, is strongly influenced by language, one of the key elements

of culture. Moreover, advertising budget and structure are based on buying habits and consumption style. Values and norms, media, and the state of the material culture, in turn, influence these variables. Theorists, including Albers-Miller, Hofstede, Pollay and Gallagher, claim that culture affects the kind of roles and the choice of themes depicted in advertising. These roles and themes are related to underlying cultural values and norms; thus, every element of culture influences each facet of marketing communication.

3) Marketing communication also influences culture, contributing to cultural borrowing and change. According to Hooker (2008), "there is no better arena for observing a culture in action than business. Cultures tend to reveal themselves in situations where much is as stake, because it is here that their resources are most needed." As more markets become global and the marketing mix standardized, the rate of cultural change will increase. Cultural changes in contemporary China illustrate this point. For instance, it was widely believed that gender identity might affect consumption behavior. However, a recent study of masculinity appeal by Emery and Tian (2003) demonstrated that American respondents and Chinese respondents acted the same. A possible explanation for this could be that the gender status in Chinese traditional culture has changed. Marketing communications by Western firms could in part account, for such a cultural change. Therefore, American marketers may succeed using the same masculine appeals to the Chinese youth market that have been used in the U.S.

Nonetheless, cultures tend to change slowly, and specific products may meet with protracted resistance. Therefore, the primary task for firms is to locate similarities in various markets and strategically make them available for entering into new intercultural markets. In intercultural communication, marketers need continually to adjust their behaviors and marketing programs to suit target markets. However, when entering foreign markets, firms frequently fall into the trap of the "self-reference" criterion, which means their business representatives might be unconsciously applying their own cultural experiences and values to marketing communication in another culture. Even more dangerous than self-reference criterion is ethnocentrism, the belief that one's own culture is superior to any other, which will ruin efforts at marketing communication.

Based on his wide experience, Gesteland (1996) identified four paired cultural models that require special attention when doing business in diverse cultural settings, and Park Myung-seok (2010) brought about the fifth pair.

1) Deal-focused vs. Relationship-focused cultures

How people solve problems differs based on what kind of culture they are in. People in a deal-focus culture (DF) focus on work itself, while people of a relationship-focus culture (RF) try to build close ties with their business partners before working with them. The work plan of a DF group is precise and concerns measurable and reproductive outcomes. On the other hand, the work plan of a RF group is flexible, taking various possible situations and changes into account. Therefore, if DF marketers work in the RF market, they will inevitably face culture clashes. RF people find DF people pushy, aggressive and rude, while a DF group thinks that a RF group is dilatory, too ambiguous and unclear to understand.

The vast majority of the world's markets are relationship oriented. When doing business in those markets, the relationship with business partners comes before principles or rules. For example, a contract consented by both parties is just a guideline that can be revised whenever necessary, rather than an agreement that must be strictly followed to the letter. People in this culture prioritize their family above the rest of society. In addition, they do business only with the people they know. So, when they have to work with strangers, they want to make sure that they get close enough to the new business partners before sealing the deal. This feature of relationship is predominant in most of Asia, Africa, the Middle East, and Latin America. In contrast, the deal-focused approach is common in only a small part of the world. Northern Europe, North America, Australia and New Zealand, in particular, have the distinctive deal-focused markets. People in these areas are quite used to doing business with strangers.

2) Formal vs. Informal business cultures

In an informal culture, such as the USA, Australia, and to some extent Canada, Denmark, Norway, and New Zealand, people believe that inequality of social status or class should be minimized. So, the hierarchy in an organization is simply based upon differences in roles. In other words, everybody has equal rights and someone's power is based only on his expertise or competitiveness. In contrast, in a formal culture, mainly in Europe and, most of Asia, the Middle East, and Latin America societies, people are treated differently in accordance with their social status, class or age. A power hierarchy is established by these elements, and it is justifiable for a person to have power and privilege based on his family connection, personal charisma or influence. In formal cultures, formalities are viewed as part of the protocol, while they are seen as something inconvenient in informal cultures. Such difference sometimes leads to the breakdown of an international trade negotiation. People from formal hierarchical cultures may be offended by the breezy familiarity of counterparts from informal, relatively egalitarian societies. On the other hand, those from informal cultures may regard their formal counterparts as distant, stuffy, pompous or arrogant.

3) Rigid-time vs. Fluid-time cultures

Time concept and time management vary from culture to culture. In a monochromic culture, time is important. Discussions follow agreed-upon agendas and move rapidly in linear fashion. In rigid time cultures, where people are expected to be punctual and perform one task at a time. They set plans and schedules in detail, and are obsessed with deadlines. Deal-focused cultures like North America, Nordic and Germanic Europe are in this category. Industrialized countries in Asia, including Korea, Japan and Singapore have relatively a rigid time concept, although they still put much significance on bonding with others.

In polychromic cultures, business discussions tend to follow their own logic rather than a fixed outline. In these cultures, relationship is more valued than deadlines. For business firms planning to negotiate in a polychromic culture, it is wise to build a substantial margin of time into agendas. In fluid time cultures, relationship between people is more important than getting things done. Therefore, even in the middle of a meeting, a person takes his calls or receives his visitors. One carries out multiple tasks at the same time. Countries in the Arabic region, most of Africa, Latin America and Southeast Asia are considered to have fluid time concept.

4) Expressive vs. Reserved cultures

The communication patterns of a reserved culture are very different from those of an expressive culture. Reserved people tend to hold back their feelings. In their culture, keeping composure is highly respected, while physical contact, exaggerated gestures and too much eye contact are avoided. Expressive people, however, communicate what they feel as freely as they want verbally, paraverbally or nonverbally. How much a person reveals his feelings is determined by the culture he has grown up in. Varying degrees of expressiveness in paraverbal and nonverbal behavior cause unexpected problems for international business people. In Japan, Thailand, many other Asian countries, Nordic and Germanic Europe, speaking loudly, revealing true feelings upon the face, or gesturing excessively are generally avoided. Therefore, people from the Mediterranean region, Latin Europe and Latin America, who feel comfortable about expressing their feelings, might have trouble doing business with those from Thailand, who are more self-controlled. On the other hand, in Egypt, a speaker generally likes to talk in a loud voice to make sure that a listener understands him. The speaker gets louder or even pounds the table when he wants to stress certain points. Otherwise, he might be ignored by the listeners. Those from North America, Australia, New Zealand, South Asia, Africa and Eastern Europe are relatively expressive.

5) Indirect vs. Direct Languages

DF and RF groups are also different in terms of the way they converse. DF people believe that, when negotiating or making conversations, they should be clear and direct about what they think. However, RF people are circuitous and indirect. They consider various situations and use a politeness strategy to avoid disagreement and disputes. Such different styles of communication often cause misunderstanding. Difficulties confronted when communicating across cultures often lead to a lot of trouble in the sales activities, negotiations, performance assessment or teamwork of a company. People who use indirect language prefer to avoid possible conflicts or confrontations, and delegate a third party to act as a mediator. In contrast, direct language users talk about the problem upfront. The nature of the two different problem-solving approaches can be summed up as harmony versus clarity.

Instead of saying a direct "no" Asian people usually say, "That will be difficult," "We will have to give that further study," or "Maybe." Direct language users such as Americans, however, misunderstand that their Asian partners are deliberately misleading or confusing them. Such expressions might be seen as an attempt to hide their intentions in negative situations. For people in a relationship-focused culture, however, the indirect language is a polite way of delivering bad or disappointing news. They are being considerate, hoping not to hurt anyone's feelings in order to maintain a good relationship. In contrast, people in a deal-focused culture believe that honesty and truth is the only and reliable way to resolve the issue. Therefore, they give negative feedback, express objection or deliver bad news as it is. (Park Myung-seok, 2010).

Although what Gesteland suggests is useful and practical, it is good to be aware of the danger of stereotyping people from other cultures. Anthropological theory suggests that it is unwise and short-sighted to project our own behavior onto substantially different cultures (Giovannini and Rosansky, 1990; Hall, 1976; Hamilton, 1987). People in different cultures have different market values and behaviors that defy typecasting by national origin alone. For example, through long observation it has been found that consuming and buying patterns and other social/economic behaviors of Chinese immigrants living in Canada are completely different from the patterns of people living in China. Therefore, business firms need to have different market communication strategies for each group (Tian, 1999). In some cases, the firms know that cultures are different, but are unable to articulate how they differ. Research is the way to find out and to know what levers to use in moving buyers/consumers. We assert that the anthropological approach is an especially effective way to carry out intercultural marketing research (Tian, 2000a; Weise, 1999).

There are many unresolved problems or issues that need to be solved and discussed by scholars and marketing professionals in theory as well as practice. In the theoretical area, the following themes and issues need to be probed and discussed:

◇ Cultural impact of markets: international versus domestic marketing communication;

◇ Standardization versus adaptation in intercultural communication;

◇ Intercultural dimensions of marketing communication research;

◇ Intercultural aspects of marketing communication mix (advertising, promotion, sales, public relations, trade shows, and commercials);

◇ Intercultural aspects of marketing communication in the service sector;

◇ Intercultural communication implications of the aftermarket;

◇ Intercultural marketing communication education and professional training.

The seven topics or themes listed above can be viewed as guidelines for further theoretical studies, although they will not be treated as exclusive for marketing scholars. More themes and topics will be discovered as the theoretical discussions proceed. As marketing professionals, we need to know clearly that although marketing principles will remain the same, there will continuously be new challenges to marketing in the new century.

Business people need to be careful so that they never underestimate the impact that culture can have on consumer buying behaviour. Developing your understanding, tolerance and acceptance of cultural differences is crucial if your international marketing objectives are to be accomplished. There are a number of key cultural elements that international marketers need to take into consideration when designing products, developing promotions and implementing distribution systems in foreign markets. These elements include values, beliefs, thought processes, symbols, traditions, religion and language. It is generally assumed that people are not born with a culture, but are born into a society in which they develop certain cultural traits and beliefs. Culture has an impact on people right from when they are born all the way into adulthood, which gives it a highly persuasive quality. In many countries, cultural traits will prevent a person from doing something that is common in another culture or encourage behaviour that is uncommon elsewhere.

It is important that international marketers pay particularly close attention to the persuasive nature of culture. You can't simply assume that people will disregard their culture just because a product you have introduced will make their life easier. Many aspects of culture have survived thousands of years and are likely to continue so long as they are being taught to children from a young age. Many countries are reluctant to let go of their culture and actively try to preserve it against foreign influence. Language is a particularly important factor to consider when developing international marketing campaigns. It might not seem like a problem at first; all you need is a good interpreter. However, language is extremely complex with significant differences occurring not just between countries, but across different regions. The best way to deal with language issues is to deal with people who grew up in your target market. They are far more adept at recognising potential issues than translators who learnt a second language later in life. Religion, tradition and local customs are also important considerations. You need to make yourself aware of the local culture to ensure that you don't accidentally or carelessly offend people. It is important that you remain sensitive and tolerant to different points of view and ensure that your brand doesn't contain any symbolism that could be offensive in the local culture.

International marketers believe that consumers would increasingly resemble each other and that they will eat the same food, wear the same clothes, watch the same television programs to an increasing proportion. But the reality is very different. Therefore, to trade in international markets, people must overcome the large cultural and economic boundaries. Different traditional beliefs, preferences, habits and customs need to be understood. Culture involves society's thoughts, words, traditions, language, materials, attitudes and feelings. One of the elements that makes culture is beliefs. Beliefs of the people in a community can show similarities. For example, four, and four times in Japan are seen as unlucky, because of which most products are sold in groups of five leads. Another element of culture, tradition, is related with non-verbal behaviour of individuals. In France the men use more cosmetic products than the women, which shows the self-conscious tradition of the French men.

As a result, learning of cultural characteristics in the analysis of consumer behavior has been an important variable in marketing, especially in market segmentation, target market and product positioning.

2.3 Cultural Impacts on International Marketing

The impact of intercultural factors on marketing is one of the issues that demands serious study. In terms of marketing practice, we suggest the following points as guidelines for marketers to minimize possible intercultural marketing mistakes:

◇ Be sensitive to do's and don'ts, taboos, and regulations. Develop cultural empathy in terms of marketing communication.

◇ Recognize, understand, and respect another's cultural difference.

◇ Be culturally neutral and realize that different is not necessarily better or worse.

◇ Never assume transferability of a concept from one culture to another.

◇ Get cultural informants involved in decision-making. Cultural informants could be local businesspeople or well trained anthropologists.

Intercultural communication is literally the communication that is taking place between two or more people from various cultural backgrounds. When we talk about intercultural marketing communication, we will change our field of focus. Not only are we going to try to obtain a good communication in general between different cultures, more specifically, we will strive for the achievement of effective communication between people from different cultural backgrounds. In other words, it's not about the message itself; it's about correctly transferring the message so that you can attain the desired effect of your message. Understanding the cultural differences among countries and peoples is extremely important for a company to develop its marketing strategy abroad. Although the aim of business may be the same everywhere, the way to do business varies considerably across countries. The advent of global markets and global companies has to some extent reduced the disparities among countries.

"Culture shock" is a potent threat to the international marketers. Cultural differences affect the applicability of the experienced marketer's professional skills directly. In a new surrounding the great marketer is no longer necessarily a successful marketer, perhaps not even a good one. The experienced marketer will often have a frustrating time getting back to the basic fundamentals of the marketing effort. When Pepsi Cola entered Japan many years ago, they selected a young executive who had been very successful in the U.S. marketplace. His age and impetuous nature, key ingredients in his American success, set back Pepsi's introduction severely. While Coca Cola gained market leadership with the help of Japanese leaders, Pepsi still has to recover from the initial mistake. This story tells us that situations can differ so drastically that experience is a misleading guide.

Cultural incompetence can easily jeopardize millions of dollars worth business through wasted negotiations, lost purchases, sales, and contracts, and poor customer relations. Furthermore, the internal efficiency of a multinational corporation may be weakened if managers and workers are not "on the same wavelength." Cultural risk is just as real as political risk in the international business arena.

In order to study cultural impacts on communication, we need first to examine culture itself. Marketing scholars define culture as that which gives people a sense of who they are, of belonging, of how they should behave, and of what they should be doing. In marketing and consumer behavior research, the concept of culture has been minimal; commonly, marketers and consumers ignore the depth and importance of the concept and its place in analyzing human behavior.

Some definitions of culture place it along a continuum, ranging from tradition-based to modernity-based. This classification incorporates and relates dimensions of economic and cultural boundedness. In this system, African, Asian, and Middle Eastern societies are categorized as tradition-based, centralized, cooperative, pre-industrialized systems. Economically, modernity-based cultures are characterized as market-driven, competitive, post-industrialized economic systems. The United States, Canada, and other Westernized societies are considered to be examples of modernity-based cultures. Regarding cultural boundedness, tradition-based cultures emphasize history and established convention. By contrast, modernity-based cultures have weaker ties to history and tradition. At the same time, conventions are ever-shifting.

The cultural boundedness of tradition-based societies produces market systems that differ markedly from market systems valorized by cultures that prioritize modernity over tradition. It is suggested that economic and social factors influence the development and adaptation of marketing institutions that relate to business transaction. Understanding the cultural boundedness of business (i.e., the degree of willingness of a culture to relinquish its traditional methods and adopt new ones) is imperative for successful international marketing communication and for marketing to ethnic populations domestically (Reese, 1998). A research conducted in a minority region in China (which is considered as "tradition-based culture") demonstrates that culture influences consumer behavior in the area of product distribution. The cultural orientation of the ethnic group consumers helped establish and maintain, through vendor loyalty, a plethora of small retailers supported by inefficient, multi-tiered distribution networks. This makes the Chinese state-owned retail business and foreign commercial institutions less profitable than they could be.

Similarly, cultural overtones in marketing operations derive, to some extent, from consumer preferences. Scholars suggest that "the cultural characteristics of a target market will be responsive to certain culturally bound channel structures, such as local stores, or bazaars..." It will be difficult for marketers from the U.S., for instance, to understand the market system in developing countries, as well as states that may value traditional community ties over "modernity" for its own sake. As an instance, U.S. marketers were hard-pressed to understand the French government's decision to restrict retail store size and protect local mom-and-pop retailers, especially when taking into consideration the success of supermarkets there. The government's decision to forego the economic efficiencies of distribution obtained by large-scale retail distribution systems is in part cultural in nature. Unless perceived and understood, profound differences in attitudes, expectations, and unworded messages will frustrate firms' efforts to do business with, for instance China, a huge and developing market that values aspects of tradition, as well as elsewhere in tradition-based cultures.

It can be argued that government intervention, as in the case of France, is intended to protect its society's culture within the existing market system or structure (Griffith and Ryans, 1995). However, in spite of some conflicts, there are societies, such as in some more areas of China, in which traditional market bazaars and modern, efficient supermarkets co-exist. This harmony is achieved only when the two systems become interdependent and supplementary. Although cultural factors affect marketing, their effect can be minimized when marketers are aware of and sensitive to cultural differences.

It is estimated that U.S. companies lose up to $4 billion annually in failed international business, in contrast of the increased revenues if companies' intercultural efforts are done properly. That is how it becomes evident why intercultural marketing research, education and knowledge are the back bones of any local company in the United States wanting to extend its local diverse customer base or wanting to extend globally. It also applies to foreign companies wanting to extend their market base in the United States.

2.4 Managing Intercultural Marketing

- **Self-reference Criterion**

Having identified the most important factors and components of cultures in intercultural marketing, we can now understand the difficulties for marketers to manage with cultural differences. Many authors worked on how companies can overcome the problem of cultural differences. James Lee (1966) used the terms self-reference criterion (SRC) to characterize our unconscious reference to our own cultural values. A four-step approach is suggested to eliminate SRC.

1) Define the problem or goal in terms of home country culture, traits, habits and norms.

2) Define the problems or goals in terms of the foreign culture, traits, habits and norms.

3) Isolate the SRC influence in the problem and examine it carefully to see how it complicates the problem.

4) Redefine the problem without the SRC influence and solve the problem for the foreign market situation.

- **Tools of Intercultural Marketing Communication (IMC)**

Following is a selection of the most important tools for intercultural marketing communication:

Written communication: the written communication is the writing style applied in for example emails sent from the company to existing clients, prospect clients, branch companies, employees, etc. The quality of the written communication is very important, as it will reflect the company' professionalism. Errors in the use of English for example will indicate untidy and unprofessional work. Furthermore, the written communication also needs a clear goal. The objective has to be reached with the correct form of communication. A choice has to be made between for example a persuasive way of writing or a rather informational form of writing.

Website: the company website is extremely important as it often is the potential customers' first acquaintance with the more extensive description of the company. The company website therefore has to be a user friendly guide in order to get the website visitor acquainted with products, projects and newsletters, etc. established by the company. The options for different languages in which the website is available will enhance the possibility for intercultural understanding and intercultural marketing communication between your company and overseas cultures.

Brochure: company brochures are also very important as they give a brief summary of company business. These brochures can for example contain projects in overseas markets. Brochures form a very strong pillar in promotion strategy of intercultural marketing communication, as it is possible to create brand awareness and brand loyalty on both the short and long term.

Exhibitions: the presence of companies at domestic or overseas exhibitions has strong mutual benefit for both the company and the visitors of the exhibition. On the one hand, strong intercultural marketing communication being applied while exhibiting company business at an overseas exhibition can create brand awareness and facilitate the integration of new overseas markets. On the other hand, the overseas business with different business culture must be addressed correctly. Correct understanding of the cultural presence in overseas exhibitions will enhance the establishment of long term relationships with the local business.

Slogan/logo: the final tool for intercultural marketing communication is the slogan and logo. The slogan and logo are a very important whole as they include the total company philosophy, mission and values in one core sentence and display. The slogan and logo have to be chosen correctly and adapted to overseas markets in order to enhance company accessibility. The use of local terms is highly recommended.

- **Intercultural Market Research**

Primary vs. Secondary Research: There are two kinds of market research: *Primary* research refers to the research that a firm conducts for its own needs (e.g., focus groups, surveys, interviews, or observation) while *secondary* research involves finding information compiled by someone else. In general, secondary research is less expensive and is faster to conduct, but it may not answer the specific questions the firm seeks to have answered (e.g., how do consumers perceive our product?), and its reliability may be in question.

Secondary Sources: A number of secondary sources of country information are available. One of the most convenient sources is an almanac, containing a great deal of country information. Some governments also publish a guide to each country, and the handbook "International Business Information". Anthropologists and economists in universities may have built up a great deal of knowledge and may be available for consulting. Consultants specializing in various regions or industries are considerably more expensive. One should be careful about relying on the opinions of expatriates (whose views may be biased or outdated) or one's own experience (which may relate to only part of a country or a certain sub-segment).

Hard vs. Soft Data: "Hard" data refers to relatively quantifiable measures such as a country's GDP, number of telephones per thousand residents, and birth rates (although even these supposedly "objective" factors may be subject to some controversy due to differing definitions and measurement approaches across countries). In contrast, "soft" data refers to more subjective issues such as country history or culture. It should be noted that while the "hard" data is often more convenient to obtain and seemingly objective, the "soft" data is frequently as important, if not more so, in understanding a market.

Data Reliability: The accuracy and objectivity of data depend on several factors. One significant factor is the motivation of the entity that releases it. For example, some countries may want to exaggerate their citizens' literacy rates owing to national pride, and an organization promoting economic development may paint an overly rosy picture in order to attract investment. Some data may be dated (e.g., a census may be conducted rarely in some regions), and some countries may lack the ability to collect data (it is difficult to reach people in the interior regions of Latin America, for example). Differences in how constructs are defined in different countries (e.g., is military personnel counted in people who are employed?) may make figures of different countries non-comparable.

Cost of Data: Much government data, or data released by organizations such as the World Bank or the United Nations, is free or inexpensive, while consultants may charge very high rates.

Issues in Primary Research: Cultural factors often influence how people respond to research. While some researchers are used to market research and tend to find this relatively un-threatening, consumers in other countries may fear that the data will be reported to the government, and may thus not give accurate responses. In some cultures, criticism or confrontation are considered rude, so consumers may not respond honestly when they dislike a product. Technology such as scanner data is not as widely available outside the United States. Local customs and geography may make it difficult to interview desired respondents; for example, in some countries, women may not be allowed to talk to strangers.

- **STP in Intercultural Marketing**

Segmentation, Targeting, and Positioning: Segmentation, in marketing, is usually done at the customer level. However, in international marketing, it may sometimes be useful to see countries as segments. This allows the decision maker to focus on common aspects of countries and avoid information overload. It should be noted that variations within some countries (e.g., Brazil) are very large and therefore, averages may not be meaningful. Country level segmentation may be done on levels such as geography—based on the belief that neighboring countries and countries with a particular type of climate or terrain tend to share similarities—, demographics (e.g., population growth, educational attainment, population age distribution), or income. Segmenting on income is tricky since the relative prices between countries may differ significantly (based, in part, on purchasing power parity measures that greatly affect the relative cost of imported and domestically produced products).

Approaches to Global Segmentation: There are two main approaches to global segmentation. At the macro level, countries are seen as segments, given that country aggregate characteristics and statistics tend to differ significantly. For example, there will only be a large market for expensive pharmaceuticals in countries with certain income levels, and entry opportunities into infant clothing will be significantly greater in countries with large and growing birthrates (in countries with smaller birthrates or stable or declining birthrates, entrenched competitors will fight hard to keep the market share).

The international product life cycle suggests that product adoption and spread in some markets may lag significantly behind those of others. Often, then, a segment that has existed for some time in an "early adopter" country such as the U.S. or Japan will emerge after several years (or even decades) in a "late adopter" country such as Britain or most developing countries.

Positioning Across Markets: Firms often have to make a tradeoff between adapting their products to the unique demands of a country market or gaining benefits of standardization such as cost savings and the maintenance of a consistent global brand image. There are no easy answers here. On the one hand, McDonald's has spent a great deal of resources to promote its global image; on the other hand, significant accommodations are made to local tastes and preferences—for example, while serving alcohol in U.S. restaurants would go against the family image of the restaurant carefully nurtured over several decades, McDonald's has accommodated this demand of European customers.

- **Standardization vs. Adaptation of the Marketing Mix**

Marketing Mix is a planned mix of the controllable elements of a product's marketing plan commonly termed as 4Ps: product, price, place, and promotion. The question of what strategy to choose: standardization or adaptation is a matter of debate since the beginning of the 1980s. In reality, almost none marketing mix is only adapted or only standardized.

◇ Standardization vs. Adaptation of Products

We define a product as anything that is offered to a market for attention, acquisition, use or consumption that might satisfy a want or need. Products include more than just tangible goods. Broadly defined, products include physical objects, services, places, organizations, ideas or mixes of these entities.

It is essential for a company to offer a product more beneficial for customers in order to create a competitive advantage and a customer loyalty. Moreover, the product has to be compatible with the culture (local customs and habits). The success of the company is determined on what marketing strategy the firm is going to use (adaptation or standardization). The decision to choose one or the other is based on business objectives but also on cultural differences (Hollensen, 2001).

According to Onkvisit & Shaw (2004), product standardization is an approach where a firm is able to export their products to international markets without any essential changes thanks to the similarities in taste and needs in global market. Product standardization is more often used for industrial goods products than customer's products and service because the latter have to be adapted to the culture of the country (Czinkota & Ronkanen, 1995).

In this way, many international companies of customer's products develop a global product which can be accepted in all countries. This product is done in international bases. By choosing this strategy, companies take into account local needs and demands. This strategy is only effective in a foreign culture close to the home company culture. Indeed, in some international markets, the company has to do modifications in the marketing mix because differences between the home culture and the foreign culture are too huge.

Table 5.1 Arguments for standardization and adaptation of product. (Adapted from Onkvisit & Shaw 2009, 247-259.)

Product standardization	Product adaptation
Simlicity: It is an easy process for executives to understand and implement. Cost-effective: Reduction of production costs Universal product image	Mandatory adaptation, due to factors such as: ● Govemment regulation ● Electrical current standards ● Measurement standards ● Product standards Optional adaptation is based on the international marketer's discretion in taking action, concerning: ● User's habits ● Cultural differences

◇ Standardization vs. Adaptation of pricing

The second component of the marketing mix is the price. In the narrowest sense, price is the amount of money charged for a product or service. More broadly, price is the sum of all the values that consumers exchange for the benefits of having or using a product or service.

Standardizing price means that the head office decides a fixed price that is applied in all international markets without taking in consideration the factors mentioned before. Standardized is more often used by companies in B2B market than in B2C market because they are less price-sensitive. When companies use this strategy, they take less risk, since as no attempt is made to respond to local conditions, no effort is made to maximize the profit either (Hollenson, 2001).

The other alternative is to adapt the price to local conditions. Managers have to establish price depending on the foreign market and foreign consumer's incomes. It doesn't mean that the price in one country will be coordinated to the price in another. Price adaption is subject to local conditions; but on the other hand; it gives the company the opportunity to take advantages of price differences that can occur when a company for example buys for lower prices and sells for a higher one (Keegan & Green, 1999).

Table 5.2 ***Comparison between pricing standardization and pricing adaptation.***

(Adapted from Doole & Lowe 2001, 420.)

Product standardization	Product adaptation
Low-risk strategy as a fixed return is guaranteed Good image of multinational firms No effort is made to maximize either profits or sales volume because they set the same price for all markets Used when selling highly specialized manufacturing plant	Profits and sales volume can increase due to different markets Lack of control because of market-differentiated pricing Bad image of multinational firms

◇ Standardization vs. Adaptation of promotion

The third component of the marketing mix is the promotion. A company's total promotion mix, also called its marketing communications mix, consists of the specific blend of advertising, sales promotion, public relations, personal selling and direct marketing tools that the company uses to persuasively communicate customer value and build customer relationships.

Issues surrounding advertising standardization tend to parallel issues surrounding product and positioning standardization. On the plus side, economies of scale are achieved, a consistent image can be established across markets, creative talent can be utilized across markets, and good ideas can be transplanted from one market to others. On the down side, cultural differences, peculiar country regulations, and differences in product life cycle stages make this approach difficult. Further, local advertising professionals may resist campaigns imposed from the outside—sometimes with good reasons and sometimes merely to preserve their own creative autonomy.

Table 5.3 ***Factors driving promotion standardization and adaptation.***

(Adapted from Doole & Lowe 2001, 338-339.)

Factors driving promotion standardization	Factors driving promotion adaptation
Improving efficiency and saving costs improving firm's image Increasing customer's trust, loyalty Trend of globalization	Customer satisfaction Cultural differences Other environmental factors such as political and legal constraints

◇ Standardization vs. Adaptation of Distribution (Place)

Choosing a type of distribution channels to use is a major decision in the development of marketing strategies. A distribution decision is a long-term decision, so when established it can be difficult to extract a firm from existing agreements. As a result, the firm needs to make a suitable and flexible distribution decision for its long-term development.

It is complicated to standardize the distribution because distribution channels vary from one country to another. Standardizing or adapting distribution depends on many factors such as the nature of market, customer characteristics, nature of product, culture, law legislation, etc. As a result, the decision-making between standardization and adaptation of the distribution is not simple. However, distribution is generally considered as the one component of marketing mix that is more often adapted. This depends on the differences in disposable incomes, purchasing habits and distribution's infrastructure. A company has to adapt for others reasons, for example when it has a sales volume, a level of involvement or a product line not ordinary. The distribution channels have a degree of adaptation or standardization depending on in which country the firm is established. The marketers and managers have to understand all the aspect of the distributions channels because it contributes to the success of the company and without this understanding the firm can't be in a leader position.

In summary, three major rules would start those Chinese companies on the route to success in intercultural marketing:

1) Recognize that a foreign customer is different—in perceptions, motivation, beliefs, and outlook. Identify, understand, accept, and respect the other's culture. Be prepared to communicate and operate on two separate and different cultural wavelengths. Don't assume sameness. One should not fall into the Self-Reference Criterion fallacy and assume that anything that is acceptable in one's own culture is necessarily acceptable in all other cultures. Familiar behaviors may have different meanings. One must adjust the pace of business to that of the people with whom one is trying to do business. One must treat everybody with whom one deals with the greatest personal respect. What one thinks of as normal or human behavior may only be cultural. Do not assume that what you meant is what was understood; do not assume that what you understood is what was meant.

2) Be culturally neutral. Being different does not denote being better or inferior. Do not cast judgment on the other party's cultural mores any more than you would want them to judge your values. It may be true that from a moral point of view, some foreign customs may appear senseless, capricious, or even cruel and insane to you. But remember you are visiting the

country as a businessman, not as a missionary. You plan to do business there, not to convert the natives to your own customs and practices. Recognize that they probably feel the same way about your culture as you do theirs. It may not be necessary to adopt their values as part of your own personal value system. All that is necessary is that you accept and respect their norms as part of their culture. Market to their culture and their mores and norms as you would want them to market to your own sensitivities.

3) Be sensitive to their cultural norms, do's, and taboos. Try to understand what they are and how your behavior may affect them even if it causes you discomfort or emotional stress. Most people do behave rationally; you just have to discover the rationale. You do not have to like or accept different behavior, but you should try to understand where it comes from in order to make peace with that behavior, or at least not react so strongly to it. It is necessary to accept, and to proceed with the business without showing distress if one wishes to come home with an agreement that is beneficial to both parties and marks the start of a long-term, healthy relationship between two companies from two cultures. One way to bridge cultural differences is to demonstrate interest in, knowledge of, respect for, and appreciation of the other side's culture.

Failure to do so can easily be interpreted as an act of cultural superiority and arrogance, a statement that the other side's culture is not significant or important. Questions about culture framed in an uncritical way show that you find the other side's culture to be interesting, important, and worth learning about. Therefore, international marketers should try to learn as much as possible about the other side's culture. Marketers should be tolerant and respectful of cultural differences. Once differences are understood, marketers should seek ways of accommodating them. Some islands of cultural commonality should be found and enjoyed together.

3. Exercises

I. Case Study on Standardization/Adaptation in Intercultural Marketing.

Case 1: Why Localization Matters: what KFC got right

Source: http://english.8168168.com/news/disp_news.asp?id=216&Class=1

Case 2: Standardizing or Adapting the Marketing Mix across Culture: A Case Study of Agatha.

Source: http://hh.diva-portal.org/smash/get/diva2:326017/FULLTEXT01.pdf

Case 3: Forbidden City Starbucks closes

Source:http://www.cbsnews.com/news/starbucks-closes-at-chinas-forbidden-city/

Case 4: Nike Faces Marketing Challenge in China: Make Running Cool

Source:http://adage.com/article/global-news/nike-faces-marketing-challenge-china-make-running-cool/230717/Published: October 31, 2011

Case 5: Brand USA: Selling Uncle Sam like Uncle Ben's

Source: www. hec. unil. ch

II. Group Discussion

High-context and low-context cultures: Gaining an edge in website localization

Posted on January 2, 2013 by Sajan

When a company's website is well-catered to its audiences' linguistic and cultural preferences, it's like a gold-paved, four-star experience that grandly ushers in customers.

Of course, no one wants the opposite effect resulting from copy that's not in your audience's native language, graphics that are offensive or confusing, or an organizational arrangement that just doesn't resonate. Any of these website localization missteps show that you don't understand the customer. Or worse, that you don't care about them.

There's no quicker way to quash a deal before it even starts.

The better you understand your audience, the more effective your website localization efforts will be in resonating with your global customers—and cultivating that all-important business relationship.

So today we want to address an aspect of intercultural communication that fosters good design and savvy website localization: the difference between low-context cultures and high-context cultures.

- **Understanding cultures: High context versus low context**

American anthropologist Edward T. Hall was known in part for identifying this notion of high-context and low-context in cultural communications. As a founding father of intercultural communication studies, Hall set up a framework of culture-based communication styles, explaining how people in different countries decode messages based on their cultural expectations.

What does all of this mean for you and your website localization initiatives? Simply knowing the key differences between high-context and low-context cultures can give you an edge in effectively designing your website so that it strikes a chord with your global audience.

High-context cultures:

◇ Japan, Arab nations and Greece, among others.

◇ Emphasis is on cultural values; this may be geared to family life or working as part of a group (collectivism over individualism).

◇ Tends to emphasize visuals over text.

◇ The message's context carries more weight than words.

◇ Communication tends to be viewed as an art form that's meant to be engaged with; it may require more time to process and decode, which the audience expects and responds to.

◇ Learning is done through demonstration and group work.

◇ Messages are rooted in the past and change is slow to come.

Low-context cultures:

◇ The United States, Germany and Scandinavian nations, among others.

◇ A person's identity tends to come from one's own accomplishments rather than from group effort (individualism over collectivism).

◇ There's an emphasis on words and text.

◇ Communication tends to be clear, direct and unambiguous.

◇ Privacy, personal space and individuality are highly valued.

◇ Learning is done through instructions and by one's attempts to perform the action.

◇Speed is prized and change happens fast.

Learning by example: IKEA and website localization

Websites localized for other countries often show glimmers of the target audience's cultural expectations, which includes the differencebetween high-and low- context cultures. IKEA's multinational website and its country-specific webpages represent a good example of this.

At left is a screen shot of the Japanese IKEA homepage (not laid out precisely right owing to the webpage crunching we did for the sake of showing as much as possible). Let's conduct a mini-assessment, shall we?

◇ Heavy use of graphics; light on copy

◇ Scrolling graphics "slideshow"

◇ Bright and colorful

◇ Visually varied and active

While there aren't any people on the website, we can see hints of why this might resonate with a high-context culture. The animal groupings evoke a communal or group sense. It's also fun and colorful, and it's generally light on text.

Now let's consider the Netherlands IKEA homepage. As you'll recall, Scandinavian countries fall into the category of low-context cultures. The differences may at first seem very subtle, but the web designers made a few key design and layout choices that point to the nature of the target audience and culture.

◇ More copy in general, plus two big, bright-red boxes featuring text to advertise sales

◇ Person featured in top box is engaged in a solitary activity

◇ No scrolling graphics

◇ With the exception of the red sales boxes, the homepage is slightly more sedate

◇ Visually orderly: stacked tables and boxes

Compared to the Japanese IKEA website, the localized Netherlands version does show some noticeable differences. The emphasis is on functional products rather than cute-looking stuffed animals (although there are a couple of those), and we see more text. The only person who appears on the homepage is shown by herself. There is also no scrolling graphics marquee as in the Japanese version.

- **Differences in design for website localization**

High-context cultures have been shown to respond very well to websites that include a lot of animations, sounds, graphics and other interactive elements. Why? There are interesting theories around this based on recent research, one theory being that people in high-context cultures appreciate interactivity in general. It makes them feel as though they are being drawn into an experience.

When we're involved in helping clients with website localization projects, we consider nuggets of insight such as this. For a Chinese website, for example, we may recommend music, flash animations or perhaps a video of an individual speaking to and welcoming the user.

In general, it's also a good practice to think about what your target audience favors with regard to web design elements, such as hierarchical structure, menu and navigation buttons and page-loading speed. Once you understand your target audience's cultural expectations for visual communication and web design, you can employ effective website localization techniques that we've explored here.

Questions:

1) What are the differences between marketing in high-and low-context cultures?

2) Your task as a global marketer or website localization specialist is always to create materials that engage the end user, preferably by appealing to their values or pain points. A large part of that is making sure your message resonates with your target audience's cultural preferences and expectations. What do you think the argument made in the article? Is the

notion of high-context versus low-context cultures useful to you in conceiving of and executing your targeted marketing materials or localized website?

III. Thinking About A Movie

The Namesake (Mira Nair, 2007)

An Indian couple emigrates from Calcutta to New York City to start a new life and a new family. Their firstborn son, Gogol Ganguli (Kal Penn), grows up rejecting his parents' Bengali culture, even though most of the family's social ties are with other Bengalis. He adopts colloquial American speech, chooses a wealthy Caucasian woman for his girlfriend, and rechristens himself "Nick." Then his father's sudden death makes him rethink his relationship to the Bengali culture.

This movie is rife with examples of culture seen from a sociological point of view. Look for the scenes in which Gogol's parents suffer culture shock after moving to New York City. Watch for examples of bilingualism as Gogol speaks to his family, switching back and forth from English to Bengali.

For Your Consideration

1) What are some of the differences between Gogol's parents' values and those of his Caucasian girlfriend?

2) How is language used in the film to reinforce feelings of a shared culture?

4. References

1. Armonstrong, G. & Kotler, P. Principles of marketing [M], 12th edition. New Jersey: Prentice Hall, 2008.
2. Cateora, P. R., & Graham, J. International Marketing [M], 10th ed. Boston: Irwin/McGraw-Hill, 1999.
3. Czinkota & Ronkanen, M. & Ronkanen, A. International marketing [M], 4t edition. Harcourt Brace and company, Florida, 1995.
4. Doole, I., Lowe, R. International marketing strategy: Analysis, development and implementation [M]. London: Thomson Learning, 2001: 214-246
5. Douglas & Craige, S.P. & Craige, C. Global marketing strategy [M]. Mc:Graw-Hill Inc, USA, 1995.
6. Doyle, P & Stern, P. Marketing Management and Strategy [M], 4th edition. Financial Times/Prentice Hall, 6 April 2006.

7. Harris, Philip R., Moran, Robert T., and Moran, Sarah V. Managing cultural differences: global leadership strategies for the 21st century: 25th anniversary edition. Amsterdam: Elsevier, 2004., 4-33
8. Hollensen, S. Global Marketing [M], 2nd edition. Pearson Education , 2001.
9. Hollensen, S. Global marketing: a decision-oriented approach [M]. 4th edtion. Harlow: Prentice Hall, 2007: 216-236.
10. Hollensen, S. Essentials of global marketing [M]. Harlow: Prentice Hall. Harcourt College Publishers, 2008: 306-309
11. Holden, N. J. Cross-cultural Management—A knowledge Management Perspective [M]. Harlow: Prentice Hall. Harcourt College Publishers, 2002.
12. Holden, N. Why marketers need a new concept of culture for the global knowledge economy [J]. *International Marketing Review, 21* (6), 2004: 563-572.
13. Kale, S.H., & McIntyre, R.P. Distribution Channel Relationships in Diverse Cultures [J]. *International Marketing Review,* vol 8, no 3, 1991: 31-45.
14. Keegan, J.K. & Green, S.M. Global Marketing [M], 6th edition. Harlow: Prentice Hall, 2010.
15. Keegan, Warren J. Global marketing management [M]. New Jersey: Pearson Education, 2002: 67-89.
16. Keegan, J.K. & Schlegelmilch, B.B. Global marketing management—A European Perspective [M]. Ashford Colour Press Ltd., Gosport, 2001.
17. Knight, G. A., & Calantone, R. J. A flexible model of consumer country-of-origin perceptions: A cross-cultural investigation [J]. *International Marketing Review, 17* (2), 2000: 127-145.
18. Kotler, P., Armstong, G. Marketing: An introduction [M], 10th edition. Harlow: Pearson, 2011.
19. Kotler, P., Wong, V., Saunders, J. & Armstrong, G. Principles of Marketing [M]. Harlow: Prentice Hall, 2008.
20. de Mooij, M. K. Global marketing and advertising: Understanding cultural paradoxes [M]. USA: Sage Publications, Inc. 2005.
21. Mueller, B. International Advertising: Communicating Across Cultures [M]. Belmont, CA: Wadsworth, 1996.
22. Mueller, B. Dynamics of International Advertising: Theoretical and Practical Perspectives [M]. New York: Peter Lang, 2004.

23. Okazaki, S. Searching the web for global brands: How American brands standardise their web sites in Europe [J]. *European Journal of Marketing, 39* (1), 2005:87-109.
24. Okazaki, S., & Alonso, J. Right messages for the right site: On-line creative strategies by Japanese multinational corporations [J]. *Journal of Marketing Communications, 9* (4), 2003: 221-239.
25. Onkvisit, S. & Shaw, John.J. 2009. International marketing: Strategy and theory. 5th edition. London: Routledge. Onkvisit & Shaw, S. & Shaw, J.J. (2004). *International marketing—Analysis and strategy, 4th European Editon.*

Chapter 6

The Application of a Case Study Methodology

I keep six honest serving men (They taught me all I knew);
Their names are What and Why and When; And How and Where and Who.

—Rudyard Kipling

"We should never denigrate any other culture but rather help people to understand the relationship between their own culture and the dominant culture. When you understand another culture or language, it does not mean that you have to lose your own culture."

—Edward T. Hall

1. Lead-in

- **Learning about the practice of strategic management is a powerful way for you to accomplish five things:**

1) Increase your understanding of what managers should and should not do in guiding a business to success.

2) Build your skills in sizing up company resource strengths and weaknesses and in conducting strategic analysis in a variety of industries and competitive situations.

3) Get valuable practice in identifying strategic issues that need to be addressed, evaluating strategic alternatives, and formulating workable plans of action.

4) Enhance your sense of business judgment, as opposed to uncritically accepting the authoritative crutch of the professor or "back-of-the-book" answers.

5) Gaining in-depth exposure to different industries and companies, thereby acquiring something close to actual business experience.

- **Case Study Samples Online**

1) http://www.caseplace.org
2) http://www.businessmajors.about.com
3) http://www.rb.com/documentdownload.axd?documentresourceid=9957
4) http://www.mckinsey.com/careers/join_us/practice_case_studies
5) http://www.csub.edu/~cbradford/documents/Case_Study_Sample_I-Elementary_School.pdf

- **Recommended Reading on Case Study Research**

1) **Yin, Robert K. (1994) *Case Study Research: Design and Methods.* London: Sage Publications Inc. 1989**

This book discusses in great detail, the entire design process of the case study, including entire chapters on collecting evidence, analyzing evidence, composing the case study report, and designing single and multiple case studies.

2) **Stake, R. E. (1995). *The Art of Case Study Research.* Thousand Oaks: Sage Publications.** This book examines case study research in education and case study methodology.

3) **Tellis. W. (1997, September). Application of a case study methodology**. *The Qualitative Report* [On-line serial], 3(3). Available:http://www.nova.edu/ssss/QR/QR3-3/tellis2.html

2. Main Text

2.1 Research Methodology for Intercultural Communication

INTERCULTURAL COMMUNICATION RESEARCH METHODS

It is well known that IC (Intercultural Communication) is influenced by many social science disciplines such as anthropology, psychology, linguistics, communication, sociology and philosophy, which IC scholars identified as the interdisciplinary characteristics. In fact, some scholars have conducted meaningful research to demonstrate the interdisciplinary characteristics of IC. As IC is a mixture of many social science disciplines, the methods to conduct IC research are various. As a matter of fact, there is no fixed pattern for the research methods of IC. As a multidimensional field, IC research has adopted the methods preferred by scholars with different academic backgrounds. Generally speaking, anthropologists tend to use the method of observation and interview to collect first-hand, holistic data, which is the qualitative method of data collection. Psychologists are keen on precise quantitative numbers and careful analysis of data, which is, in their opinion, more reliable and persuasive. Linguists collect specific language data to reveal problems that appear in the process of IC, and communication scholars are interested in the exploration of theories about IC. When studying IC, it is recommended by some scholars that more than one method be adopted to achieve a comparatively more comprehensive result. As there is no definite research method for IC research, it is held that the empirical nature of any kind of research, be it intercultural or not, is just the same and the traditional qualitative and quantitative methods used in social science research are also applied to the study of IC.

The influence of quantitative methodologies on studies about intercultural communication was hegemonic until the 1990s, when the publication of the journal *International and Intercultural Communication Annual* began to promote methodological pluralism, opening the doors to the use of qualitative methodology.

In most intercultural business communication courses, cases are used extensively as a teaching tool. Case studies are stories. They present realistic, complex, and contextually rich situations and often involve a dilemma, conflict, or problem that one or more of the characters in the case must negotiate. Although they have been used most extensively in the teaching of medicine, law and business, case studies can be an effective teaching tool in any number of disciplines. As an instructional strategy, case studies have a number of virtues. They bridge the gap between theory and practice and between the academy and the workplace. They also give students practice identifying the parameters of a problem, recognizing and articulating positions, evaluating courses of action, and arguing different points of view.

DIFFERENT TYPES OF INTERCULTURAL COMPARISON METHODS

Nowadays there are many types of intercultural comparisons. One method is comparison of case studies. Controlled comparison among variants of a common derivation is another form of comparison. Typically anthropologists and other social scientists favour the third type called intercultural studies, which uses field data from many societies to examine the scope of human behaviour and to test hypotheses about human behaviour and culture.

Controlled comparison examines similar characteristics of a few societies while intercultural studies uses a sufficiently large sample that statistical analysis can be made to show relationships or lack of relationships between certain traits in question. The anthropological method of holocultural analysis or worldwide intercultural analysis is designed to test or develop a proposition through the statistical analysis of data on a sample of ten or more nonliterate societies from three or more geographical regions of the world. In this approach, cultural traits are taken out of the context of the whole culture and are compared with cultural traits in widely diverse cultures to determine patterns of regularities and differences within the broad base of the study.

AIMS OF INTERCULTURAL ANALYSIS

Intercultural communication looks at how people from different cultural backgrounds try to communicate. It also tries to produce some guidelines, which help people from different cultures to better communicate with each other.

Culture has an interpretative function for the members of a group, who share that particular culture. Although all members of a group or society might share their culture, expressions of culture-resultant behaviour are modified by the individuals' personality, upbringing and life-experience to a considerable degree. Intercultural analysis aims at harnessing this utilitarian function of culture as a tool for increasing human adaptation and improving communication.

Intercultural management is seen as a discipline of international management focusing on cultural encounters, which aims to discover tools to handle cultural differences seen as sources of conflict or miscommunication.

2.2 What Is a Case Study

A case study is a description of an actual administrative situation involving a decision to be made or a problem to be solved. It relates a real situation that actually happened just as described, or some portions have been disguised for reasons of privacy. Most case studies are written in such a way that the reader takes the place of the manager whose responsibility is to make decisions to help solve the problem. In almost all case studies, a decision must be made, although that decision might be to leave the situation as it is and do nothing.

Case studies are multi-perspectival analyses. This means that the researcher considers not just the voice and perspective of the actors, but also of the relevant groups of actors and the interaction between them. They give a voice to the powerless and voiceless. When sociological investigations present many studies of the homeless and powerless, they do so from the viewpoint of the elite.

Case study is known as a triangulated research strategy. Triangulation can occur with data, investigators, theories, and even methodologies. The protocols that are used to ensure accuracy and alternative explanations are called triangulation. The need for triangulation arises from the ethical need to confirm the validity of the processes. In case studies, this could be done by using multiple sources of data. The problem in case studies is to establish meaning rather than location.

When students are presented with a case, they place themselves in the role of the decision maker as they read through the situation and identify the problem they are faced with. The next step is to perform the necessary analysis—examining the causes and considering alternative courses of actions to come to a set of recommendations. To get the most out of cases, students read and reflect on the case, and then meet in learning teams before class to "warm up" and discuss their findings with other classmates. In class—under the questioning and guidance of the professor—students probe underlying issues, compare different alternatives, and finally, suggest courses of action in light of the organization's objectives. With a case study being unfold in class, students do 85 percent of the talking, as the professor steers the conversation by making occasional observations and asking questions.

TYPES OF CASE STUDIES

There are various types of case studies. Case studies vary in length and detail, and can be used in a number of ways, depending on the case itself and on the instructor's goals. They can be short (a few paragraphs) or long (e.g. 20+ pages). They can be used in lecture-based or discussion-based classes. They can be real, with all the detail drawn from actual people and circumstances, or simply realistic. They can provide all the relevant data students need to discuss and resolve the central issue, or only some of it, requiring students to identify, and possibly fill in (via outside research) the missing information. They can require students to examine multiple aspects of a problem, or just a circumscribed piece. They can require students to propose a solution for the case or simply to identify the parameters of the problem.

Yin (1993) has identified some specific types of case studies, namely Exploratory, Explanatory, and Descriptive. Stake (1995) included three others: Intrinsic—when the researcher has an interest in the case; Instrumental—when the case is used to understand more than what is obvious to the observer; Collective—when a group of cases is studied. Exploratory cases are sometimes considered as a prelude to social research. Explanatory case studies may be used for doing causal investigations. Descriptive cases require a descriptive theory to be developed before starting the project. Pyecha (1988) used this methodology in a special education study, using a pattern-matching procedure. In all of the above types of case studies, there can be single-case or multiple-case applications.

Under the more generalized category of case study exist several subdivisions, each of which is custom selected for use depending upon the goals and/or objectives of the investigator. These types of case study include the following:

Illustrative Case Studies: These are primarily descriptive studies. They typically utilize one or two instances of an event to show what a situation is like. Illustrative case studies serve primarily to make the unfamiliar familiar and to give readers a common language about the topic in question.

Exploratory (or pilot) Case Studies: These are condensed case studies performed before implementing a large scale investigation. Their basic function is to help identify questions and select types of measurement prior to the main investigation. The primary pitfall of this type of study is that initial findings may seem convincing enough to be released prematurely as conclusions.

Cumulative Case Studies: These serve to aggregate information from several sites collected at different times. The idea behind these studies is the collection of past studies will allow for greater generalization without additional cost or time being expended on new, possibly repetitive studies.

Critical Instance Case Studies: These examine one or more sites for either the purpose of examining a situation of unique interest with little to no interest in generalizability, or to call into question or challenge a highly generalized or universal assertion. This method is useful for answering cause and effect questions.

ELEMENTS OF A CASE STUDY

Element:	**Description:**
Introduction	The introduction defines the problem to be examined and explains the parameters or limitations of the situation.
Overview/Analysis	The overview/analysis provides a scenario of the situation and offers more detail about the various players in the scenario, including the organization, its employees or other people involved with the issue in question. It may also mention professional, technical or theoretical issues that arise from the situation. It might also include graphic or visual aids such as budgets, organizational charts, mission statements or technical specifications, as relevant. In complex case studies, the overview and analysis may be presented separately.

Status report	The status report describes the organization's actions, on the matter. It may include statements from managers or employees about their intentions for resolving the issue.
Case problems	In many case studies, the status report may end with one or two case problems, which require the learner to analyse or solve a particular question. Case problems generally take one of three forms: 1. Give a situation and ask learners what they would do next. 2. Set a task, such as asking learners to prepare a report recommending an action for review by a key official. 3. Illustrate a scenario and ask learners to analyse the faults and recommend how it should have been handled.
Appendices	The case study may include as many appendices as necessary to ensure learners understand the case scenario and have the necessary information to solve the case problems, including exhibit copies of documents, charts, technical specifications and so on.

2.3 How to Use Case Studies

FOR INSTRUCTORS

Instructors adopt different approaches in their application of the case analysis method. Some require active learners/students to use a specific analytical procedure to examine an organization; others provide less structure, expecting students to learn by developing their own unique analytical method. Still other instructors believe that a moderately structured framework should be used to analyze a firm's situation and make appropriate recommendations. Your professor will determine the specific approach you take. The approach we are presenting to you is a moderately structured framework.

How to use case studies will depend on the goals, as well as on the format, of your course. If it is a large lecture course, for example, you might use a case study to illustrate and enrich the lecture material. Also in a large class you might consider breaking the class into small groups or pairs to discuss a relevant case. If your class is a smaller, discussion-format course, you will be able to use more detailed and complex cases, to explore the perspectives introduced in the case in greater depth, and perhaps integrate other instructional strategies, such as role playing or debate.

Regardless of the format in which you employ case studies, it is important that you, as the instructor, know all the issues involved in the case, prepare questions and prompts in advance, and anticipate where students might run into problems. Finally, consider who your students are and how you might productively draw on their backgrounds, experiences, personalities, etc., to enhance the discussion.

While there are many variations in how case studies can be used, these six steps provide a general framework for how to lead a case-based discussion:

1) Give students ample time to read and think about the case. If the case is long, assign it as homework with a set of questions for students to consider (e.g., What is the nature of the problem the central character is facing? What are some possible courses of action? What are the potential obstacles?)

2) Introduce the case briefly and provide some guidelines for how to approach it. Clarify how you want students to think about the case (e.g., "Approach this case as if you were the presiding judge" or "You are a consultant hired by this company. What would you recommend?") Break down the steps you want students to take in analyzing the case (e.g., "First, identify the constraints each character in the case was operating under and the opportunities s/he had. Second, evaluate the decisions each character made and their implications. Finally, explain what you would have done differently and why."). If you would like students to disregard or focus on certain information, specify that as well (e.g., "I want you to ignore the political affiliation of the characters described and simply distinguish their positions on stem-cell research as they are articulated here.")

3) Create groups and monitor them to make sure everyone is involved. Breaking the full class into smaller groups gives individual students more opportunities for participation and interaction. However, small groups can drift off track if you do not provide structure. Thus, it is a good idea to make the task of the group very concrete and clear (e.g., "You are to identify three potential courses of action and outline the pros and cons of each from a public relations standpoint"). You may also want to designate roles within each group: for example, one individual might be charged with keeping the others on task and watching the time; a second individual's role might be to question the assumptions or interpretations of the group and probe for deeper analysis; a third individual's role might be to record the group's thoughts and report their decision to the class. Alternatively, group members could be assigned broad perspectives (e.g., liberal, conservative, libertarian) to represent, or asked to speak for the various "stake-holders" in the case study.

4) Have groups present their solutions/reasoning: If groups know they are responsible for producing something (a decision, rationale, analysis) to present to the class, they will approach the discussion with greater focus and seriousness. Write their conclusions on the board so that you can return to them in the discussion that follows.

5) Ask questions for clarification and to move discussion to another level. One of the challenges for a case-based discussion leader is to guide the discussion and probe for deeper

analysis without over-directing. As the discussion unfolds, ask questions that call for students to examine their own assumptions, substantiate their claims, provide illustrations, etc.

6) Synthesize issues raised. Be sure to bring the various strands of the discussion back together at the end, so that students see what they have learned and take those lessons with them. The job of synthesizing need not necessarily fall to the instructor, however; one or more students can be given this task.

Some variations on this general method include having students do outside research (individually or in groups) to bring to bear on the case in question, and comparing the actual outcome of a real-life dilemma to the solutions generated in class.

FOR STUDENTS

Beforehand (usually a week before), you will get:

1) the case study,
2) (often) some guiding questions that will need to be answered, and
3) (sometimes) some reading assignments that have some relevance to the case subject.

Your work in completing the case can be divided up into three components:

1) what you do to prepare before the class discussion,
2) what takes place in the class discussion of the case, and
3) anything required after the class discussion has taken place.

- **Case Analysis Method**

As an active learner, your preparation is critical to successful use of the case analysis method. Without careful study and analysis, active learners lack the insights required to participate fully in the discussion of a firm's situation and the strategic actions that are appropriate.

Table 6.1 Consequences of Student Involvement with the Case Method

1. Case analysis requires students to practice important managerial skills—diagnosing, making decisions, observing, listening, and persuading—while preparing for a case discussion.
2. Cases require students to relate analysis and action, to develop realistic and concrete actions despite the complexity and partial knowledge characterizing the situation being studied.
3. Students must confront the *intractability of reality*—complete with absence of needed information, an imbalance between needs and available resources, and conflicts among competing objectives.
4. Students develop a general managerial point of view—where responsibility is sensitive to action in a diverse environmental context.

(**Source:** C.C. Lundberg and C. Enz, 1993, A framework for student case preperation, *Case Research Journal* 13 (summer): 134.)

As Table 6.1 suggests, the case method can help you develop your analytical and judgment skills. Case analysis also helps you learn how to ask the right questions—that is, the questions that focus on the core strategic issues included within a case. Students aspiring to be managers can improve their ability to identify underlying problems, rather than focusing on superficial symptoms, through development of the skills required to ask probing, yet appropriate, questions. The particular set of cases your instructor chooses to assign the class can expose you to a wide variety of organizations and managerial situations. This approach vicariously broadens your experience base and provides insights into many types of managerial situations, tasks, and responsibilities. Such indirect experience can help you make a more informed career decision about the industry and managerial situation you believe will prove to be challenging and satisfying. Finally, experience in analyzing cases definitely enhances your problem- solving skills.

Furthermore, when your instructor requires oral and written presentations, your communication skills will be honed through use of the case method. Of course, these added skills depend on your preparation as well as your instructor's facilitation of learning. However, the primary responsibility for learning is yours. The quality of case discussion is generally acknowledged to require, at a minimum, a thorough mastery of case facts and some independent analysis of them. The case method therefore first requires that you read and think carefully about each case.

- **Student Preparation For Case Discussion**

If you are inexperienced with the case method, you may need to alter your study habits. A lecture-oriented course may not require you to do intensive preparation for each class period. In such a course, you have the latitude to work through assigned readings and review lecture notes according to your own schedule. However, an assigned case requires significant and conscientious preparation before class. Without it, you will be unable to contribute meaningfully to in-class discussion. Therefore, careful reading and thinking about case facts, as well as reasoned analyses and the development of alternative solutions to case problems, are essential. Recommended alternatives should flow logically from core problems identified through study of the case. Table 6.2 shows a set of steps that can help you develop familiarity with a case, identify problems, and propose strategic actions that increase the probability that a firm will achieve strategic competitiveness and earn above-average returns.

Table 6.2 An Effective Case Analysis Process

Step 1:	a. In general—determine who, what, how, where and when (the critical facts in a case).
Gaining Familiarity	b. In detail—identify the places, persons, activities, and contexts of the situation.
	c. Recognize the degree of certainty/uncertainty of acquired information.
Step 2:	a. List all indicators (including stated "problems") that something is not as expected or as desired.
Recognizing Symptoms	b. Ensure that symptoms are not assumed to be the problem (symptoms should lead to identification of the problem).
Step 3:	a. Identify critical statements by major parties (e.g., people, groups, the work unit, etc.).
Identifying goals	b. List all goals of the major parties that exist or can be reasonably inferred.
Step 4:	a. Decide which ideas, models, and theories seem useful.
Conducting the Analysis	b. Apply these conceptual tools to the situation.
	c. As new information is revealed, cycle back to substeps a and b.
Step 5:	a. Identify predicaments (goal inconsistencies).
Making the Diagnosis	b. Identify problems (descrepancies between goals and performance).
	c. Prioritize predicaments/problems regarding timing, importance, etc.
Step 6:	a. Specify and prioritize the criteria used to choose action alternatives.
Doing the Action Planning	b. Discover or invent feasible action alternatives.
	c. Examine the probable consequences of action alternatives.
	d. Select a course of action.
	e. Design an implementation plan/schedule.
	f. Create a plan for assessing the action to be implemented.

(**Source:** C.C. Lundberg and C. Enz, 1993, A framework for student case preperation, *Case Research Journal* 13 (summer): 144.)

• What to Expect From In-Class Case Discussions

Classroom discussions of cases differ significantly from lectures. The case method calls for instructors to guide the discussion, encourage student participation, and solicit alternative views. When alternative views are not forthcoming, instructors typically adopt one view so students can be challenged to respond thoughtfully to it. Often students' work is evaluated in terms of both the quantity and the quality of their contributions to in-class case discussions. Students benefit by having their views judged against those of their peers and by responding to challenges by other class members and/or the instructor.

During case discussions, instructors listen, question, and probe to extend the analysis of case issues. In the course of these actions, peers or the instructor may challenge an individual's views and the validity of alternative perspectives that have been expressed. These challenges are offered in a constructive manner; their intent is to help students develop their analytical and communication skills. Commonly instructors encourage students to be innovative and original in the development and presentation of their ideas. Over the course of an individual discussion, students can develop a more complex view of the case, benefiting from the diverse inputs of their peers and instructor. Among other benefits, experience with multiple case discussions should help students increase their knowledge of the advantages and disadvantages of group decision-making processes.

The case analysis process described above can help you prepare to effectively discuss a case during class meetings. Adherence to this process results in consideration of the issues required to identify a focal firm's problems and to propose strategic actions through which the firm can increase the probability it will achieve strategic competitiveness. In some instances, your instructor may ask you to prepare either an oral or a written analysis of a particular case. Typically, such an assignment demands even more thorough study and analysis of the case contents. At your instructor's discretion, oral and written analyses may be completed by individuals or by groups of two or more people. The information and insights gained through completing the six steps shown in Table 6.2 often are of value in the development of an oral or a written analysis. However, when preparing an oral or written presentation, you must consider the overall framework in which your information and inputs will be presented.

- **Preparing An Oral/Written Case Presentation**

Experience shows that two types of thinking, analysis and synthesis, are necessary to develop an effective oral or written presentation. Usually your presentation may contain up to eight parts.

1) Investigate and Analyze the Company's History and Growth. A company's past can greatly affect the present and future state of the organization. To begin your case study analysis, investigate the company's founding, critical incidents, structure, and growth. Go through the

case twice, once for a quick overview and once to gain full command of the facts; then take care to explore the information in every one of the case exhibits. Make a complete list of the problems and issues that the company's management needs to address.

2) Identify Strengths and Weaknesses Within the Company. Using the information you gathered in step one, continue your case study analysis by examining and making a list of the value creation functions of the company. For example, the company may be weak in product development, but strong in marketing. Look for opportunities to apply the concepts and analytical tools in the text chapters—all of the cases in the book have very definite ties to the material in one or more of the text chapters.

3) Gather Information on the External Environment. The third step in a case study analysis involves identifying opportunities and threats within the company's external environment. Special items to note include competition within the industry, bargaining powers, and the threat of substitute products.

4) Analyze Your Findings. Using the information in steps two and three, you will need to create an evaluation for this portion of your case study analysis. Compare the strengths and weaknesses within the company to the external threats and opportunities. Determine if the company is in a strong competitive position and decide if it can continue at its current pace successfully.

5) Identify Corporate Level Strategy. To identify a company's corporate level strategy for your case study analysis, you will need to identify and evaluate the company's mission, goals, and corporate strategy. Analyze the company's line of business and its subsidiaries and acquisitions. You will also want to debate the pros and cons of the company strategy.

6) Identify Business Level Strategy. Thus far, your case study analysis has identified the company's corporate level strategy. To perform a complete analysis, you will need to identify the company's business level strategy. (Note: if it is a single business, the corporate strategy and the business level strategy will be the same.) For this part of the case study analysis, you should identify and analyze each company's competitive strategy, marketing strategy, costs, and general focus.

7) Analyze Implementations. This portion of the case study analysis requires that you identify and analyze the structure and control systems that the company is using to implement its business strategies. Evaluate organizational change, levels of hierarchy, employee rewards, conflicts, and other issues that are important to the company you are analyzing.

8) Make Recommendations. The final part of your case study analysis should include

your recommendations for the company. Every recommendation you make should be based on and supported by the context of your case study analysis. Prioritize your recommendations and make sure they can be carried out in an acceptable time frame with the available resources. Support each recommendation with persuasive argument and reasons as to why it makes sense and should result in improved company performance. Review your recommended action plan to see if it addresses all of the problems and issues you identified—any set of recommendations that does not address all of the issues and problems you identified is incomplete and insufficient. Avoid recommending any course of action that could have disastrous consequences if it doesn't work out as planned; therefore, be as alert to the downside risks of your recommendations as you are to their upside potential and appeal.

Table 6.3 outlines the sections that should be included in either an oral or a written presentation: introduction (strategic profile and purpose), situation analysis, statements of strengths/weaknesses and opportunities/threats, strategy formulation, and implementation. These sections, which can be completed only through use of the two types of thinking, are described in the following discussion.

Table 6.3 General Outline for an Oral or Written Presentation

I.	Strategic Profile and Case Analysis Purpose	
II.	Situation Analysis	
		A. General environmental analysis
		B. Industry analysis
		C. Competitive environmental analysis
		D. Internal analysis
III.	Identification of Environmental Opportunities and Threats and Firm Strengths and Weaknesses (SWOT Analysis)	
IV.	Strategy Formulation	
		A. Strategic alternatives
		B. Alternative evaluation
		C. Alternative choice
V.	Strategic Alternative Implementation	
		A. Action items
		B. Action plan

(**Source:** http://www.swlearning.com/management/hitt/hitt_student/case_analysis_2.html#table3)

In the oral presentation, there are several things you can do on your own to be good and look good as a participant in class discussions:

➢ Although you should do your own independent work and independent thinking, don't hesitate before (and after) class to discuss the case with other students. In real life, managers often discuss the company's problems and situation with other people to refine their own thinking.

➢ In participating in the discussion, make a conscious effort to contribute, rather than just talk. There is a big difference between saying something that builds the discussion and offering a long-winded, off-the-cuff remark that leaves the class wondering what the point was.

➢ Avoid the use of "I think," "I believe," and "I feel"; instead, say, "My analysis shows—" and "The company should do ________, because ________." Always give supporting reasons and evidence for your views; then your instructor won't have to ask you "Why?" every time you make a comment.

➢ In making your points, assume that everyone has read the case and knows what it says; avoid reciting and rehashing information in the case—instead, use the data and information to explain your assessment of the situation and to support your position.

➢ Bring the printouts of the work you've done on the case or the notes you've prepared (usually two or three pages' worth) to class and rely on them extensively when you speak. There's no way you can remember everything off the top of your head—especially the results of your number crunching. To reel off the numbers or to present all five reasons why, instead of one, you will need good notes. When you have prepared thoughtful answers to the study questions and use them as the basis for your comments, everybody in the room will know you are well prepared, and your contribution to the case discussion will stand out.

● **Structure of the Written Report**

Yin (Case Study Research—Design and Methods, Sage, 2003) lists six different types of structure:

1) *Linear analytic*: this is a very common approach, and adopts the viewpoint of the researcher, dealing with issue/problem being studied, literature review, methods used, findings, conclusions.

2) *Comparative*: the case study is looked at from a number of viewpoints to consider which gives the best explanation.

3) *Chronological*: case study evidence is presented in chronological order.

4) *Theory-building*: case study is presented in the context of a particular theory.

5) *Suspense*: opposite to analysis, the outcome is given first and then the explanation.

6) *Unsequenced*: the structure follow no particular logic.

Different Instructors will require different formats for case reports, but they should all have roughly the same general content. For this course, the report should have the following sections in this order:

1) Title page
2) Table of contents
3) Executive summary
4) Problem (Issue) statement
5) Data analysis
6) Key Decision Criteria
7) Alternatives analysis
8) Recommendations
9) Action and Implementation Plan
10) Exhibits

DATA COLLECTION

There are many different sources of data and what you use will depend on your research design. No one source of data is complete and it is important to triangulate by having more than one source. Here is a brief summary of some important sources:

Documentation: this includes primary sources, i.e. from the unit of analysis itself, e.g. emails, letters, meeting minutes and agendas, project proposals, press releases, advertising texts, annual reports, and secondary sources in the form of other published studies, market intelligence reports and press cuttings.

Archival records: probably from the company's databases, e.g. customer records, organization charts, lists, survey data (e.g. if the unit of analysis was evaluated), personal records (e.g. diaries, wall calendars, etc.)

Interviews: especially with key informants, e.g. the directors responsible for the decisions exemplified in the case. These can be open-ended, where the informant is probed for his or her version of events, or semi-structured, where the interrogator has a number of pre-selected questions (the difference here from a written survey is that the questions are more likely to be open than closed, intended to probe in further depth than would be possible in a survey).

Questionnaires: may also be used for a particular population sample, as in the Dutch heart health study considered as an example, or for a range of people involved in the case who are too numerous to be interviewed individually.

Direct observation: for example, you might observe people using new technology, or users using a new library system. Videos are often used here.

Participant observation: here, observation is based on actual involvement in the process, say as a staff member.

Physical artifacts: these represent physical evidence of the case. For example, if one was studying what use is made of a new software program, printouts or screen shots of how people had used the software would constitute physical evidence.

Your final collection of data, which will incorporate original documents, your own notes, videos, audio cassettes, reports of interviews, should be kept in a well-organized database so that subsequently they can be easily retrieved, and accessed when you are providing references for your conclusions. As stated earlier, you should always triangulate one type of data evidence with others; it is reasonably easy to do this with case studies as by their very nature they are very amenable to different research approaches and data sources.

Table 6.4 Strengths and Weaknesses of Data Collection Methods

Source of Evidence	Strengths	Weaknesses
Documentation	• stable—repeated review • unobtrusive—exist prior to case study • exact—names etc. • broad coverage—extended time span	• retrievability—difficult • biased selectivity • reporting bias—reflects author bias • access—may be blocked
Archival Records	• same as above • precise and quantitative	• same as above • privacy issue might inhibit access
Interviews	• targeted—focuses on case study topic • insightful—provides perceived causal inferences	• bias due to poor questions • response bias • incomplete recollection • reflexivity—interviewee expresses what interviewer wants to hear
Direct Observation	• reality—covers events in real time • contextual—covers event context	• time-consuming • selectivity—might miss facts • reflexivity—observer's presence might cause change • cost—observers need time

continued

Source of Evidence	Strengths	Weaknesses
Participant Observation	• same as above • insightful into interpersonal behavior	• same as above • bias due to investigator's actions
Physical Artifacts	• insightful into cultural features • insightful into technical operations	• selectivity • availability

(**Source**: Yin, 1994, p. 80)

COMMENTARY ON CASE STUDIES

Researchers often debate the relative merits of particular methods.

• Strengths of Case Studies

Most case study advocates point out that case studies produce much more detailed information than what is available through a statistical analysis. Advocates also hold that while statistical methods might be able to deal with situations where behavior is homogeneous and routine, case studies are needed to deal with creativity, innovation, and context.

Flexibility: The case study approach is a comparatively flexible method of scientific research. Because its project designs seem to emphasize exploration rather than prescription or prediction, researchers are comparatively freer to discover and address issues as they arise in their experiments. In addition, the looser format of case studies allows researchers to begin with broad questions and narrow their focus as their experiment progresses rather than attempt to predict every possible outcome before the experiment is conducted.

Emphasis on Context: By seeking to understand as much as possible about a single subject or small group of subjects, case studies specialize in "deep data," or "thick description"—information based on particular contexts that can give research results a more human face. This emphasis can help bridge the gap between abstract research and concrete practice by allowing researchers to compare their firsthand observations with the quantitative results obtained through other methods of research.

• Weaknesses of Case Studies

Inherent Subjectivity: The case study has long been stereotyped as the weak sibling among social science methods, and is often criticized as being too subjective and even pseudo-scientific. Likewise, "investigators who do case studies are often regarded as having deviated from their academic disciplines, and their investigations as having insufficient precision (that is, quantification), objectivity and rigor" (Yin 1989). Opponents cite opportunities for subjectivity in the implementation, presentation, and evaluation of case study research. The approach relies on personal interpretation of data and inferences. Results may not be generalizable, are difficult to test for validity, and rarely offer a problem-solving prescription. Simply put, relying on one or a few subjects as a basis for cognitive extrapolations runs the risk of inferring too much from what might be circumstance.

High Investment: Case studies can involve learning more about the subjects being tested than most researchers would care to know—their educational background, emotional background, perceptions of themselves and their surroundings, their likes, dislikes and so on. Because of its emphasis on "deep data," the case study is out of reach for many large-scale research projects which look at a subject pool in the tens of thousands. A budget request of $10,000 to examine 200 subjects sounds more efficient than a similar request to examine four subjects.

Ethical Considerations: Researchers conducting case studies should consider certain ethical issues. For example, many educational case studies are often financed by people who have, either directly or indirectly, power over both those being studied and those conducting the investigation. This conflict of interests can hinder the credibility of the study. The personal integrity, sensitivity, and possible prejudices and/or biases of the investigators need to be taken into consideration as well. Personal biases can creep into how the research is conducted, alternative research methods used, and the preparation of surveys and questionnaires.

A common complaint in case study research is that investigators change direction during the course of the study unaware that their original research design was inadequate for the revised investigation. Thus, the researchers leave unknown gaps and biases in the study. To avoid this, researchers should report preliminary findings so that the likelihood of bias will be reduced.

SOURCES OF CASES

It is possible to write your own case studies, although it is not a simple task. The material for a case study can be drawn from your own professional experiences (e.g., negotiating a labor dispute at a local corporation or navigating the rocky shoals of a political campaign), from current events (e.g., a high-profile medical ethics case or a diplomatic conundrum), from historical sources (e.g., a legal debate or military predicament), etc. It is also possible to find published cases from books and on-line case study collections. Whatever the source, an effective case study is one that,

◇ tells a "real" and engaging story
◇ raises a thought-provoking issue
◇ has elements of conflict
◇ promotes empathy with the central characters
◇ lacks an obvious or clear-cut right answer
◇ encourages students to think and take a position
◇ portrays actors in moments of decision
◇ provides plenty of data about character, location, context, actions
◇ is relatively concise

Business cases that can be used in a classroom are published by various outlets, universities and publishers alike. Three main large-scale case warehouses exist in the world, which distribute cases for a fee (based on the student number in a course). Ivey and Harvard cross-distribute their cases.

- **HBS (Harvard Business School)**

Harvard Business School, a part of Harvard University, located in Boston, MA, USA, distributes over 18,000 cases via its *Harvard Business Review* portal. About 2,000 of them are Ivey cases. HBR cases are generally more expensive than Ivey cases. Harvard Business Publishing does not sell HBS case studies directly to libraries. Due to these restrictions, libraries cannot purchase HBS case studies or put them on reserve.

Students may purchase case studies at the Harvard Business Publishing site for a small fee. Instructors may apply for Educator's Access. Harvard Business Publishing also offers case studies from other sources. The Harvard Business Review, available through the Business Source Complete database, publishes one case study per issue. HBR's cases are about fictional companies, present common managerial dilemmas and offer concrete solutions from experts.

◇ HBS Case Studies via Harvard Business Publishing
◇ Case Studies in Harvard Business Review

- **ECCH (European Case Clearing House)**

The world's largest collection of 62,000+ management case studies and journal article reprints; includes cases from the major case producing schools worldwide. Cases are available to students for a nominal fee.

Unlike Ivey and Harvard, ECCH is not attached to any university. It's a non-profit member based organization which offers the largest number of case studies (almost 45,000) written by a variety of writers. Cases submitted directly to ECCH don't undergo a peer review and not necessarily have teaching notes. A part of its warehouse represents cases from Harvard and Ivey, and other university publishers. ECCH case prices are similar to those of Ivey. Use ECCH search to locate case studies from participating organizations and individuals.

◇ ECCH

◇ ECCH Case Collections

● **Ivey Publishing**

The Richard Ivey School of Business, the University of Western Ontario, is the second largest producer of business case studies and the largest producer of Asian cases in the world. Ivey Publishing is located at the Richard Ivey School of Business at the Western University (formerly the University of Western Ontario), Canada. It published over 8,000 cases written by Ivey School of Business faculty and associated researchers and writers. Ivey cases are peer-reviewed and accompanied by a Teaching Note facilitating preparation of teaching a case in the classroom. A special service for instructors is matching your favorite textbook with cases from the database (CaseMate). Overall, Ivey distributes almost 23,000 cases. You can search for cases and access abstracts for free. To view the full texts, you need to register at *Ivey Publishing. Ivey Publishing* has special distribution rates for emerging markets.

● **Free Case Studies**

◇ MIT Sloan Teaching Innovation Resources: MIT Sloan Teaching Innovation Resources (MSTIR) is a collection of teaching materials, including case studies, simulations, deep dives, and industry, business and country overviews that MIT Sloan provides as a free teaching resource open and available to the world.

◇ Case Place: An initiative of the Aspen Institute's Center for Business Education which provides cases that focus on "mainstream business issues and incorporate ethical, social, environmental, values-based and governance issues."

◇ Glassmeyer/McNamee Center for Digital Strategies, Tuck School of Business at Dartmouth

◇ Case Studies in the Vincent L. LaCorte Case Series

◇ The Times 100 Case Studies

◇ World Business Council for Sustainable Development Case Studies

◇ BELL Case Studies from World Resource Institute: BELL teaching cases explore sustainability related business challenges and capture business decisions that identify environmental challenges as business development opportunities.

- **Additional Fee-based Sources**

These case studies may be located and purchased through ECCH and Harvard Business Publishing or directly from a publisher.

◇ Darden Business Publishing

◇ Standford Graduate School of Business

◇ Kellogg Case Collection

◇ ICMR Center for Management Research, India

◇ Thunderbird School of Global Management

◇ Asia Case Research Center

The following Websites are particularly good locations for company and industry information:

◇ Securities and Exchange Commission EDGAR database (contains company 10-Ks, 10-Qs, etc.) http://www.sec.gov/cgi-bin/srch-edgar

◇ CNN Money http://money.cnn.com

◇ Hoover's http://hoovers.com

◇ The Wall Street Journal Interactive Edition http://www.wsj.com

◇ Business Week http://www.businessweek.com

◇ Fortune http://www.fortune.com

◇ MSN Money Central http://moneycentral.msn.com

◇ Yahoo! Finance http://fi nance.yahoo.com/

- **Sources for Industry and Competitor Analysis**

Table 6.5 Sources for Industry and Competitor Analysis

Abstracts and Indexes	
Periodicals	ABI/*Inform*
	Business Periodicals Index
	InfoTrac (CD-ROM computer multidiscipline index)
	Investext (CD-ROM)
	Predicasts F&S Index United States
	Predicasts Overview of Markets and Technology (PROMT)

continued

	Predicasts R&S Index Europe
	Predicasts R&S Index International
	Public Affairs Information Service Bulletin (PAIS)
	Reader's Guide to Periodical Literature
Newspapers	*NewsBank*
	Business NewsBank
	New York Times Index
	Wall Street Journal Index
	Wall Street Journal/Barron's Index
	Washington Post Index
Bibliographies	
	Encyclopedia of Business Information Sources
	Handbook of Business Information
Directories	
Companies—General	*America's Corporate Families and International Affiliates*
	Hoover's Handbook of American Business
	Hoover's Handbook of World Business
	Million Dollar Directory
	Standard & Poor's Corporation Records
	Standard & Poor's Register of Corporations, Directors, and Executives
	Ward's Business Directory
Companies—International	*America's Corporate Families and International Affiliates*
	Business Asia
	Business China
	Business Eastern Europe
	Business Europe

continued

Bibliographies	
	Business International
	Business International Money Report
	Business Latin America
	Directory of American Firms Operating in Foreign Countries
	Directory of Foreign Firms Operating in the United States
	Hoover's Handbook of World Business
	International Directory of Company Histories
	Moody's Manuals, International (2 volumes)
	Who Owns Whom
Companies—Manufacturers	Manufacturing USA: *Industry Analyses, Statistics, and Leading Companies*
	Thomas Register of American Manufacturers
	U.S. Office of Management and Budget, Executive Office of the President, *Standard Industrial Classification Manual*
	U.S. *Manufacturer's Directory*
Companies—Private	*Million Dollar Directory*
	Ward's Directory
Companies—Public	Annual Reports and 10-K Reports
	Disclosure(corporate reports)
	Q-File
	Moody's Manuals:
	• *Moody's Bank and Finance Manual* • *Moody's Industrial Manual* • *Moody's International Manual* • *Moody's Municipal and Government Manual* • *Moody's OTC Industrial Manual* • *Moody's OTC Unlisted Manual* • *Moody's Public Utility Manual* • *Moody's Transportation Manual*

continued

	Standard & Poor Corporation, *Standard Corporation Descriptions:*
	• *Standard & Poor's Handbook* • *Standard & Poor's Industry Surveys* • *Standard & Poor's Investment Advisory Service* • *Standard & Poor's Outlook* • *Standard & Poor's Statistical Service*
Companies—Subsidiaries and Affiliates	*America's Corporate Families and International Affiliates*
	Ward's Directory
	Who Owns Whom
	Moody's Industry Review
	Standard & Poor's Analyst's Handbook
	Standard & Poor's Industry Report Service
	Standard & Poor's Industry Surveys (2 volumes)
	U.S. Department of Commerce, *U.S. Industrial Outlook*
Industry Ratios	
	Dun & Bradstreet, *Industry Norms and Key Business Ratios*
	Robert Morris Associates Annual Statement Studies
	Troy Almanac of Business and Industrial Financial Ratios
Industry Forecasts	
	International Trade Administration, *U.S. Industrial Outlook Predicasts Forecasts*
Rankings & Ratings	
	Annual Report on American Industry in *Forbes*
	Business Rankings and Salaries

continued

	Business One Irwin Business and Investment Almanac
	Corporate and Industry Research Reports (CIRR)
	Dun's Business Rankings
	Moody's Industrial Review
	Rating Guide to Franchises
	Standard & Poor's Industry Report Service
	Value Line Investment Survey
	Ward's Business Directory
Statistics	
	American Statistics Index (ASI) Bureau of the Census, U.S. Department of Commerce, *Economic Census Publications*
	Bureau of the Census, U.S. Department of Commerce, *Statistical Abstract of the United States*
	Bureau of Economic Analysis, U.S. Department of Commerce, *Survey of Current Business*
	Internal Revenue Service, U.S. Treasury Department, *Statistics of Income: Corporation Income Tax Returns*
	Statistical Reference Index (SRI)

(**Source**: http://www.swlearning.com/management/hitt/hitt_student/appendix_1.html)

EXAMPLES OF CASE ANALYSIS WRITING

A good way of getting good at writing case studies is by looking at other examples. A lot of case study examples can be found on the websites:

◇ *http://lilt.ilstu.edu/main/*

◇ *http://lilt.ilstu.edu/rcringer/mqm383/assignments%20and%20cases/example%20of%20case% 20analysis%20writing.pdf*

◇ *http://olc.spsd.sk.ca/DE/PD/instr/strats/casestd/casestds.pdf*

◇ *http://www.emeraldinsight.com/authors/guides/write/case.htm?part=4&PHPSESSID=vjuqisuaolf933ukkjpooe4tk5*

It is very important to remember that a case study should not be a mere narrative of events, but should seek to study genuine research issues and find the answers to real questions. A sample set of research questions is like this:

"The research questions (RQ) for this study are based on the discussion above and focus on the following co-branding issues:

RQ1. What objectives underpinned the corporate co-brand?

RQ2. How were brand values deployed to establish the corporate co-brand within particular discourse contexts?

RQ3. How was the desired rearticulation promoted to stakeholders?

RQ4. What are the sources of corporate co-brand equity?"

Before you can write up your case study, you have to analyse the data. The initial question is likely to be important here. The most common methods of analysis currently used are:

***Pattern matching*:** It is used where a set of results is predicted, and then compared with the actual ones.

***Explanation building*:** It is used where a particular explanation is used to analyse data about a case. The explanation may be influenced by a particular theoretical stance, for example discourse theory may explain aspects of branding practice.

***Time-series analysis*:** This method looks at trends over time, matching them with possible explanations, for example, looking at road deaths over a particular period and deciding whether an apparent initial reduction in deaths is caused by reduction in the speed limit or just a temporary fluctuation, or whether the flourishing of industry sectors in a small area is to do with proactive practices. A **complex time series analysis** would cover a case where there was more than one significant trend.

***Logic models*:** This stipulates a complex chain of events over time, and looks at the interplay between independent variables (causes) and dependent variables (events). The latter are predicted and then compared with actual events. It's similar to pattern matching (see above) but differs from it because of importance of sequence of events.

Cross-case synthesis: Findings are analysed across cases and generalizations are made.

Table 6.6 **FORMAT FOR WRITTEN CASE ANALYSIS**

Required Sections	Guidelines
I. Executive Summary	• One to two paragraphs in length • On cover page of the report • Briefly identify the major problems facing the manager/key person • Summarize the recommended plan of action and include a brief justification of the recommended plan

continued

Required Sections	Guidelines
II. Statement of the Problem	• State the problems facing the manager/key person • Identify and link the symptoms and root causes of the problems • Differentiate short term from long term problems • Conclude with the decision facing the manager/key person
III. Causes of the Problem	• Provide a detailed analysis of the problems identified in the Statement of the Problem • In the analysis, apply theories and models from the text and/or readings • Support conclusions and /or assumptions with specific references to the case and/or the readings
IV. Decision Criteria and Alternative Solutions	• Identify criteria against which you evaluate alternative solutions (i.e. time for implementation, tangible costs, acceptability to management) • Include two or three possible alternative solutions • Evaluate the pros and cons of each alternative against the criteria listed • Suggest additional pros/cons if appropriate
V. Recommended Solution, Implementation and Justification	• Identify who, what, when, and how in your recommended plan of action • Solution and implementation should address the problems and causes identified in the previous section • The recommended plan should include a contingency plan(s) to back up the "ideal" course of action • Using models and theories, identify why you chose the recommended plan of action—why it's the best and why it would work
VI. External Sourcing	• 5 external sources (in addition to your textbook) should be referenced to back up your recommendations or to identify issues. This information would be ideally sourced in current journals, magazines and newspapers and should reflect current management thought or practice with respect to the issues identified.
VII. Spelling Grammar and Presentation	• Your case analysis should: • Include the 5 sections listed in the outline • Be double spaced and the pages should be numbered • Have 1inch margins—top bottom left and right • Use 12 point font size • Be free of spelling errors • Use an established referencing system • Present the executive summary on the first page of the assignment along with your name (s), student number(s), course section and due date

(**Source**: http://r.search.yahoo.com/_ylt=AwrBT7uOao5UMMEAEttXNyoA;_ylu=X3oDMTEzO TFsdTN uBHNlYwNzcgRwb3MDMQRjb2xvA2JmMQR2dGlkA1NNRTM5OV8x/RV=2/RE=1418648335/RO=10/RU= http%3a%2f%2fusers.ipfw.edu%2ftodorovz%2fcaseformat.doc/RK=0/RS=.U1WzXjCzdkG2MHgv2Y1LgYfBFI-)

3. Exercises

I. Self-assessment *(These twenty-four statements concerning your feelings about communicating with other people. Please indicate in the space provided the degree to which each statement applies to you by marking whether you (1) Strongly Agree, (2) Agree, (3) Are Undecided, (4) Disagree, or (5) Strongly Disagree with each statement. There are no right or wrong answers. Many of the statements are similar to other statements. Do not be concerned about this. Work quickly; just record your first impressions.)*

______1. I dislike participating in group discussions.

______2. Generally, I am comfortable while participating in group discussions.

______3. I am tense and nervous while participating in group discussions.

______4. I like to get involved in group discussions.

______5. Engaging in group discussion with new people makes me tense and nervous.

______6. I am calm and relaxed while participating in group discussions.

______7. Generally, I am nervous when I have to participate in group discussions.

______8. Usually I am calm and relaxed while participating in meetings.

______9. I am very calm and relaxed when I am called upon to express an opinion at a meeting.

______10. I am afraid to express myself at meetings.

______11. Communicating at meetings usually makes me uncomfortable.

______12. I am very relaxed when answering questions at a meeting.

______13. While participating in a conversation with a new acquaintance, I feel very nervous.

______14. I have no fear of speaking up in conversations.

______15. Ordinarily I am very tense and nervous in conversations.

______16. Ordinarily I am very calm and relaxed in conversations.

______17. When conversing with a new acquaintance, I feel very relaxed.

______18. I am afraid to speak up in conversations.

______19. I have no fear of giving a speech.

______20. Certain parts of my body feel very tense and rigid while giving a speech.

______21. I feel relaxed while giving a speech.

______22. My thoughts become confused and jumbled when I am giving a speech.

______23. I face the prospect of giving a speech with confidence.

______24. While giving a speech, I get so nervous I forget facts I really know.

(Score Analysis is available on PPT attached.)

II. Thinking About A Movie

Smoke Signals (Chris Eyre, 1998)

Lanky, geeky Thomas Builds-the-Fire (Evan Adams) and athletic Victor Joseph (Adam Beach) live on a Coeur d'Alene Indian reservation in Idaho. Thomas's parents died in a fire when he was a baby; he was saved by Victor's father. After hearing that Victor's father has died in Phoenix, the two decide to take a road trip to learn more about the man who played such a pivotal role in their lives. At first Victor does not want his nerdy sidekick's company, but Thomas has saved enough money to bankroll the trip. The two grow closer as they learn more about themselves and their lost patriarch.

This movie portrays the subculture of contemporary Coeur d'Alene Indians who live in the mainstream culture but hold on to their Native American norms and values. Watch for the scene in which Victor tells Thomas how to act "properly stoic," demonstrating how members of the tribe reinforce the norms of their subculture.

For Your Consideration

1) What informal norms of the Coeur d'Alene culture does the movie show?

2) How do Thomas and Victor deal with the representations of Native American tribal people presented in mainstream films and television?

III. CASE ANALYSIS

Case 1: A businesswoman from the United States is in Germany for contract negotiations between her employer and a large German bank. The meeting is scheduled for nine o'clock in the morning. When she arrives to the meeting a few minutes before its start time, she is amazed that all her German counterparts are already seated and ready to begin the meeting. A few days later, upon her arrival back to the United States, she remarks to her American colleagues her experience with German culture. In particular, she notes their level of attentiveness to punctuality and planning and says, "I thought we were punctual here in the U.S.! It's nothing compared to how Germans view punctuality."

Case 2: ***IKEA Marketing in China.***

(Source: *http://english.8168168.com/news/disp_news.asp?id=20&Class=1*)

Case 3: ***Initial Adjustment Issues Faced By Foreign Teachers in China***

(Source: *http://www.transitionsabroad.com/listings/living/articles/culture_shock_in_china.shtml*)

Questions:

1) What main cultural differences did foreign teachers experience in China?

2) What kind of role do Chinese students can play in foreign teachers' adjustment to

Chinese culture?

4. References

1. Aczel, A. Complete business statistics [M]. New York: Richard Irwin, 1996.
2. Barkley, E. F, Cross, K. P. & Major, C. H. Collaborative Learning Techniques: A Handbook for College Faculty [M]. San-Francisco: Jossey-Bass, 2005.
3. C.C. Lundberg and C. Enz. A framework for student case preparation [J], *Case Research Journal* 13 (summer), 1993: 134.
4. Chen, G.M., and Starosta, W.J. Foundations of Intercultural Communication [M]. Boston: Allyn and Bacon, 1998.
5. Christensen, C. R. Teaching By the Case Method [M]. Boston: Harvard Business School, 1981.
6. Davis, B. G. Tools for Teaching [M]. San Francisco: Jossey-Bass, 1993.
7. Denzin, N. The research act [M]. Englewood Cliffs, NJ: Prentice Hall, 1984.
8. Erskine, Leenders, & Mauffette-Leenders. Learning with Cases, by published by the Richard Ivey School of Business, The University of Western Ontario, 1997.
9. Feagin, J., Orum, A., & Sjoberg, G. (Eds.). A case for case study [M]. Chapel Hill, NC: University of North Carolina Press, 1991.
10. Lomas, Carlos; Osorio, Andres & Tusón, Amparo. *Ciencias del lenguaje, competencia comunicativas y enseñanza de la lengua*. Barcelona: Paidós, 1993.
11. Pyecha, J. A case study of the application of noncategorical special education in two states [M]. Chapel Hill, NC: Research Triangle Institute, 1988.
12. Stake, R. The art of case research [M]. Newbury Park, CA: Sage Publications, 1995.
13. Yin, R. Case Study Research: Design and Methods (Applied Social Research Methods) [M]. Thousand Oaks, CA: Sage Publishing, 1989.
14. Yin, R. Applications of Case Study Research [M]. Thousand Oaks, CA: Sage Publishing, 1993.
15. Yin, R. Case study research: Design and methods [M], 2nd ed. Thousand Oaks, CA: Sage Publishing, 1994.
16. Yin, R. Case Study Research—Design and Methods [M]. CA: Sage Publishing, 2003.

